INSIDE THE MYTH

Inside the Myth

Orwell: Views From the Left

edited by
CHRISTOPHER NORRIS

LAWRENCE AND WISHART
LONDON

Lawrence and Wishart Limited
39 Museum Street
London WC1A 1LQ

This edition first published 1984
© Lawrence and Wishart, 1984

Each essay © the author

Photoset in North Wales by
Derek Doyle & Associates, Mold, Clwyd
Printed and bound in Great Britain by
Oxford University Press

Contents

Christopher Norris

Introduction

Few readers will need to be warned in advance that this book is no pious celebration of Orwell in the wake of his *annus mirabilis*. 'Orwell and the Left' is a violently disjunctive coupling, as many of these essays make clear. They focus on the ways in which Orwell has been kidnapped by the forces of reaction, taken over triumphantly by those who hold him up as *the* great example of a socialist who finally saw the light. No matter how ambivalent (or downright contradictory) his writings, Orwell is now firmly established as the voice and conscience of 'liberal' values against everything perceived as a threat to consensus democracy. The fact that such consensus is largely manufactured – and by methods which Orwell clearly foretold – is an irony which socialist readers will recognise but hardly relish. The prophecies lent themselves all too readily to the kind of right-wing recuperative reading which has turned Orwell into the patron saint of current Cold-War doublethink. One can imagine his misery and revulsion had Orwell lived to read some of the subtle and not-so-subtle propaganda put out in his name during 1984. The ghost must still be dancing on his grave in a fury of impotent scorn. But the fact that his writings are subject to such gross appropriation is evidence of their deeper complicity with those who would so use them.

Alan Brown shows this process very strikingly at work in the school examination system, where *Animal Farm* and *Nineteen Eighty-Four* are among the perennial O and A Level texts, with students left in no doubt as to what kind of model answer the examiners are looking for. The simplest-seeming questions

conceal a whole rhetoric of loaded politcal values. Malcolm
Evans extends a similar analysis to the way that 'Orwell' has
been processed by the popular media as a handy source of
images and slogans for various propaganda purposes. That
these are often crude interpretations – strategic *misreadings* at
some crucial point – doesn't alter the fact of Orwell's being
constantly available for just such uses. Stephen Sedley makes
this point very firmly in his discussion of the weaknesses of
Animal Farm, whether judged as political tract or narrative
fiction. The deep-laid conservative cast of Orwell's writing
goes along with the repeated assertions that everything he
wrote was devoted to defending 'democratic socialism' against
all forms of totalitarian threat. Nowadays he is cited as chief
witness for a form of repressive 'consensus' politics which finds
no need for the cruder methods predicted in *Nineteen
Eighty-Four*. This, more than anything, requires that the left
should address itself to analysing the Orwell myth in all its
latter-day manifestations.

We need to demythologize Orwell so as to see more clearly
the nature of that 'common-sense' ideology which lends itself
so willingly to propaganda purposes. A number of
contributors here – Easthope, Evans, Norris – draw upon
recent (post-structuralist) theories of language as a means of
relating that covert ideology to Orwell's style and narrative
stance. But to leave the analysis there would be to give Orwell
up into the hands of a dominant consensus reading utterly
indifferent to such challenges. 'Theory', after all, is a
well-known affliction of left-wing ideologues, deprived of the
common-sense wisdom that comes of accepting things as they
are. This attitude is doubtless reinforced by the fact that most
varieties of 'left' criticism tend to take a negative or strongly
demythologizing view of whatever they interpret. In Orwell's
case, such a reading would point to the delusions of a
common-sense empiricist idiom that sets itself up as a
knowledge independent of language, ideology and politics.
One can hardly begin to take account of the Orwell
phenomenon unless by way of this negative critique. But
clearly there is something more to be said if one wants to go on
and *reclaim* Orwell's writing – some of it at least – for the
purposes of socialist critique.

Fredric Jameson makes this the central issue of his book *The Political Unconscious* (1980). The negative labour of demystification is a necessary stage but the *first stage only* in what Jameson sees as the project of Marxist criticism.

> A Marxist negative hermeneutic, a Marxist practice of ideological analysis proper, must in the practical work of reading and interpretation be exercised *simultaneously* with a Marxist positive hermeneutic, or a decipherment of the Utopian impulses of these same still ideological cultural texts.

Jameson writes in passing of *Nineteen Eighty-Four* as a 'counter-revolutionary' text, but one which possesses the disruptive potential to undermine confidently orthodox readings. This merest of hints is amplified here by Antony Easthope, whose essay develops a strategy of reading to discover (by way of the Lacanian unconscious) what textual symptoms are repressed or occluded in the authorized version. Lynette Hunter's is also a redemptive reading, though one which places more faith on Orwell's *conscious* management of narrative technique. She sees the novels as developing steadily from an immature stage of confusedly subjective self-assertion to a point of more sophisticated narrative control where 'characters' assume a certain credible autonomy of viewpoint. There is an obvious tension between Hunter's reading and the argument (implicit in Easthope and Evans) that any such talk of the 'autonomous' individual is falling directly into Orwell's ideological trap. What these essays share is a clear understanding that the 'honest George' style of plain, no-nonsense *reportage* has to be patiently deconstructed if we want to resist its more insidious rhetorical effects. Otherwise that style will continue to impose its bogus common-sense 'values' in the service of every kind of reactionary populist creed.

The left has need of theory in its task of challenging the apparently self-evident truths of consensus politics. One effect of Orwell's style was to institute a certain idea of documentary realism which sounded very much (in Raymond Williams's phrase) like a man 'bumping up against experience' and setting down the facts in a straightforward, truth-telling way. But this

raises the question of how to draw a line between
'documentary' texts (like *The Road To Wigan Pier*) and those of
Orwell's novels which exploit the same devices of style and
narrative stance. To point out such signs of rhetorical
convergence between Orwellian 'fact' and 'fiction' is to throw a
very sizeable paradox into the myth of Orwell as an unbiased
partisan of social and historical truth. This myth has been
constructed around the twin presumptions of his factual
accuracy as a recorder of events and his *authenticity* as the
intellectual 'conscience of an age'. It is a view which finds
classic expression in the well-known essay by Lionel Trilling,
where Orwell's style is taken on trust as the very embodiment
of political good faith against the pressures of conformist
ideology. Hence the desire of these essays to read Orwell's texts
against the grain of their own clearly-marked values and
assumptions. This in turn means pressing hard on the
distinction between novel and documentary modes, since it is
here – in the tensions necessarily ignored by wholesale
admirers and ideologues – that Orwell's writing comes up
against the limits of its own contradictory project.

Other contributors are not so much concerned with matters
of language, ideology and representation. They focus more
specifically on the ways in which Orwell either falsified the
documentary record or allowed mere prejudice to pass for
objective fact. Bill Alexander, who fought in Spain with the
International Brigades, challenges Orwell's version of events
on various points of detailed historical accuracy. His
conclusion is that *Homage to Catalonia* not only treats the record
selectively but practises a form of systematic distortion wholly
in keeping with Orwell's anti-Communist bias. Robert
Stradling likewise casts a cold eye on *Homage* and the other,
more overtly polemical writings which came out of Orwell's
Spanish experience. As an historian of the period, with
knowledge of other contemporary sources, Stradling is
prompted to reflect on the ambiguous status of Orwell's text,
its failures in point of historical accuracy going along with its
almost novelistic sense of worked-up narrative involvement.
But of course it is impossible to criticise Orwell on
documentary grounds without believing that there is, after all,
an historical truth of the matter which his writings more or less

consciously distort. None of these essays can be taken to deny that belief, whatever their suspicions of the form it took in Orwell's plain-dealing literary style.

His treatment of women gives further cause to look at the forms of ingrained prejudice which skewed Orwell's vision in novels and documentary writing alike. Deirdre Beddoe brings out the very marked sexual politics which effectively confines his female characters to a role of passive dependence or (like Dorothy in *A Clergyman's Daughter*) short-lived domestic rebellion. Beatrix Campbell pursues this analysis into Orwell's failure to understand the politics of working-class sexual and family life, as portrayed with such offensive disdain in *Wigan Pier* and elsewhere.

In the end – as Alaric Jacob remarks in his essay – the reader is brought up against the same negativity, the same despairing upshot to every line of thought in Orwell's political writing. It is for critics on the left to point out the varieties of false logic and crudely stereotyped thinking that produced this vision of terminal gloom. Thus Stuart Hall, for one, brings out the mixture of half-truths and predisposed pessimist conclusions which characterized Orwell's thinking on the origins and logic of the modern totalitarian state. From a different but related angle, Andy Croft places *Nineteen Eighty-Four* in the company of other, less celebrated works of political fiction which held out against the Orwellian malaise. Either they preserved some measure of utopian commitment, or – failing that – they diagnosed contemporary dangers and evils with a force and acuity wholly lacking in Orwell. It is too much to hope that *Nineteen Eighty-Four*, like 1984, will soon be consigned to the dusty annals of Cold-War cultural propaganda. Celebrations may cease upon the stroke of twelve, but there will still be many whose interests it suits to go on mistaking the Orwellian pumpkin for a Natopolitan coach-and-six.

Malcolm Evans

Text, Theory, Criticism: Twenty Things You Never Knew About George Orwell

1. In his essay 'Boys' Weeklies', Orwell maintained that the two basic political assumptions of publications like the *Gem* and *Magnet* were 'nothing ever changes, and foreigners are funny',[1] illustrating the second with an account of some popular conventions:

> FRENCHMAN: Excitable. Wears beard, gesticulates wildly.
> SPANIARD, MEXICAN etc.: Sinister, treacherous.
> ARAB, AFGHAN etc.: Sinister, treacherous.
> CHINESE: Sinister, treacherous. Wears pigtail.
> ITALIAN: Excitable. Grinds barrel-organ or carries stiletto.
> SWEDE, DANE etc.: Kind-hearted, stupid.
> NEGRO: Comic, very faithful. (*CEJL*, Vol. 1, p. 517)

In response to this and Orwell's broader critique, Frank Richards, the editor of *Magnet* and doyen of the genre, argued that barring a few temporary mutations, such as the craze for lipstick and modernist literary 'muck', nothing ever does change: 'Decency seems to have gone – but it will come again.' As for the comic qualities of foreigners, Richards goes on,

> I must shock Mr Orwell by telling him that foreigners *are* funny. They lack the sense of humour which is the special gift of our chosen nation: and people without a sense of humour are always unconsciously funny. (*CEJL*, Vol. 1, p. 538)

Thus Orwell's comments on the conservatism, snobbishness and insularity of the weeklies constitute, for Richards, an attack on a typically English decency and geniality which it is incumbent on the writer of popular fiction to nurture, so protecting the nation's youth from overwrought foreign 'duds' like Ibsen and Chekhov, and from intellectuals, like Orwell himself, preoccupied with sex, class, strikes and politics. The function of the boys' writer is to entertain, turn the reader's mind to 'healthy pursuits', give him a feeling of 'cheerful security', and to avoid at all costs any engagement with politics or an incitement to 'unhealthy introspection', both of which are harmful to the young: 'If there is a Chekhov among my readers, I fervently hope that the effect of *Magnet* will be to turn him into a Bob Cherry!' (*CEJL*, Vol. 1, p. 540)

*   *   *

2. This exchange, published in Cyril Connolly's *Horizon* in March and May 1940, sketches a theoretical conflict which remains unresolved. While Richards promotes 'pure' entertainment, decency and an unchanging human nature, Orwell focuses on popular literature's reproduction of hegemonic constructions of class, race, manliness and the distinctively 'English'. Stripped of Richards's overt prudishness and his willingness to *declare* assumptions about foreigners, some of the basic positions outlined in the two essays might reappear in a contemporary debate on 'professionalism', ideology and popular demand between a producer of television comedy, for example, and a researcher in Cultural or Communication Studies, disciplines anticipated to a degree in Orwell's writing on popular culture. But this conflict also shapes Orwell's own practice in fiction, his comments on more conventionally literary topics, and the contention of critical discourses within which his criticism and fiction are themselves now reproduced and evaluated. Frank Richards's defence of a fiction which is 'outside politics', which deals with matters ultimately more 'human' and 'fundamental', is a demotic analogue of the 'disinterested' criticism dominant in English schools and universities from the 1920s to the mid-1970s, in which the 'literary' is constructed precisely in terms of its *transcendence*, in

the last analysis, of the ephemeral, the ideological, the propagandist. Before this tradition was isolated by contemporary feminist, post-structuralist and post-Althusserian criticisms, and its own ideological interests disclosed, it was already subject to the challenge of a series of propositions popularized by Orwell – 'All art is propaganda', 'All issues are political issues', 'The opinion that art should have nothing to do with politics is itself a political attitude'[2] – and a critical practice which implicitly questioned formalism, aestheticism and the fetishization of the 'literary' by returning to history, politics, material factors operating in the text's production and reception, and the conditions of its reproduction in criticism and commentary. When Orwell writes about Shakespeare, Dickens or Henry Miller, no less than in his work on boys' weeklies and comic postcards, there is a call for something more than 'literary' criticism, a gesture toward articulating 'literature' itself within a larger theory of discourse and ideology. The need for this articulation to continue, against the inertia of the loosely contextualized and nominally apolitical discourses that constitute traditionalist literary studies, is nowhere clearer than in the problems posed by reading Orwell in 1984.

*   *   *

3. The 'Orwellian future' became the present and soon the past, the preoccupation with prophecy giving way to an examination of the forces that sustained its vitality for so long and in the face of so much evidence to the contrary. Orwell predicted, at various times, that the Stock Exchange would be pulled down after World War II and the country houses turned into children's holiday camps, that the Conservative Party would win the 1945 election, and that England would be blown off the map by atomic weapons before 1967. He imagined that he would end up in a concentration camp.[3] Even these miscalculations pale beside the vision in *Nineteen Eighty-Four* of *The Times* as an organ of Ingsoc ('English Socialism' in Oldspeak). But this, as Orwell insisted in his comments on the novel,[4] was not so much a prophecy as part of a satirical warning, a *possible* scenario itself engaged in the fight against

totalitarianism and its own imaginary future. So what could have been another wildly inaccurate prediction becomes a successfully self-negating projection, a minor landmark on the road to Rupert Murdoch's ownership of *The Times* in 1984 and to that paper's financial and ideological alliance, linking both ends of the 'free market' in information, with the *News of the World* ('all human life is here') and the *Sun* ('the place where there is no darkness').

* * *

4. The literary text, as Pierre Macherey argues,[5] is impenetrably encrusted with its criticism, commentary and other nominally secondary discourses, which all become assimilated to it as part of its material history. For this reason Britain's best-selling daily newspaper was essential reading for Orwell scholars in 1984. The *Sun*'s consideration for slow readers, in underlining, italicizing or capitalizing all essential phrases, has the useful side-effect of producing a sketch-map of ideological landscapes less clearly visible through the 'balances' and superior 'textuality' of more reputable institutions (*The Times*, the BBC). Here, in its refreshing simplicity, is an uncluttered version of hegemony, and a key to discourses that have continually reworked *Nineteen Eighty-Four* since 1949. The *Sun*'s first leader page of the new year was, predictably, devoted to an oblique celebration of Orwell's work under the headline '1984: What we must do to keep Big Brother at bay.' (2 January 1984, p.6) The prose is urgent and concise, almost as clear as a window-pane, producing a world which is readable, incontestable, *out there*. Orwell foresaw 'an England dominated by Marxist tyranny', but Margaret Thatcher, at the passing of the old year, 'spoke of the reality of 1984 as a time of liberty and hope.' While accepting 'the truth of her words', set against Orwell's 'fictional view', the *Sun* insists that its readers must maintain their customary standard of critical awareness. Orwell 'saw Marxism leading inevitably to what he described as a foot stamping constantly on the human countenance.' This has happened in Russia, 'where Yuri Andropov presides like some invisible Big Brother' denying freedom and privacy:

IT HAS HAPPENED in Poland, where basic human rights are regarded as a crime against the state.

IT HAS HAPPENED in China, under the lunatic Red Guards.

IT HAS HAPPENED everywhere in the third of the world that now lies under the Communist heel.

Moving back from this boys' weeklies site of sinister and treacherous foreigners, the editorial warns that the threat diagnosed by Orwell comes 'not just from the military power of Russia but from the enemy within.' The Opposition's programme for the 1983 General Election was 'Marxist in everything but name', and had it prevailed 'we would have been taken so far down the path to the Corporate State, there could have been no turning back.' The Labour Party spent much of 1983 purging itself of socialists but it remains, in spite of its 'cosmetic treatment', in the hands of 'all manner of extremists', while the 'ugly face of Socialism' is still shown by 'industrial bullies who try to take away men's livelihood if they are not in a union.' The piece concludes with a guarded optimism:

> As 1984 opens, we have been spared the Orwell nightmare. We have liberty under Margaret Thatcher. We have hope of a better tomorrow.
>
> Yet all these things are not automatic.
>
> *We have to deserve them. We have to earn them.*
>
> *We must be vigilant every day in 1984 and beyond to preserve them from any assault.*

*   *   *

5. Here 'Socialist' slides into 'Communist' via the intermediary term 'Marxist' to constitute a 'lunatic' and 'nightmare' order directly opposed to 'liberty', 'hope', 'truth', 'human rights', 'Margaret Thatcher' and to what 'we' must strive for and preserve according to the choric exhortation which blends the *Sun*'s public discourse with the private voices its antagonists in Russia, the British unions and the Labour Party would seek to silence. This basic opposition, in all its banality, is validated by the authority of astringent prophecy and literary canonization,

and establishes the frame for an accompanying feature – '20 THINGS YOU NEVER KNEW ABOUT GEORGE ORWELL'.[6] Most of these you knew already. Orwell, whose real name was Eric Blair (1), was the son of a 'minor civil servant' (2), served in the Imperial Police in Burma instead of going to university (6), became 'fiercely anti-Communist' during the Spanish Civil War (12), married twice (10,18), smoked too much (17) and, mostly in circumstances of financial hardship, wrote books that became 'modern classics' (14,20). These items establish Big Brother's paternity and produce for the author a history and a private life in no way incompatible with the leader writer's appropriation of *Nineteen Eighty-Four*. There is even leeway for some faint traces of the 'left' Orwell – his formative experiences at St Cyprian's (3) and sense of social inferiority at Eton (4) – and for an acknowledgement of other factors contributing to the 'nightmare' qualities of his last novel, which ' "wouldn't have been so gloomy if I hadn't been so ill" ' (18). Such details add an element of 'complexity' and a solidity of specification which vouches for the metonymic realism of the pivotal, editorial construction of 'Orwell-in-1984'. But this, like any other text signifies as much through its strategic silences as by what it makes manifest,[7] and there are at least twenty other things the ideal *Sun* reader never knew about George Orwell, each of which would tend to decentre the text, disclose its contrivance, and displace its evasively tendentious subject. This silenced discourse, largely Orwell's own, includes:

a)   The writer who specifically refuted any interpretation of *Nineteen Eighty-Four* as an attack on socialism or the British Labour Party and who claimed, in 1947, that all his serious work during the previous decade had been written '*against* totalitarianism and *for* democratic Socialism, as I understand it.' (*CEJL*, Vol. 4, p. 566; Vol. 1, p. 28)

b)   Orwell's ability to distinguish socialism or communism from the prospect of Soviet state capitalism. (*CEJL*, Vol. 1, p. 369)

c)   His belief in the need for revolution in England, coupled with his contempt for the small percentage of the population in control of the country's wealth and land – people who, historically, 'seized it by force, afterwards hiring lawyers to provide them with title-deeds', and whose privileged descendants are 'just about as useful as so many tapeworms.' (*CEJL*, Vol. 2, pp. 105-134; Vol. 3, pp. 241-2)

d)   Orwell's acceptance, along with 'most enlightened people', of 'the Communist thesis that pure freedom will only exist in a classless society, and that one is most nearly free when one is working to bring such a society about.' (*CEJL*, Vol. 4, p. 84)

e)   'Those who now call themselves Conservatives are either Liberals [the 'wets' of 1984], fascists or the accomplices of fascists.' (*CEJL*, Vol. 2, p. 228)

f)   Journalists who wish to retain their integrity are frustrated by 'the concentration of the Press in the hands of a few very rich men' [1984 revision: '... and multinational corporations']. 'The freedom of the press in Britain was always something of a fake because, in the last resort, money controls opinion.' (*CEJL*, Vol. 4, p. 82; Vol. 1, p. 373)

The *Sun*'s catalogue could also be extended by 'human interest' elements. The fact that Orwell's father – the 'minor civil servant' – was, more specifically, a Sub-Deputy Agent in the Opium Department of the British Raj, involved in the narcotics trade with China, legalized, since 1860, as a government monopoly, adds a historical resonance to editorial comments on the 'lunatic' Red Guards.[8] The list might also specify the side on which Orwell fought in the Spanish Civil War, and the confirmation of his socialism in Barcelona. It can, of course, go on almost indefinitely. It ends with the Orwell of 'Boys' Weeklies', well qualified to read another 'Orwell' out of this now familiar type of propaganda, with the critic who could distinguish a truly popular culture, in England 'something that goes on beneath the surface, unofficially and more or less frowned on by the authorities' (*CEJL*, Vol. 2, p. 78) from an administered '*prolefeed*' – 'rubbish entertainment and spurious news'.[9]

*   *   *

6. For Orwell the aesthetic response was something of a luxury, albeit one finally subject to democratic validation. If you are hungry, frightened or suffering, *King Lear* is no better than *Peter Pan*. (*CEJL*, Vol. 4, p. 258) At the best of times there is no way of definitively proving that one writer is 'good', another 'bad' (*CEJL*, Vol. 4, pp. 334-5), and there is ultimately only one test of literary merit. Against Tolstoy, who compared the popularity of Shakespeare to such 'epidemic suggestions' as the Crusades, the quest for the Philosopher's Stone and the Dutch mania for tulip growing, Orwell argued the criterion of *survival*, itself an 'index of majority opinion' confirmed by the Shakespearean fragments scattered throughout vernacular English. (*CEJL*, Vol. 4, pp. 335, 345-6) In the case of what he considered the major works of modern literature – *Ulysses*, Maugham's *Of Human Bondage*, most of Lawrence's early writing and Eliot's poems up to 1930 – he was prepared, as early as 1940, to provisionally affirm that they *had* survived and to remove the question of their value from the sphere of an academic and journalistic debate which he viewed only in terms of an insoluble struggle between a theory of 'art for art's sake' on the one hand and reductive evaluations of 'ideas' in relation to formalized systems of thought such as Marxism or Catholicism on the other.[10]

*   *   *

7. According to this test of time, particularly the shortened version of it employed in 'Inside the Whale', the status of *Animal Farm* and *Nineteen Eighty-Four* as 'modern classics' can go unquestioned, adding Orwell's seal of 'majority opinion' to the great commercial and ideological feast centred on his work in 1984. But the check on this aesthetic idealism endorsed by what seems the most empirical and 'natural' of tests emerges from the contradictions in Orwell's own writing. 'Anything worth reading always "dates" ', he claims elsewhere in reference to Twain's *Roughing It* (*CEJL*, Vol. 1, p. 62), and the literary language which gains majority approval by filtering into the vernacular is not inevitably from work of the highest quality: 'The phrases and neologisms which we take over and use without remembering their origin do not always come

from writers we admire.' (*CEJL*, Vol. 2, p. 224) Isaac Deutscher's extension of Orwell's remark on Kipling to the reception of *Nineteen Eighty-Four* makes it clear that, in certain cases at least, survival may be related less to a spontaneous majority taste than to the business of cultural and ideological reproduction. A book that lends itself to 'adventitious exploitation', Deutscher suggests, needs not be 'a literary masterpiece or even an important and original work,' and a great poet's words are not easily transformed into 'slogans' and 'hypnotizing bogies'. They enter the language 'by a process of slow, almost imperceptible infiltration, not by frantic incursion.'[11]

* * *

8. The survival through four decades of Big Brother and his vocabulary, and their apotheosis in 1984, represent, of course, a very special case. *Twenty-One Eighty-Four* would, for obvious reasons, have received less attention not only in political speeches and tabloid journalism, on television and in the pulpit, but in reviews, books and academic articles, and on British O and A Level syllabuses. As 'literature' (or what gets taught on literature courses), Orwell's work survives in defiance of his own estimation of it, ranging from the acknowledged shortcomings of *Nineteen Eighty-Four* (*CEJL*, Vol. 4 pp. 507-536) to the view of his *oeuvre* as a historically determined abdication from 'art' and 'aesthetic enthusiasm' – 'I am not really a novelist anyway', 'I have been forced into becoming a sort of pamphleteer.' (*CEJL* Vol. 4, p. 478; Vol. 1, p. 26) It also survives despite his conviction of 'the *impossibility* of any major literature until the world has shaken itself into its new shape.' (*CEJL* Vol. 1, p. 578) But as work which is only marginally literary, writing not altogether 'good',[12] the longevity of which is located outside the 'aesthetic' function, Orwell's fiction, particularly in 1984, *makes visible* the principle more easy concealed closer to the discursive centre of 'literature': that the test of time is also a test of the range of ideological apparatuses and discourses whose work the more naïve formulations of literary survival, including those by Orwell himself, would attempt to eclipse.

* * *

9. This principle, which moves from an aesthetic idealism to the material production within ideology of a body of texts *deemed* 'aesthetic' and valuable, also emerges in another Orwellian persona, that of the hard-pressed and hard-bitten professional writer. As a critic Orwell is quite capable of lapsing back into judgments that idealise 'literature' as a universal dialogue of free spirits. Even Shakespeare receives a mild reprimand for refusing to challenge the rich and powerful, 'flattering them in the most servile way' and allowing subversive opinions to be expressed only by fools and mad people – points Kenneth Muir despatches succinctly with reference to the conditions of production in the English theatre, most notably censorship and the screening of all play-texts by the Master of the Revels.[13] But Orwell's comments on his own experience of publishing and on the practical determinants of reputation and survivability trace a network of relations which is the obverse of this idealist coin. Few modern texts have a more illuminating *institutional* genesis than *Animal Farm* for example: rejected by Dial Press because it was 'impossible to sell animal stories in the USA' (*CEJL*, Vol. 4, p. 138) and by T.S. Eliot at Faber because 'we have no conviction ... that this is the right point of view from which to criticise the political situation at the present time', translated into Ukrainian for dissemination in the USSR, then seized by the American authorities in Munich (1,500 copies) and handed over to Soviet officials. (*CEJL* Vol. 4, pp. 433-4) These episodes are an ironic prelude to the policy changes that sustained a reverse censorship of *Animal Farm* and *Nineteen Eighty-Four*, a positive discrimination accompanying their incorporation into Cold War polemic.[14] Orwell was also familiar with the detail of more mundane forms of institutional boosting and neglect. These include publishers' advertising, its effect on reviewing,[15] and the negotiations of literary reviewers who are also authors – 'You scratch my back, I'll scratch yours.' (Orwell to Connolly)[16] They extend, more crucially, to the *teaching* of literature, and its links with publishing and the arbitration of taste. Gordon Comstock's contempt for 'those moneyed young beasts who glide so gracefully from Eton to Cambridge and from Cambridge to the literary reviews'[17] is only slightly modulated in Orwell's attack on 'the *Criterion-Scrutiny*

assumption that literature is a game of back-scratching (claws
in or out according to circumstances) between tiny cliques of
highbrows.' (*CEJL*, Vol. 1, p. 285) At St Cyprian's the young
Eric Blair's spare-time reading was determined by the
requirements of the English Paper (*CEJL*, Vol. 1, p. 386) and
one of Orwell's last pieces of published jouranlism, a review of
The Great Tradition, hints at the tightening noose that binds
literature and pedagogy. Leavis, in this account, aims to induce
in the reader 'a feeling of due reverence towards the "great"
and of due irreverence towards everybody else', implying that
one should read 'with one eye on the scale of values, like a
wine-drinker reminding himself of the price per bottle at every
sip.' Thus Austen, George Eliot, James and Conrad are 'great'
while the remaining English novelists appear 'not only inferior
but ... reprehensible', and behind it all is the magisterial voice
which says 'Remember boys' and 'I was once a boy myself':
'But though the boys know that this must be true, they are not
altogether reassured. They can still hear the chilly rustle of the
gown, and they are aware that there is a cane under the desk
which will be produced on not very much provocation.'[18]
Given the expansion, and complexion, of English Studies in
the 1950s and 1960s, this is Orwell at his most prophetic, a
passage to be recalled by anyone who first encountered *Animal
Farm* and *Nineteen Eighty-Four*, along with Golding's *Lord of the
Flies* perhaps, amid chalk-dust, the innate corruption of
human nature, and the impossibility of significant change.

*   *   *

10. EITHER
(a)   'Orwell is concerned to show how revolutionary ideals of
       justice, equality and fraternity always shatter in the event.'
       (A.E. Dyson)
       'With *Animal Farm* he led the wavering lefties out of the
       pink mists of Left Land into the clear daylight.'
       (Wyndham Lewis)
       Do you agree?
OR
(b)   'Ultimately there is no test of literary merit except
       survival.' (George Orwell)

Discuss with detailed reference to texts which have not survived.

* * *

11. The project that suggests itself then is to recover from Orwell's work the fragments of a theory of ideology focusing on 'literary' and cultural *production*; to re-centre the 'distinctively Orwellian' in the work on popular culture and the moments in other essays where questions of interpretation and form are fused with concerns relegated in the dominant academic criticisms to a secondary, purely supplementary, 'sociology of literature'. Such a project might emphasize the relative autonomy of (and contradiction within) the institutions, rituals and discursive fields of a cultural production determined only in the last instance by the economic base.[19] Orwell's comments on the distortion of his own preferences as a writer lend support to this reformulation of the 'centre' of his work, which coincides with the best means of describing it. In a letter to Geoffrey Gorer (April 1940) he recommends 'Boys' Weeklies', the Dickens essay and 'Inside the Whale', and adds: 'I find this kind of semi-sociological literary criticism very interesting & I'd like to do a lot of other writers, but unfortunately there's no money in it.' (*CEJL* Vol. 1, p. 579)

* * *

12. But a marriage of Orwell and Althusser seems, in other ways, preposterous and the objections to such a project are manifold. Not least of these is Orwell's apparent belief in something like 'the sanctity of the individual imaginative response'. His view of the novel as 'a Protestant form of Art' inaccessible to Marxists and Catholics (*CEJL*, Vol. 1, p. 568) parallels his compulsive need, in fiction and in criticism, to be located outside 'the smelly little orthodoxies.' (*CEJL*, Vol. 1, p. 504) His account of *Practical Criticism*, a book he recommends to 'anyone who wants a good laugh', *endorses* the rite which compels students to 'respond' without prejudice to a text shorn of all marks of a political or historical context. His analysis dwells not on the questionable assumptions of I.A.

Richards but on the success of his 'experiment', which reveals the shortcomings of taste in Cambridge undergraduates who have 'no more notion of distinguishing between a good poem and a bad one than a dog has of arithmetic.' (*CEJL*, Vol. 3, p. 171) The business of 'recuperating Orwell for the right' involves, in many cases, no more than reasonable argument backed up by a mountain of evidence. This process of recuperation also has a distinguished history which goes back at least as far as 1940, when Q.D. Leavis claimed that 'nature didn't intend him to be a novelist' but that Orwell's criticism was almost up to the *Scrutiny* mark: 'potentially a good critic', 'without having scholarship or an academic background he yet gives the impression of knowing a surprising amount about books and authors', 'an alert intelligence', 'his pages are not cluttered up with academic "scholarship" ', 'what he knows is live information, not card-index rubbish'.[20] If there is a more progressive discourse at work in Orwell's text it is constantly interrupted by this strain of conservative empiricism, which emerges again in his love of a 'transparent' language (prose 'like a window-pane') of 'the surface of the earth', of 'solid objects and scraps of useless information'. (*CEJL*, Vol. 1, pp. 28-30) It surfaces too in the adherence to a common-sense aesthetic: the test of time as proof of literary merit; the state of being most 'alive' outside theory; the form-content division which generates insights of the 'Dali, though a brilliant draughtsman, is a dirty little scoundrel' variety (*CEJL*, Vol. 3, p. 185), while deploring the separation between 'ideas' criticism and 'art for art's sake' which they implicitly perpetuate.

* * *

13. Literary theory and questions of how we should read lead inevitably back to the political issues. Four months after Frank Richards, in the name of 'Englishness' and 'decency', cast his antagonist in the role of a dogmatic left-wing theorist, Q.D. Leavis upheld the 'responsible, adult and decent' stamp of Orwell's work in diametrically opposite terms: 'he can see through the Marxist theory, and being innately decent (he displays and approves of bourgeois morality) he is disgusted

with the callous theorising inhumanity of the pro-Marxists ...
he isn't the usual parlour-Bolshevik seeing literature through
political glasses.'[21] Of the struggle against fascism Orwell
wrote, quoting Nietzsche, 'He who fights too long against
dragons becomes a dragon himself: and if thou gaze too long
into the abyss, the abyss will gaze into thee' (*CEJL*, Vol. III,
p. 267) – a remark amplified in the Wigan Pier *Diary* with
reference to the working man who becomes a trade-union
official or a Labour politician: 'by fighting against the
bourgeoisie he becomes bourgeois.' (*CEJL*, Vol. 1, p. 198) This
principle of exchange has a peculiar force in relation to
Orwell. Nothing in the *Critical Heritage* volume devoted to his
work resembles Q.D. Leavis's vituperative tone, dependence
on jargon and conviction of grace more than the *Pravda* review
of *Nineteen Eighty-Four*.[22] And the 'Frank Richards' constructed
in 'Boys' Weeklies' and the reply to it is in many ways more like
'Orwell' than Eric Blair himself.

* * *

14. Orwell too, in other places, is content to caricature
foreigners and is concerned with the nature of 'Englishness'.
'Spaniards are cruel to animals, Italians can do nothing
without making a deafening noise, the Chinese are addicted to
gambling.' (*CEJL*, Vol. 2, p. 76) The 'typically English'
characteristics are, in contrast, strikingly close to his own
'not-really-a-novelist-anyway' and anti-theoretical modes: the
English 'are not gifted artistically' and 'are not intellectual',
more specifically they have 'a horror of abstract thought, they
feel no need for any philosophy or systematic "world view".'
(*CEJL*, Vol. 2, p. 77) Where theory or an analytical system
suggests one course of action, an intuitive 'Englishness'
inevitably intervenes. The English working class, for example,
has never been able to think internationally except for the brief
success of the 'Hands off Russia' movement in 1920. (*CEJL*,
Vol. 2, p. 85) Orwell's Englishmen *are* finally Bob Cherries,
sturdy individuals with a sense of fair play who oppose
twentieth-century political theories with 'not another theory of
their own, but a moral quality which must be vaguely
described as decency.' (*CEJL*, Vol. 3, p. 28) Here Orwell meets

Frank Richards again, also the magisterially 'responsible, adult and decent' Leavises, and sets off on the trail of a notoriously vague and untheorized 'decency' which is the central thread of his more conservative discourse. Much has been written on this topic in general terms but it merits closer atention. 'Decency' is fundamental to Byron's poems (*CEJL*, Vol. 1, p. 121) but 'thinking and decent people' are generally not too keen on Kipling. (*CEJL*, Vol. 1, p. 225) Shakespeare's wish to ingratiate himself with the rich and powerful is not quite decent, while Dickens admires *nothing but* 'common decency'. (*CEJL*, Vol. 1, p. 457) For Orwell 'decency' is synonymous with what Marxists call 'bourgeois morality' (*CEJL*, Vol. 3, p. 22) but it also pertains to the 'decent, labouring poor'. (*CEJL*, Vol. 1, p 77) All 'decent' people want a classless society (*CEJL*, Vol. 4, p. 187) but the means for accomplishing this are difficult to imagine as it almost seems, to Orwell, that 'men are only decent when they are powerless.' (*CEJL*, Vol. 1, p. 372) The recipe that emerges is for political quietism coupled perhaps with revolutionary fantasy, and the baggy definition of 'decent', in these instances and throughout Orwell's work, comes uncomfortably close to his definition of 'English'.[23] Neither category entertains many prospects of change. In 1984 such terms are the preserve of a right-wing, right-minded doublethink. Without them it would be difficult to escalate the arms race and claim '*We* are the Peace Movement',[24] or to accept (or rather disguise) a figure of $4\frac{1}{2}$ million unemployed while justifying the institution of a small police-state in Nottinghamshire as a defence of the miners' right to work. It may be that Orwell was *really* a decent enough type while the Thatcher/Brittan/Heseltine uses of 'decent' are, in fact, indecent. Small consolation. '[Language] becomes ugly and inaccurate because our thoughts are foolish, but the slovenliness of our language makes it easier for us to have foolish thoughts.' (*CEJL*, Vol. 4, p. 157)[25] The Newspeak C vocabulary would do well to limit 'decent' to accommodation and cups of tea.[26]

*   *   *

15. Orwell and Frank Richards concur to some extent on

foreigners and Englishness, they are joined by the Leavises for 'decency' and unease about theory, and they all assemble again on the idealization of a lost past. The world of Greyfriars, Bob Cherry and Billy Bunter is stuck at 1910, writes Orwell (*CEJL*, Vol. 2, pp. 616, 518), a criticism muted by a nostalgia for the Edwardian period which haunts much of his own work, fiction and non-fiction. This is the time before mass-slaughter, totalitarianism and the 'horror of politics' (*CEJL*, Vol. 2, p. 39), the time of a genuine literaray criticism 'of the older kind – criticism that is really judicious, scrupulous, fair-minded, treating a work of art as a thing of value in itself.' (*CEJL*, Vol. 2, p. 149) This indistinct past also holds the very possibility of the 'literature' denied to a present of partisanship and pamphleteering. After his first dream of the Golden Country, Winston Smith wakes up 'with the word 'Shakespeare' on his lips.' (*1984*, p. 31) Orwell's self-conscious nostalgia differs markedly from the more earnest and cerebral pastoralism of F.R. Leavis's 'organic community'.[27] But from the two contrasting myths of the past there issues a common rhetoric of independence, responsibility and the 'concrete', a stewardship of 'humane' values and decency against a pressing reductivism and dehumanization. Orwell's 'criticism of the older kind' is the conservative strain in his own criticism. It is also *Scrutiny* criticism and the correct method of reading as laid down by a British government report published in 1921. Orwell, as Q.D. Leavis noted, was not an academic critic, and his marginal status in this respect seems to have kept him unaware of the fact that to be disinterested, untheoretical and fearlessly unorthodox was becoming just about as orthodox as you could get.

* * *

16. The Newbolt Committee's report to the British Board of Education on *The Teaching of English in England* (1921) is beginning to receive the attention it merits,[28] and there is room here only to give the barest synopsis. English appears as a relatively recent invention, the first chairs in the subject having been established at Cambridge as late as 1878 and at Oxford in 1885. The task at hand is to promote English literature in

education as a basis of 'humane culture', a 'great source of national pride' and a potential bond of national unity.[29] To this end, literature is to be viewed as a 'record of the experiences of the greatest minds' (p. 149), one which has a historical dimension but which is to be studied primarily for its 'nobler, more eternal and universal element.' (p. 205) In the tradition of Matthew Arnold, the report's 'apostle of culture' (p. 259), this body of work will 'civilize' in ways that transcend theoretical and political considerations, being part of 'a disinterested endeavour to learn and propagate the best that is known and thought in the world', and 'to see the object as in itself it really is.'[30] There is much here that might have engaged the more conservative Orwell, with his nostalgia for an 'older' criticism which treats the work 'as a thing of value in itself'. The Newbolt Report also bends the discourse which links Arnold, the Leavises and the future of literary studies in England up to the 1970s towards a construction of the 'Englishness' which preoccupied Orwell too, and which marks in his work a limit of the theoretical, and a privileged site of the empirical, the intuitive and the 'decent'.[31] But the report's analysis of literature, pedagogy, and their relation to English society strays into areas that acknowledge pressing historical and political considerations, and touch on aspects of the ideological determination of what 'literature' is and how it functions which are lost in a blind spot in Orwell's criticism, between the sketchy comments on literature and schooling at the edge of his 'semi-sociological', quasi-materialist mode, and the more orthodox strain of 'fearless distinterestedness' and the imaginative response. By coincidence Orwell's own work and these areas of the Newbolt Report intersect at a significant, if idiosyncratic, point – Tolstoy's attack on *King Lear*. Orwell makes Tolstoy's essay the occasion for a confrontation between dogmatic stringency and the organic vitality of a uniquely gifted imagination. Shakespeare, typically English, 'was not a philosopher or a scientist, but he did have curiosity, he loved the surface of the earth and the process of life.' (*CEJL*, Vol. 4, p. 345)[32] Tolstoy, in contrast, is a spiritual bully, 'a moralist attacking an artist', one who fails to recognize that Shakespeare 'can no more be debunked by such methods than you can destroy a flower by preaching a sermon at it.'

(*CEJL*, Vol. 2, p. 157) Behind this presentation of the central conflict there is a triple renunciation – Lear's, mirrored in Tolstoy's,[33] which reflects in turn Orwell's self-professed sacrifice of a disinterested 'art' (Shakespeare) to the pressure of conscience (Tolstoy) and the fate of the pamphleteer: 'Forty years later, Shakespeare is still there, completely unaffected, and of the attempt to demolish him nothing remains except the yellowing pages of a pamphlet which hardly anyone has read ...' (*CEJL*, Vol. 4, p. 348) But one author of the Newbolt Report *had* read Tolstoy's pamphlet,[34] and exploited it with a startling disingenuousness as an instance of the doctrinaire rejection of art 'now prevalent in Bolshevist Russia.' (p. 254) This attack on the Soviet Union, like the one in the *Sun*'s celebration of Orwell sixty-three years later, is largely for domestic consumption, aimed at 'the enemy within'. 'The working classes, especially those belonging to organised labour movements' are, the report claims, 'antagonistic to, and contemptuous of, literature', associating it with 'antimacassars, fish-knives and other unintelligible and futile trivialities of "middle-class culture" ', and rejecting academic literary study as an attempt ' "to side-track the working-class movement".' The committee concludes that 'the nation of which a considerable portion rejects this means of grace, and despises this great spiritual influence, must assuredly be heading to disaster.' (p. 252) For the class whose culture is represented in the Newbolt Report as 'Culture' itself, this disaster came close to arriving only five years later, with the 1926 General Strike.

* * *

17. In the blind spot of Orwell's criticism there are at least twenty things he never knew, or failed to interrelate, that would have rendered problematic his unwitting affirmation of the Arnold-Newbolt-Leavis line. These include the impact of the 'Hands Off Russia' movement on the Newbolt Report's attempt to produce a focus of national unity in the distinterested pursuit of literary culture; the origin of academic English Literature as a 'poor man's Classics' in the WEA colleges; Engels's comments on the role of such innovations in establishing a 'labour aristocracy' which would co-operate

with the bourgeoisie in times of crisis; the 1926 sell-out when trade union leaders capitulated to government at the moment when the General Strike was gathering momentum and trade unionists on strike committees up and down the country were gaining control of towns and villages in the face of 'every organ of local and central government, the police and army, radio and press, scabs, employers and fascists united as one instrument against the labour movement';[35] the recognition on the left, in the aftermath of the strike, of a failure to educate workers *politically* – in the theory and history of working-class struggle;[36] and finally Sir Henry Newbolt's direct appeal, in his presidential address to the English Association in 1928 and in the wake of 'our nine days' civil war', for a sense of national unity based not on social equality but on everyone *forgetting* that classes existed.[37] In the event 'literature', as an ideological formation centred in education, did not go the way of antimacassars, now rarely seen outside the first-class compartments on British Rail. Recent work by Renée Balibar, Dominique Laport, Etienne Balibar and Pierre Macherey confirms the part played by literary study in the education system's reproduction of the relations of production, a process which includes not only access to the riches of 'culture' for the successful minority but also the perpetuation, within the dominant ideology, of a class ejected from the system at an early stage which can experience the 'national' language and culture only in terms of an exclusion and a state of being tongue-tied to a 'basic' fragment.[38] This *process* of 'literature' remains, as Terry Eagleton argues, 'a crucial mechanism by which the language and ideology of an imperialist class establishes its hegemony.'[39] During this mechanism's great period of consolidation, Orwell appears in the guise of a classically-trained Old Etonian innocent abroad, loosely aware of the relationship between literature and state pedagogy but not of its extent and intricacy, nor of the concealed ideological work of the personal and 'disinterested' response. He sees Arnold only as a proponent of 'art for art's sake', instrumental in re-establishing links between English culture and the European mainstream. (*CEJL*, Vol. 2, p. 151) Newbolt appears only as the unintentionally comic minor poet of 'play up and play the game'. (*CEJL*, Vol. 1, pp. 561, 592) Leavis is the shadowy pedant, less implicated in the academy's *production* of 'literature' than in impeding what Orwell sees as the literary and critical imagination's natural course. There are only random observations and a failure, finally, to connect. The *Wigan Pier* proles are commended for their ability to 'see through ['education'] and reject it by a healthy instinct',[40] but elsewhere Orwell notes with approval that the standard of public education in England has risen. (*CEJL*, Vol. 2, p. 97) He recognizes, with Wyndham Lewis, that the English working class are 'branded on the tongue' (*CEJL*, Vol. 3, p. 19), but makes no connection between this and the hegemonic construction of a 'national' language and literary culture. Meanwhile, in another part of the Newbolt Report, the Divisional Inspector of Schools is pleased to announce that teachers of phonetics and voice production 'have gone some way towards getting rid of undesirable forms of London speech.' (p. 165)

* * *

18. Blair's legacy to criticism is the two discourses, each periodically displacing the other and offering no prospect of synthesis beyond continuing his own project of constructing a literary/historical subject 'Orwell' whose humanity and integrity rest in a refusal of the openly theoretical – the man who is more significant than his work,[41] the quirky combination of 'committed socialist' and 'conservative eccentric',[42] 'the wintry conscience of a generation',[43] the mythic bearer of an 'implacable honesty' which is 'an English characteristic – an honesty which is humorous, obstinate if not pig-headed, and, above all, somehow *sweet*.'[44] Whether this sweet English decency is to be recuperated by the right or reclaimed by the left is now largely immaterial. There are other ways of contesting 'Orwell' which refuse to refurbish the category of the autonomous subject in this way, and which may acknowledge, with Foucault or Derrida, that the rediscovery of *writing*, text, discourse implies a fading of 'man' as the privileged, transcendental signified – an assimilation of Blair, Kenneth Miles and P.S. Burton, perhaps, into the divided,

eternal and omni-directional 'H. Lewis Allways', Orwell unbound.[45]

*   *   *

19. Such critical practices would negate themselves by seeking Orwell's posthumous approval. And there is no doubt that any successor in *Nineteen Eighty-Four* to the liberal academy might well have borne at least a strong superficial resemblance to the multi-disciplinary field loosely defined in 1984 as contemporary critical theory. The Lacanian and Althusserian subject moves towards confirming Orwell's fear that what he called 'the autonomous individual' was going to be 'stamped out of existence' (*CEJL*, Vol. 1, p. 576), questioning the integrity of 'the few cubic centimetres inside your skull' considered inviolable by Winston Smith, 'the last man in Europe.' (*1984*, pp. 27,234) A number of other key oppositions present themselves: Orwell's anxieties about the disappearance of an objective history against the contemporary view of historical discourse as inevitably a production of the past *for* the present;[46] Derridean *écriture* or Barthes's view of writing as 'an intransitive verb' against Orwell's wish to move writing closer to speech and the prophetic reply of the insufferable youth in 'Inside the Whale' – 'My dear aunt ... one doesn't write *about* anything, one just *writes*';[47] 'The Prevention of Literature' and the Macherey/Balibar prevention of just such a concept as literature from functioning 'naturally' and obscuring its own work as an ideological form; Orwell's view of ideology as a dogmatic system of ideas, against an ideology which pervades the subject's consciousness as a lived, imaginary relation to the real conditions of existence.[48] Beyond these areas of contention are the stereotypes that pop up in Orwell's text like tin ducks in a shooting-gallery, joining theory, intellectualism, socialism and ideas of sexual aberration in the broad category of the 'left-wing trendy', which remains powerfully operative while right-wing trendies from *Scrutiny* to Scruton pass theoretically invisible and relatively unmolested.[49] This series of moving targets includes 'Pinks', 'pansies', feminists,[50] Quakers, 'shock-headed Marxists chewing polysyllables', bearded vegetarians, fruit-juice drinkers, proponents of birth-control

and homeopathic medicines, nudists, pacifists, 'Labour Party backstairs crawlers', people who do yoga and live in Welwyn Garden City, and those who wear pistachio-coloured shirts or the ubiquitous sandals so detested by the man H.G. Wells described as 'an English Trotskyist writer with enormous feet.'[51] Somewhere in this list there will be a random hit against anyone involved, however marginally, in the present transition from an increasingly discredited tradition of 'disinterested' Eng. Lit. to the study of language, ideology and cultural forms anticipated in Orwell's 'semi-sociological' work. But the damage is in the past, and this handing of ammunition to what Orwell regarded elsewhere as the class-enemy is well documented.[53] The best course after 1984 is to take what is useful from Orwell's more progressive criticism, use it to contextualize the conservative strain, and look to your footwear: 'My kid made sure he was some kind of enemy agent ... She spotted he was wearing a funny kind of shoes – said she'd never seen anyone wearing shoes like that before ... Pretty smart for a nipper of seven, eh?' (*1984*, p. 53)

* * *

20. He sat back. A sense of complete helplessness had descended upon him. To begin with, he did not know with any certainty that this *was* 1984. It must be round about that date, since he was fairly sure that his age was thirty-nine, and he believed that he had been born in 1944 or 1945 but it was never possible nowadays to pin down any date within a year or two. (*1984*, pp. 11-12)

Perhaps it was 1985 after all, or 1986 – another year or two to drag out the commercial and critical Orwellfest, a stay of execution for tabloid Big Brother nightmares, and then? On the leader page of the *Sun* for 2 January 1984, to the left of 'What we must all do to keep Big Brother at bay' and above '20 THINGS YOU NEVER KNEW ABOUT GEORGE ORWELL', there is a cartoon. Three women gossip and drink tea, ignoring a diminutive vicar. On the left, spread across a settee and snoring, is an unshaven man in his vest, toes protruding through the holes in his socks and left hand trailing between beer-can, cigarette packet and ashtray. A fat woman in slippers and apron is saying: 'IF BIG BROTHER IS WATCHING MY HUSBAND, HE'S IN FOR A BORING YEAR!' British workers are shiftless anyway, so if this one is unemployed he is probably not too concerned. Women go on nattering and drinking tea. These people would not repay the trouble of communist police-state surveillance but, through the vigilance of their betters, it will not happen anyway. This is England. Big Brother is not watching. 'While literary critics have been cultivating sensibility in the minority,' writes Terry Eagleton, 'large segments of the media have been busy trying to devastate it in the majority.'[53] It is no longer enough to assume that a reading of *Nineteen Eighty-Four* (or *Animal Farm*, or *Romeo and Juliet* for that matter) will refine the sensibilities and enhance the critical awareness of English students – particularly the large majority who will not enter higher education – or equip them to read *against* the *Sun*, television commercials, ITN News and the whole range of discourses mobilized within the culture industry. And when Orwell's *annus mirabilis* is finally over there should be no further recourse to questions solely concerned with what he 'really meant', the weakness of his characteriz-ation, the tendency of politics to interfere with the story – the sort of normative academic exercise which accomplishes its own form of devastation.[54] 1984 will intervene, the century's most textualized year, and one which re-presents Orwell's text as an incrustation of discourses and practices constituted as new objects of study for a post-post-Newbolt English: the language of the Data Protection Bill and DHSS leaflets;[55] the reporting of Cruise, the Greenham Common peace camps and the miners' strike; the final capitulation of the Soviet state broadcasting system to the allure of 'The Benny Hill Show'; and the historic alliance of the High Court, *The Times* and the National Front to protect 'academic order and disinterested teaching'[56] in the Humanities Faculty of North London Polytechnic. In this new, more fluid canon there will be room, at least temporarily, for the cartoon on the *Sun*'s first editorial page of 1984, which has a density and intertextuality of its own. At one level it blocks the saturnalian release and subversion attributed by Orwell to truly 'popular' versions of this type of art (*CEJL*, Vol. 2, pp. 193-4), simply reaffirming the dominant constructions of morality, class and political freedom. But it also reaches into the areas repressed in the text around it – into the twenty things you never knew about George Orwell that you are never likely to read about in the *Sun*. The cartoon is a pastiche of the style described by Orwell in 'The Art of Donald McGill', with its 'heavy lines and empty spaces', 'grotesque, staring, blatant quality', 'overwhelming vulgarity', and 'utter lowness of mental atmosphere'. (*CEJL*, Vol. 2, pp. 184-5) The same pot-bellied husband appears in any number of seaside postcards of the 1920s and 30s, peering across the sand and saying 'I can't see my little Willy'. His wife is one of McGill's 'monstrously parodied' women 'with bottoms like Hottentots' (*CEJL*, Vol. 2, p. 184), idealized by Orwell in *Nineteen Eighty-Four* as the indomitable spirit of the English working class: 'a monstrous woman ... with heavy red forearms', 'no mind ... only strong arms, a warm heart, and a fertile belly', 'powerful mare-like buttocks', ' "She's beautiful", he murmured', 'Out of these mighty loins a race of conscious beings must one day come' (*1984*, pp. 123, 187-8). The cartoon pursues these references relentlessly, in the stuffed seagull which decorates the hat of one of the visiting women ('deliberately ugly, the faces grinning and vacuous,' *CEJL*, Vol. 2, p. 185), the imbecile, midget clergyman ('always a nervous idiot' *CEJL*, Vol. 2, p. 187), and the naming of Big Brother himself within an inversion of the 'warm, decent, deeply human atmosphere' of Orwell's sentimentalized working-class interiors:

> ... the fire glows in the open range and dances mirrored in the steel fender ... Father, in shirt sleeves, sits in the rocking chair at one side of the fire reading the racing finals, and Mother sits on the other side with her sewing, and the children are happy with a pennorth of mint humbugs, and the dog lolls roasting himself on the rag mat. (*Wigan Pier*, p. 104)

In the cartoon, Mother no longer knows her place, and the sleeping Father, newspaper open at a page which bears a remarkable resemblance to the one we are looking at, now reads the *Sun*. Such self-reference may well bring a minor burst of *jouissance* to the refined deconstructed sensibility, a pleasure in textuality or in the *Sun* as 'literature'. But it is only the first step on a path which leads back to the *political* imperative of Orwell's best criticism in the 1930s and 1940s, and then forward to the conjunction of theory and sign-breaking his work never fully achieved: 'no denunciation without an appropriate method of detailed analysis, no semiology which cannot, in the last analysis, be acknowledged as *semioclasm*.'[57]

Notes

1 In S. Orwell and I. Angus (eds.) *The Collected Essays, Journalism and Letters of George Orwell*, Vol. 1, Harmondsworth, 1970, p. 516. Referred to hereafter as '*CEJL*'.

2 *CEJL*, Vol. 1, p. 26; Vol. 4, p. 167; Vol. 1, p. 492.

3 *CEJL*, Vol. 2, p. 99; Vol. 3, pp. 431-2, Vol. 4, pp. 441-2; Vol. 1, pp. 366, 392 and 421.

4 *CEJL*, Vol. 4, p. 464.

5 C. Mercer and J. Radford (eds.), 'An Interview with Pierre Macherey', *Red Letters*, No. 5, pp. 6-9.

6 'Judy Wade', *Sun*, 2 January 1984, p.6.

7 See P. Macherey, *A Theory of Literary Production* (tr.G.Wall), London, 1978, pp. 85-90.

8 B. Crick, *George Orwell: A Life,* Harmondsworth, 1982, p. 45.

9 *Nineteen Eighty-Four*, Harmondsworth, 1983, p. 263.

10 *CEJL*, Vol. 1, pp. 491-2, 557-61; Vol. 2, pp. 149 ff.

11 I. Deutscher, '1984 – The Mysticism of Cruelty', in S. Hynes (ed.), *Twentieth Century Interpretations of 1984*, Englewood Cliffs, 1971, p. 30.

12 See below notes 41 and 54.

13 *CEJL*, Vol. 4, p. 435; Kenneth Muir, 'Shakespeare and Politics', in A. Kettle (ed.), *Shakespeare in a Changing World*, London, 1964, p. 74.

14 See J. Meyers (ed.),*George Orwell: The Critical Heritage*, London, 1975, pp. 19-20; Conor Cruise O'Brien, *Writers and Politics*, London, 1965, p. 32.

15 See *CEJL*, Vol. 1, pp. 348, 366; Vol. 4, pp. 215-8.

16 Letter dated 14 March 1938 (*CEJL*, Vol. 1, p. 343)

17 *Keep the Aspidistra Flying*, Harmondsworth, 1962, p. 13.

18 'Exclusive Club', *Observer*, 6 February 1949, p. 3. Not included in *CEJL*.

19 See L. Althusser, 'Ideology and Ideological State Apparatuses', *Lenin and Philosophy*, (tr.B.Brewster), London, 1971, pp. 134-136, *passim*.

20 Q.D. Leavis, *Scrutiny* review included in Meyers (ed.), op.cit., p. 188.

21 Ibid., pp. 187-188.

22 Q.D. Leavis's venom is directed towards Stephen Spender and *Criterion* in particular. See also I. Ansimov's review (*Pravda*, 12 May 1950) in Meyers (ed.), op.cit., pp. 282-283.

23 See Conor Cruise O'Brien, review of *CEJL* in Meyers (ed.), op.cit., pp. 346-348.

24 Cf. Raymond Williams, '*Nineteen Eighty-Four* in 1984', *Marxism Today*, January 1984, p.14; P. Chilton, 'Newspeak: It's the Real Thing', in C. Aubrey and Chilton (eds.), *Nineteen Eighty-Four in 1984*, London, 1983, pp. 36-41.

25 My intention here is to turn Orwell's text against itself, not to endorse this view of the relationship between 'language' and 'thought'.

26 See *Nineteen Eighty-Four*, pp. 265-266.

27 See Francis Mulhern, *The Moment of Scrutiny*, London, 1979, pp. 57-63; Terry Eagleton, *Criticism and Ideology*, London, 1976, pp. 24, 40.

28 See C. Baldick, *The Social Mission of English Studies*, Oxford, 1983, pp. 89-107; B. Doyle, 'The Hidden History of English Studies', in P. Widdowson (ed.), *Re-reading English*, London, 1982, p. 17ff. T. Hawkes, 'Telmah: To the Sunderland Station', *Encounter*, April 1983, pp. 50-60.

29 Board of Education, *The Teaching of English in England*, London, 1921, p. 202.

30 Matthew Arnold, *Complete Prose Works*, Vol. III, R.H. Super (ed.), Ann Arbor, 1962, pp. 258, 282.

31 This does not exclude New Criticism. See T. Hawkes, *Structuralism and Semiotics*, London, 1977, pp. 151-156.

32 cf., 'Shakespeare was like most Englishmen in having a code of conduct, but no world view, no philosophical faculty.' (*CEJL*, Vol. 2, p. 155)

33 See *CEJL*, Vol. 4, pp. 340-3.

34 John Dover Wilson. See Hawkes, art.cit., pp. 55-57.

35 J. Foster, 'British Imperialism and the Labour Aristocracy', in J. Skelley (ed.), *The General Strike 1926*, London, 1976, p. 3.

36 H. Francis, 'South Wales', in Skelley (ed.), op.cit., p. 232.

37 P. Howarth, *Play Up and Play the Game*, London, 1973, p. 12.

38 E. Balibar and P. Macherey, 'On Literature as an Ideological Form', in R. Young (ed.), *Untying the Text: A Post-Structuralist Anthology*, London, 1981, pp. 79-99; R. Balibar, *Les Français Fictifs*, Paris, 1974; R. Balibar and D. Laporte, *Le Français National*, Paris, 1974.

39 Eagleton, op.cit., p 55.

40 *The Road to Wigan Pier*, Harmondsworth, 1962, p. 103. Referred to hereafter as '*Wigan Pier*'.

41 See A. Zwerdling, *Orwell and the Left*, New Haven and London, 1974, p. 143; R. Williams, *Orwell*, London, 1971, pp. 52, 94. cf. *CEJL*, Vol. I, p. 23.

42 Conor Cruise O'Brien, op.cit., p. 33.

43 V.S. Pritchett's *New Statesmen* obituary, in Meyers (ed.), op.cit., p. 294.

44 Malcolm Muggeridge, *Esquire* review of *CEJL* (March 1969), in Meyers (ed.), op.cit., p. 360.

45 In November 1932, before the publication of *Down and Out in Paris and London*, Blair offered 'Miles', 'Burton', 'Orwell' and 'Allways' to Gollancz as a choice of pseudonyms. P. Stansky and W. Abrahams, *The Unknown Orwell*, London, 1972, p. 254. See also M. Foucault, *The Order of Things*, London, 1970, pp. 385-387; J. Derrida, *Writing and Difference*, (tr. A.

Bass), London, 1978, pp. 279-280, 293.

46 See *Homage to Catalonia*, Harmondsworth, 1962, pp. 233-7. cf. C. Lévi-Strauss, *The Savage Mind*, London, 1972, pp. 256-9, and Terry Eagleton, *Walter Benjamin*, London, 1981, pp.51-52.

47 *CEJL*, Vol. 3, p. 165; Vol. 1, p. 557.

48 Althusser, art.cit., p. 187.

49 There is only one reference to *Scrutiny* in the four volumes of *CEJL*, and none to Q.D. or F.R. Leavis.

50 Readers interested in Orwell and feminism should take *CEJL*, Vol. 1, p. 160 and Vol. 2, p. 191, n.20 into account, also *Nineteen Eighty-Four*, pp. 110-112, 126-127 and Jenny Taylor, 'Desire is Thoughtcrime', in Aubrey and Chilton (eds.), op.cit., pp. 24-32.

51 See *Wigan Pier*, pp. 152, 195-196; *CEJL*, Vol. 1, pp. 245-6, and numerous index entries on 'Pinks', Intelligensia, left-wing etc.

52 O'Brien, op.cit., pp. 32-33; E.P. Thompson, *Out of Apathy*, London, 1960, pp. 158ff. Orwell's sceptical view of historical materialism, the 'pea-and-thimble trick with those three mysterious entities, thesis, antithesis and synthesis' leads not to an escape from theory but to the conservatism of a cyclical view of history and the truism 'power corrupts': see *CEJL*, Vol. 1, pp. 489-9; Zwerdling, op.cit., pp. 27-28; and G. Woodcock, *The Crystal Spirit*, Harmondsworth, 1970, p. 128.

53 Terry Eagleton, *Literary Theory*, Oxford, 1983, pp. 215-216.

54 ' "The political message is constantly getting in the way of the story and this diminishes its interest and excitement." How far do you agree with this view of *1984*?' (London A Level English Literature paper, Summer 1972); ' "Characterisation in this novel is negligible: it is completely subordinated to the political message." Do you agree?' (London A Level, Winter 1973). This type of Orwell question, reaffirming a particular ideology of 'literature' rather than a *directly* political propaganda, predominates in public examination papers.

55 See Chilton, art.cit. and other essays in the 'Communications' and 'Technologies' sections of Aubrey and Chilton (eds.), op.cit.

56 See 'Totalitarian Nursery', *The Times*, 18 May 1984, p. 11 and Roger Scruton, 'The Enemy in the Classroom', *The Times*, 22 May 1984, p. 14. This list covers only the first half of 1984.

57 Roland Barthes, *Mythologies*, (tr. A. Lavers), London, 1973, p. 9.

Alan Brown

Examining Orwell: Political and Literary Values in Education

A good deal of hard work has gone into producing the 'George Orwell' who has featured so large in the 'macabre celebrations' of 1984.[1] The earliest efforts were put in by Eric Blair, whose choice of a pseudonym was one element in the construction of a literary voice. From Blair into Orwell is a road well trodden by biographers: a personal journey which traces the evolving values of an individual. But biographical criticism can take us only so far in an understanding of the 'Orwell' phenomenon. Concerned with the 'raw material' of Orwell's life and times, it has little to say about how this material has been selectively forged into a powerful instrument of political dogma.

There is a certain continuity between much that Orwell wrote and the outlines of a later, 'Orwellian' voice, but the latter did not become part of political culture without going through the mills of mass media, of the education system: institutions of 'learning' and 'taste'. The significance of 'Orwell' as a weapon of Cold War propaganda, as a means of persuading a generation of the essential futility of radical social change, go far beyond the intentions of a single biography. Rather than seeking out the details of Orwell's existence, we need to look again at the necessity of his invention.

Focusing on the use of Orwell's texts in education both restricts and expands the topic of this essay. It cuts out a range of media, but it brings to the foreground questions about the political content of teaching practices. This is particularly important in dealing with a subject, 'literature', which works through techniques of dialogue and persuasion. It may be acceptable to convince year upon year of examinees that Shakespeare's tragic characters are brought down by a 'flaw' in their nature, less so to teach *Animal Farm* as the artistic evidence of a 'tragic flaw' in political idealism. The politics of literature teaching are not, in any case, confined to interventions on 'political' topics. In its very form, literary education can be a subtle and coercive medium for instilling beliefs and values.

Discussions of literature in schools are tied to examinations. This may not exhaust the possibilities of teaching but it always defines them. Students are required to attain a certain level, to succeed, as in any competitive environment. They are also required to enter into a language of 'personal response', 'self-expression', to have 'opinions' and 'tastes'. They are at the same time being instructed and being asked to supply the positive content of their instruction. This can be an exciting and creative process – equally it can be a manipulative form of 'thought policing'.

At their worst, the masonic rituals of literary criticism work to persuade students to reproduce acceptable ideas *as* personal response, to internalise attitudes received from above as subjective points of view. Certainly, there is enough outward motivation for examinees to perform this 'doublethink', and if the ideas and values are themselves presented as simple common sense, resistance becomes hard to imagine.

It is characteristic of the 'Orwell' persona that it conveys a neutral, received wisdom, of 'objective' and 'human' truths. Ideas of Orwell as 'the man of good will', 'the conscience of an age',[2] are supported by a vocabulary of belief which passes for self-evidence and everyday language. If the techniques of persuasion familiar to literary criticism can be termed 'masonic', this is not because they rest on arcane symbols understood only by an élite. The very opposite, popular critical wisdom is spoken in a language which 'goes without saying'. Its apparent proximity to common sense invites us to adopt it, uncritically, as our own.

Orwell's popularity as material for school study makes him unique amongst his contemporaries. In the present, exceptional year, his work appears on all of the Examining Boards at O or A Level, but his presence throughout the post-war decades has been constant. In putting together a profile of Orwell in the education system, I have relied on two main sources: examination questions drawn from the different Boards over the past thirty years and a wide selection of Study Aids, primarily on *Animal Farm* and *Nineteen Eighty-Four*.[3] I would not claim that the Study Aids reproduce the details of teaching Orwell in any given or likely situation. What they offer is an uncontroversial reading of plots and themes, a fund of typicality in a language without questions. The remarkable unanimity of views across these different books is the strongest reason for taking their arguments seriously. They provide an adequate complement to the preoccupations of exam questions on Orwell as they have emerged across the Boards and over the years.

There is no suggestion here of a 'conspiracy' in the production of an 'Orwell' myth. To believe in a conscious, hidden intention behind the consensus of views would lead to totalitarian fantasies of the kind which *Nineteen Eighty-Four* deals in. A vital part of the development of political myths in a democratic, pluralist society consists in the form of debate: not in the willful suppression of contrary views but in the persistence of shared and unexamined assumptions.

There is a wide plurality of views on Orwell from conflicting political stances. The most popular account, amply expressed by Lionel Trilling's introduction to *Homage to Catalonia*,[4] presents the writer as a personification of moral values. But there is no shortage of other, more sceptical, iconoclastic versions.[5] Should these latter accounts of Orwell succeed in dominating the literary-political consensus, another version will be passed on to successive generations, as the truth about Orwell, as 'Orwell' himself.

At the basis of the myth, it is taken for granted that we are dealing with a single personality. In so far as we reflect on the political world in which Orwell wrote, this is in order to judge the veracity of his account. By placing the 'personal' before the 'political' in this way, by stressing from all sides the primary significance of Orwell as individual, the consensus of views receives its grounding. Arguments about Orwell's 'honesty', 'realism', 'stamina',[6] all work to strengthen the politically debilitating assumption that social conflict is secondary, beyond the individual. This cheap transcendence is the mundane work of literary criticism. It sets the agenda for debate and ensures that our perceptions of history and subjectivity are mediated by unchanging, timeless 'truths', of human nature, morality and fate. The price of such wisdom is a studied ignorance of the ways in which 'timeless truths' are themselves fabricated through political culture.

Inside the Myth

As a proportion of the exam questions on Orwell at O and A Level, those which deal with the author himself are in a minority. The largest group deals with *Animal Farm* and, at O Level, the emphasis is more on the characters of donkeys and dictators than on the author as such. Nevertheless, I begin with a reading of the author as character because the myth of 'Orwellian' values bears directly on the teaching of primary texts.

Questions about the author derive from a limited selection of essays and autobiographical accounts which have appeared on syllabuses: *Inside the Whale and Other Essays, Homage to Catalonia, Selected Writings*.[7] The following are taken from the Associated Examining Board, 1971-2 and deal with *Inside the Whale*:

What impression have you formed of George Orwell from your reading of this book? Illustrate your answer by careful reference to his work ...

Orwell has been called 'the social conscience of his age'. Explain this remark and comment on it ...

Orwell has been praised for his 'wide sympathies'. Illustrate this by comparing two essays from this collection.

The second and third questions help to suggest the right way of answering the first. Orwell is an embracing figure of 'conscience' and 'sympathies'. This is not simply open to discussion. The last question asks for illustrations of 'wide sympathies' which are assumed to be in evidence. The concern with Orwell as representative of an epoch is paralleled by interest in his personal qualities:

> Do you think that Orwell emerges from *Homage to Catalonia* as a brave man or not?[8]

The oscillation between individual and social characteristics has a purpose. If Orwell is to act as the representative voice for an entire generation, his credentials must first be established:

> He was an observer, keeping as fair-minded as possible about what he saw, remaining responsible to objective truth. (*York Notes, Nineteen Eighty-Four*, p. 8)
> In short, throughout his adult life and work, George Orwell remained a fiercely honest man, even with himself. (*Coles Notes, Animal Farm*, p. 5)
> Orwell was sociable and home-loving, believing in family life ... Orwell was selfless, naturally mild and gentle ... Orwell loved animals ... Exaggeratedly perhaps, but significantly, one of his friends called him a 'saint'. (*Brodies Notes, Animal Farm*, pp. 12-13)

The 'Orwell' myth involves a type of canonisation. A version of the individual as embodiment of human values leads inevitably to his status as a 'trustworthy guide'.[9] It is a curious rhetorical mixture: moral values of 'bravery', 'honesty', 'sympathy' are linked directly to criteria of 'objectivity' and 'straightforward fact'. Implicit here is the belief that moral purity is inseparable from truth as such. If we want to know the 'facts' of an era we must seek out its saints:

> The writer, as Orwell sees him, especially the prose writer, is the guardian of simplicity, objectivity and straightforward fact, and so, in our age, he becomes the protector of the human spirit. (*York Notes, Nineteen Eighty-Four*, p. 8)

The binding together of morality and objectivity works to erase our sense of a point of view in reading Orwell. Given the mixture of truth to fact and truth to self, statements attributed to the author take on an oracular and incontestable value. In the following extract, the neutrality of this 'Orwellian' voice is put to a political use:

> Basing his argument on personal experience and commonsense, but mostly on observed fact, Orwell comes to the conclusion that the socialism of his time was mostly unrealistic and irrelevant. (*York Notes, Animal Farm*, p. 8)

Who can contradict 'commonsense', 'fact', 'experience'? The author's authority is conveyed by an insistence on personal experience and impartial knowledge. We are led back to Eton and Burma, Wigan, Spain and Paris, across the *curriculum vitae* of the writer's 'experience'. The authenticity of what is lived is counterbalanced by a language of detachment – 'observed fact'. Orwell 'lived' the socialism of his time, applied his normative mind to its traits and 'comes to the conclusion ...' Led along by the empiricist appeal of this argument it becomes hard to refute Orwell's verdict. This at least would be so for students approaching the politics of Orwell's generation for the first time. The total absence of doubt or qualification must incline them to swallow opinion and even bigotry as acceptable truth. The following notorious extract from *The Road to Wigan Pier* is a reminder of Orwell's manner of discussing the socialist 'type':

> ... that dreary tribe of high-minded women and sandal-wearers and bearded fruit-juice drinkers who come flocking towards the smell of 'progress' like bluebottles to a dead cat.[10]

A further aspect of the personality myth stresses 'realism', the pain of truth. Experience is not merely travel; it is also, in its religious sense, suffering through knowledge. 'Orwell' is characterised across the range of biographical glosses in Study Aids as a stoic figure, seeing the truth (the worst) and refusing to flinch from it:

> Orwell never deluded himself ... His burning love of truth, as he saw it, made him an uncomfortable goad to the indifferent, complacent or malevolent. (*Brodies Notes, Animal Farm*, pp. 11-12)

... when in 1941 many people were praising the cleverness of Stalin's foreign policy ... Orwell condemned it as treacherous and opportunistic. Nor would he silence his criticisms when the Soviet Union entered the Second World War on the side of the allies. This was precisely the moment when he wrote *Animal Farm*. (*Longmans Study Text, Animal Farm*, p. xxii)

There is no suggestion here that words such as 'treacherous' and 'opportunistic' might be insufficient, even misleading as an account of Soviet foreign policy. Everything encourages us to read history as a morality play, a melodrama of extremes: honesty versus treachery. Adjectives such as 'burning' colour the picture of Orwell's commitment to truth as religious in nature and intensity. His speaking-out of unpalatable truths is an imperative, a vocation. There is no pause to reflect on the politics of his interpretations; we are led back once more to the individual source from which they stem.

In this way, the 'eternal' role of the artist as truth-teller is harnessed to a political function. Experience, common sense, realism and honesty are each facets of a total and manufactured personality. Taken together, they provide a platform from which political attitudes can be put across in education without suspicion of bias or indoctrination. Putting 'Orwell's' point of view (that of reason and decency) is not really putting a point of view at all. It is a way of seeing behind the transience of political conflict to the more basic truths of human nature and morality.

The reduction of politics to personality moves from comments on specific historical moments to embrace Orwell's wider 'philosophy'. Here, the individual is all-pervasive:

The chief theoretical difficulty for Orwell was caused by his awareness of individual human differences, which interfere with the abstract group philosophy of socialism. He was himself a courageous individualist, and he feared the loss of freedom that he knew socialism involved. (*Coles Notes, Nineteen Eighty-Four*, pp. 7-8)

Reading through the pathos of the 'Orwellian' dilemma we may not pick up the damaging assumptions on which the argument rests. Socialism as 'abstract', as 'the loss of individual freedom' is presented as 'known' and 'feared'. The value of elevating Orwell to heroic and mythical proportions is nothing so much as this: politics are reduced to the stage on which the writer performs and, following the writer, we make few complaints about the scenery.

Seeing the world through the eyes of an individual creates a world of personal values. At the extreme, these values are used to embrace the whole political field. Orwell as the representative voice of an age is shown to contain the differing and contradictory strands of his time. The conflicting elements achieve a precarious harmony in the 'Orwell' persona: socialist/critic of socialism, idealist/realist, subjective participant/objective observer. It is left to the figure of 'Orwell', finally, to resolve the great debates of left and right, to assert a middle way between ideologies and conflicting forces:

> ... creativity for him [Orwell] was first and foremost a matter of being able to see things as they are. Because socialism often considered that freedom was a possible danger to the movement, Orwell came to feel that socialism could easily have a kind of fascism inside it ... To Orwell the freedom to be different within society was what mattered. It is the main theme of *Nineteen Eighty-Four*. (*York Notes, Nineteen Eighty-Four*, p. 11)

> Orwell came to believe that socialism could easily have a type of fascism in it ... to Orwell the freedom to be different within one's society was all important. This feature of socialism, of having an inbuilt fascism inside it, can be seen in *Animal Farm* ... (*York Notes, Animal Farm*, pp. 10-11)

> Orwell thus revealed the psychological sameness of communism and fascism and did not shrink from criticising the abuse of socialism ... (*Longmans Study Text, Animal Farm*, pp.xxii-xxiii)

Violently opposed political theories and practices are here reduced to a 'psychological sameness', that is, to a dismissive value-judgement based on no more than a hypothetical model of human nature. Having dissolved the contradictions between 'communism' and 'fascism' in either a historical or theoretical form, the way is open for a socialism itself devoid of content. Orwell's socialism can be reduced to a Victorian value of 'concern' and charity towards others, to a moral subjectivism which calls for no more than a sentimental response:

> Typically, Orwell related every experience back to his overriding concern for the poor. (*Longmans Study Text, Animal Farm*, p. xvii)

Socialism as moral piety is perfectly acceptable inside the Orwell myth. But any attempt to conceive of society and subjectivity as susceptible to organised change must be perceived solely as 'threat'. Socialism is assimilated to fascism; 'Orwell' does not shrink from the 'fact', nor do the 'facts' prevent him from being a socialist. The moral fable within which history and ideology are suspended applies equally well to *Animal Farm* and *Nineteen Eighty-Four*.[11] The song remains the same: human nature is constant and its finest embodiment in the 'Orwell' persona serves only to remind us of this intractable truth of the status quo.

I am not attacking the 'lived life' of Eric Blair at this point. How much he actually personified the virtues attributed to him in popular myth seems to me a question both impossible to answer and unhelpful to pursue. My concern is with the political work carried out beneath the banner of 'Orwellian' values. The fantasy of his human attributes, refined to a point of perfection, provides an absolute standard against which political events and beliefs can be judged. The reader is urged to identify his or her self with the innate values of 'Orwell', and to espouse the belief in the primacy of the individual which he represents. All roads lead back to the human subject in isolation, above history and (in Orwell's case) above criticism. Questions of Soviet history, of the Spanish Civil War, the Depression, the 'nature' of communism, socialism, fascism, can then be answered from a viewpoint which systematically erases the tracks of its own political bias. Teaching Orwell for examinations will not be a matter of overt dogma, but rather a process of filtering the political field through the categories of orthodox literary criticism.

If, as the 'Orwell' persona asserts, the good writer is the 'true' writer, then an appreciation of literary qualities will be tied to a view of political reality. This reality is not presented in political terms. Devoid of conflict, of theoretical content and historical detail, it is expressed as the fund of established truths, natural and unchanging: truths of character, morality, of irony, of 'life' itself:

> It is the business of the satirist to expose the follies of mankind and to remind us all of our essential humanity.[12]

The art of satire, of common sense, of the 'Orwell' industry, is to remind us of what we know already and to resign us to its inevitability. If political change is an illusion, we must derive our comfort from an aesthetics of constancy and inertia.

The ABC of Apathy

Animal Farm is the most popular of Orwell's texts with examiners. It is set almost exclusively for O Level study, *Nineteen Eighty-Four* being largely reserved for A Level study. *Animal Farm*, so the story goes, can be read either as political satire or, on its own terms, as a 'thoroughly entertaining story'.[13] This might seem to recommend its use as an introductory text for O Level literature students, the qualities of 'simplicity' and 'charm' making the book inherently readable. However, any student who approaches the exam with knowledge only of the plot and pleasure in the story is unlikely to fare well. An ability to regurgitate the equations of a Cold War wisdom is taken for granted in most exams. The demand is either stated overtly or couched in a language of 'symbolic meaning' and 'satirical purpose'. Below are four questions on *Animal Farm* taken consecutively from the London Board, O Level, summer and winter 1964:

Summer 1964:

a) A fable is defined as 'a story especially with animals as characters, conveying a moral by indirect means'. By reference to *three* episodes or characters show how far *Animal Farm* fits this definition of a fable.

b) Give an account of the building of the Windmill and its interruptions; show how far this affected the animals and what, in real life, it is meant to represent.

Winter 1964:

a) Describe the origin of the seven commandments, and give an account of the changes they underwent later. What was Orwell's satire directed against in this part of the book?

b) Write an essay defending *Animal Farm* against a reader who tells you that it is 'merely anti-communist propaganda'. Illustrate your answer with detailed reference to the book.

It is possible to answer the first of these questions without specific reference to Russian politics; the fable can be stressed as about 'revolution in general'. This reading, which relies on a prior knowledge of the Russian 'example', is looked at more closely further on. The second question asserts that 'real life' is behind the book and might be answered by reference to Soviet industrialisation and the Five Year Plans. The third question is looking for details of propaganda techniques and the rewriting of history, as attributed to the 'communist state'. With the final question, the student's grasp of 'real life' is taken as read and the task is to say what *more* than 'anti-communist propaganda' the book is. Students are not invited to advance the 'propaganda' argument, but only to refute it.

The political effectiveness of *Animal Farm* derives largely from its allegorical form. If, as is assumed in much educational material on the book, an allegory is a simple equivalence between the 'symbolic' and the 'real' (Napoleon=Stalin, Manor Farm=Russia), then the student's task will be primarily one of rote-learning. The ticking off of relations is at the lowest level what is required. What is simply asserted is that the correspondences are valid, that

Old Major's speech corresponds to the thought of Marx ...
Battle of the Cowshed: corresponds to the counter-revolutionary war which raged in Russia ... The sale of timber to Fredrick of Pinchfield: corresponds to the Nazi-Soviet pact of 1939 ... (*York Notes, Animal Farm*, p. 30)

But this entire exercise, heavily documented across the different 'crib' books, heavily encouraged by the form of questions, is not in itself adequate as an instrument of political dogma. The skeleton of correspondences needs to be supported by a wider critical account, of Marx, of communism, of revolution in general:

> Marx was an idealist, dreaming of a paradise on earth in which all men were free and equal and enjoyed a good standard of living. (*Coles Notes, Animal Farm*, pp. 9-10)

> ... communism is idealistic. Its ideas are mainly the inspiration of Karl Marx, a German economist, and he was an idealist, dreaming of a utopian paradise in which all men should be free and equal. (*Longmans Study Text, Animal Farm*, pp. xx-xxi)

The characterisation of Marx operates at a very crude level of argument. Words such as 'dreaming' and 'idealistic' carry the weight of what argument there is. But the caricature becomes more effective when embodied in episodes from the text. The coherence and detail of the fable create an impression of substance. Early in *Animal Farm*, Old Major the prize Boar recounts his 'dream'. He calls on the animals to struggle for their freedom and reminds them of their equality:

> His [Major's] speech is a wonderfully concise account of Marxist socialist theory. The idealistic nature of this theory is cleverly pointed to in the tiny episode of the rats. While Major is speaking four rats appear from their holes and the dogs rush at them ... (*York Notes, Animal Farm*, p. 14)

The student is urged to identify Marxist theory with a short speech in an animal fable and to appreciate the skill of its refutation in an incident from 'Tom and Jerry'. The stupidity of this account should not blind us to its effective force. There is something very reassuring in this oscillation between human and animal 'nature', and, with no further context of judgement likely, students may have little incentive to go beyond the level of their instruction.

Why is *Animal Farm* taught in this way? It could be argued that if questions are centred on a version of Russian history, on a critique of communism, of revolution in general, this is as it should be. Its author intended it as such. How else than as a damning allegory of Soviet communism could the book be taught? The apparent fairness of this appeal to the author's intentions begs several questions about teaching practices and the idea of an author's 'purpose'.

If Orwell's intentions are cited as justification for the political slant in teaching *Animal Farm*, they must be admitted to bear on an external, historical world. This must certainly be the case for an author who, by all accounts, was concerned to 'expose the myth' about recent Soviet history. If *Animal Farm* is read, with its author's assumed purposes in mind, as an attempt to counter the widespread pro-Russian feeling which was then current,[14] the context has manifestly changed since 1945. If the book was designed to present a different viewpoint, the difference no longer exists as such. In a Cold War world, Orwell's polemic reproduces rather than counters popular myth and, in the absence of its polemical context, the author's intentions cannot be treated as simply portable.

Lacking an alternative viewpoint against which to be read, the book's argument reads as soliloquy, its 'truths' as no more than a reinforcement of views which can be gleaned from most tabloid papers, most of the time. No attempt is made in the range of Study Aids (nor encouraged by the form of exam questions) to debate the account of history portrayed in *Animal Farm*. The relation between book and reality is conveyed as a simple parallelism, with the student required to pick off points of correspondence. This practice, which cannot be called other than indoctrination, is unjustifiable in terms of authorial intention. Nor can it be claimed that it would be too much for O Level students to wrestle with the complexities of Russian history and Marxist theory. This might be an argument against setting the book at all, but if the students are 'old enough' to be indoctrinated, they are old enough to be permitted to think.

The wholesale rejection of Marxism which is set out in readings of *Animal Farm* reduces to a basic formula: Marx was an idealist, nature is unalterable, Marx was wrong. So what is wrong with idealism?

So what is wrong with idealism? Why should Orwell want to condemn these dreams of a utopia? The answer is that this very

> idealism allowed for the emergence of a frightening and repressive
> dictatorship in Russia every bit as bad as the dictatorships
> established by Hitler and Mussolini ... (*Longmans Study Text,
> Animal Farm*, p. xxi)

Effectively, Marx's writings, communism *per se*, and by
implication socialism, are presented as idealism (theory) =
tyranny (practice). An occasional paragraph is reserved for
Marx's economic analyses but these marginalia are swept aside
by the continuous assertion that Marxism-communism is both
naive/cynical and idealistic/violent. The logic of this account is
paradoxical and this is a vital part of its persuasive power.

In the discussion of 'Orwell' as personality, it was argued
that oppositions are set up and mediated by the authorial
persona. Individualism/socialism, pessimism/idealism, subjective experience/objective fact: these category-pairs are
established and then harmonised in the overarching persona of
an individual. A parallel technique develops here: the
assimilation of opposing forces, communism to fascism,
idealism to tyranny, prepares the ground for a middle way.
The simple negation and transcendence of artificially presented
oppositions draws on a rhetoric of 'experience', 'realism' and
'nature', implying that above and beyond extremes there is a
realm of political common sense, of day-to-day living. The
neutrality of this implied position is presented as the point
from which the writer writes and the reader reads: a standing
back from conflict, an overview from which the individual
human subject looks down on but is not defined by political
struggle.

The persuasiveness of the 'Orwell' myth rests then on a
logical strategy. Political myth as described here is a type of
machine for suppressing social contradictions. This argument
bears resemblance to a structuralist account of myth,[15] but
differs in its approach to the logic at work. Formal
structuralism, as associated with Lévi-Strauss, tends to see the
principles of logic as the reflexive object of the myths
themselves. It is the logical organisation of human thought
which is reified in mythical forms. Rather than placing logic
above or prior to society, we can see it emerging through
specific forms of political and 'aesthetic' language. The

resolving of logical contradictions is thus not a formal dance of discrete elements, but a specific intervention in a field of conflict. The 'Orwell' myth pacifies readers; contradictory theories, factions, values and vocabularies are mediated by a strategy of mutual exclusion and emerge as a harmony of truths which exceed the political field.

The strategy is not confined to 'crib' books on Orwell. The following extract from a *Guardian* article on Orwell develops a similar argument:

> The year which he made famous is now upon us, but nowhere in the democratic world has his monstrous vision of it come to pass. Instead, the kingdom of ends has lost some of its sway, the totalitarian temptation has receded with the imaginative grip of the socialist idea.[16]

The rhetoric carries us beyond a totalitarian/socialist equivalence towards a 'post-ideological' world. Means are substituted for 'ends' and the threat of radical social change is warded off. The attractions of this argument stem from its capacity to reduce the conflict of ideas and forces to a language of political realism. Yet this realism is sustained by little more than the negation of theories as 'extremes' and the refusal to consider its own theoretical basis. In its literary context, the argument stresses the now familiar values of 'human nature', 'fate' and the cheaper aesthetics of irony:

> Animalism, Communism, Fascism – what you will – so far as the mass of people is concerned, turns out to be a hollow progress, a barren achievement. (*Brodies Notes, Animal Farm*, p. 24)

> The time will come when the details of Russian history that aroused Orwell's anger will be forgotten, and *Animal Farm* will be remembered for its bitter, ironic analysis of the stages all revolutions tend to go through. (*York Notes, Animal Farm*, p. 31)

> It probably will not matter if the anti-Communist satire of *Animal Farm* remains intelligible. Already the specifics of its protest against Stalinism require considerable explanation for the younger generation, but its satire on corrupted revolution and the

misuse of power remains completely clear. Given human nature, it will unfortunately remain clear as long as society resembles anything in the world today. (*Coles Notes, Animal Farm*, p. 8)

To the student required to say what more than anti-communist propaganda the novel is, here is the model answer. Moving past versions of Soviet history and Marxist theory, reducing all 'isms' to a meaningless continuum, the argument leans back onto a language of timeless disillusion and 'home truth'.

There is some irony in the final assertions that Russian 'history' is ultimately irrelevant: mere detail. A good deal of effort goes into stressing detail as to the content and accuracy of *Animal Farm*'s account. All the same, it is a necessary step for a literary-critical approach which works to erase the marks of its political interest. History and politics must be dealt with, but in a form which appears as neither politically nor historically limited. This is achieved by a logical twist in which politics are both discussed and not discussed, being merely the context in which wider 'non-political' truths are found.

The success of this formula makes the activity of literary criticism appear as an endless sequence of pyrrhic victories. The same values are 'discovered', reiterated across the widest range of texts. Words such as 'irony' fill the vacuum created when political struggle has itself been emptied of meaning. What is offered is an intellectual Nirvana: political struggle is represented as an eternal contradiction (idealism=tyranny), the reader is invited to step back from the friction of thought and to survey a 'human comedy' of critical judgement. This uneasy marriage between literary and political values appears innocently, but effectively as a language of 'make believe'.

Nineteen Eighty-Four

I have again and again committed the very faults I am protesting against.[17]

Moving from educational material on *Animal Farm* to its counterpart on *Nineteen Eighty-Four* can give a sense of *déjà vu* to the reader. The broad outlines of an attack on communism, socialism and the idea of political change remain largely intact; the formula which sets human values against the image of a

totally alien political process is expressed in terms so general
that it passes easily from one text to another. There are
however, major differences in critical discussion of the two
works. These can be treated in part as a response to inherent
differences in the works themselves, in part as the result of a
switch from O Level modes of criticism to the requirements of
A Level.[18]

Tasks at O Level consist mainly in recording details of plot
and character within a tightly drawn critical framework. Value
judgements are often invited, but rarely in a form which makes
them problematic. At A Level, issues of critical discrimination
come to the fore. Students must assess the conformity between
set texts and literary standards. They must define terms and
relate these definitions to instances of interpretation.

The more overt preoccupation with value-judgements at A
Level emerges in the treatment of *Nineteen Eighty-Four* as a set
of problems related to the book's structure and purpose.
Where *Animal Farm* 'can' be regarded as a unified, morally
didactic fable, raising few problems of form or meaning,
Orwell's final novel presents immediate complications of
structure, meaning, characterisation. *Nineteen Eighty-Four*
combines the conventions of realist fiction with those of the
scientific romance; it includes a lengthy extract from
Goldstein's 'book', as well as the appendix on Newspeak.

The unorthodox construction of Orwell's novel presents a
problem for critical response. If rigid critical expectations as
regards the unity of a work of art, the requirements of plot and
character, are brought to bear, then *Nineteen Eighty-Four* must
be regarded as a 'flawed' work. Exam questions show a marked
tendency to reproduce these standards and thus to pose the
question of the novel's failure. The failure in turn is seen in
terms of a conflict between 'literary' qualities and political
purposes:

' "1984" is unashamedly a book with a message'. Do you consider
that this diminishes its merits as a novel?

'The political message is constantly getting in the way of the story,
and this diminishes its interest and excitement.' Do you agree with
this view of '1984'?

'Characterisation in this novel is negligible. It is completely subordinated to the political message.' Do you agree?[19]

Although it is possible for examinees to refute these verdicts, they are inevitably forced to organise their answers within the framework of debate which the questions establish. This means that they must discriminate between conflicting values; they must be able to differentiate between 'literary' standards and an implied threat from the political 'message'. Yet it is quite unclear how this distinction should be made.

If we take the third of the above questions, on 'character', this could be answered in a number of ways. It could be argued that indeed, the figure of Winston lacks credibility, Julia is presented as a crude, sexist stereotype, O'Brien is no more than a personification of the totalitarian fantasy. This might suggest a weakness in the novel but does little to show why the weakness results from excessive focus on the 'message'. Equally, it could be said that characters are weak and undeveloped because, in a totalitarian society, that is how 'characters' are.[20] This would require us to accept the literary weakness as an accurate representation of an imagined political truth; an argument which is impossible to verify and which, again, does little to clarify the supposed conflict between political and aesthetic values. In the absence of any decisive criteria for distinguishing between the two areas, arguments like the above can be reproduced in various forms without touching the nub of the question.

The failure of examinees to make the necessary judgements and discriminations is recorded in the following extract from an Examiners' Report. The relevant books are *Nineteen Eighty-Four* and *Brave New World*:

Essays on Orwell and Huxley tended to be historical or political or sociological or psychological rather than literary in their approach. Both writers are, of course, interesting from these points of view, but it is surprising that when they have been prescribed for papers on literature, their literary qualities have been ignored.[21]

Yet it is not so surprising. On the one hand, questions on

Orwell repeatedly stress the importance of political over aesthetic considerations in the novel. On the other hand, the broader background of discussion of Orwell's work does little to promote an understanding of the issues involved.

There are two specific ways in which the relation between artistic and political value is presented in exam questions and Study Aids. The first is to see the two terms as complementary. In discussions of *Animal Farm* and the 'Orwell' persona, this involves stressing the 'truth' and 'clarity' of a writer's account. The artist who tells the truth honestly and in plain language satisfies the demands of both aesthetic and political standards. This approach rationalises the two elements but it does so by effectively cancelling out the latter term. Political reality is conceived as a superstructure, built on moral and psychological values and reducible to them. Literary qualities, by comparison, are regarded as the necessary counterpart of personal qualities. There is no need for a theory of aesthetics to map out the technical aspects of literature; artistic excellence is simply moral virtue translated into 'prose ... like a window pane.'[22]

Reducing political meanings to subjective norms creates an impasse, not only for an understanding of history and theory, but for any coherent description of literary value. Values are located in the pre-verbal realm, inaccessible to anything other than tautological accounts. It follows that any work which directly questions the sacrosanct status of the individual human subject will be seen in negative terms, as a deviation from implicit standards.

Nineteen Eighty-Four, with its lack of distinctive 'characters', its reduction of subjectivity to coercive norms of behaviour, is a case in point. The problems which this novel poses are more than those of subject-matter; the novel's form proves to be inseparable from the ideas it contains. Intentionally or not, the novel undermines the political assumptions of realist fiction:

> For realism is not just a matter of literary form. It is the common-sense expression in aesthetic terms of an ideology in which the unified human subject 'makes sense' of his/her world by negotiation with external forces – Nature, Society, etc., which presupposes a world that *can* be made sense of and an always

potentially self-determining human subject.[23]

By seeking to give a plausible account of the death of the
'individual', Orwell necessarily moves into areas which violate
the premises of realist fiction. In order to understand why this
violation should be seen in terms of the 'political message', we
need to look at the second way in which art and politics are
conceived in educational material on Orwell.

In contrast to a stress on the harmony of literary/political
values, there is an account which asserts their absolute division.
The political field is characterised as inherently alien, abstract;
as an essential threat to human freedom. If politics cannot be
assimilated to subjectivity, it must be regarded as a threat to
subjectivity itself. The seeds of this extreme viewpoint are
found, for example, in earlier accounts of *Animal Farm*, where
political struggle is portrayed as a timeless futility and the State
as an external 'fact'. They can be traced through the account of
socialism as 'abstract group philosophy',[24] and as an essential
threat to individual liberty. They find their fullest expression in
the many accounts of *Nineteen Eighty-Four* which adopt Orwell's
fictional model of the absolute, totalitarian State as if it was a
descriptive account of modern political reality.

Between the two extremes of political and aesthetic value
there is little to choose. To reduce politics to an aesthetic of
personal values, or to treat politics as a totally alien force
amounts to the same. In either case it becomes impossible to
discriminate between conflicting areas of value, each being
defined solely as the rejection or assimilation of the other. The
major effect of these opposing-complementary stances is to
mystify the notions of value in reading Orwell and to present
this mystification as a 'fact of life'.

Any attempt to go beyond this impasse, to theorise the
relation between subjects and society according to a different
model, would be regarded as a threat to the 'individual'. This
is true both for Orwell himself and for the tradition which
reproduces him. In his account of 'change' in Orwell's writings
Frank Gloversmith makes the following point:

Any change that is backed by articulated theory ... is anathema to
Orwell. He attempts to dismiss intellectuals (of any class), to

dismantle theories of change as intrinsically authoritarian, and to redefine socialism by locating it inside his experience of the northern working class ...[25]

The resistance to theory predictably opposes personal values ('experience') to abstraction. More than this it sees theory as 'intrinsically authoritarian'. In effect, theory is personified as 'totalitarianism'; as an attempt to confine the individual within an autonomous, alien frame.

The association between these two terms, 'totalitarianism' and 'theory', may well be 'false' but it continues to produce effects. A theoretical treatment of subjective values would indeed spell the death of the 'individual', if by 'individual' we mean that self-determined subject which haunts the pages of 'Orwell' criticism. The fantasy of totalitarianism expresses this threat. Change can only be seen as for the worst – of all possible worlds. Unless, that is, it is confined to the 'change of heart'.

In the absence of any theoretical shift in the approach to Orwell, students will continue to be systematically confused by 'literary' and 'political' values. The standards of orthodox literary criticism reproduce rather than clarify this confusion and it is an essential element of their existence that the problem should remain. It is a mark of the distance which literary criticism has failed to travel, that Orwell's resistance to theory should be presented to students of his work as a positive virtue.

Notes

1 Raymond Williams, 'Orwell's 1984 and Ours', *Morning Star*, 3 January 1984.
2 Frank H. Thompson Jr., *Orwell's Image of the Man of Good Will, College English* xxii, No. 4, January 1961. Reprinted in *Coles Notes, Nineteen Eighty-Four*, Toronto, 1982.
3 The following Study Aids have been used: *Brodies Notes, Animal Farm*, Suffolk, 1978; *Coles Notes, Animal Farm*, Toronto, 1982; Robert Welch (ed.), *York Notes, Animal Farm*, Hong Kong, 1980; Robert Wilson (ed.), *Longman Study Text, Animal Farm*, Hong Kong, 1983; *Brodies Notes, Nineteen Eighty-Four*, Suffolk, 1977; *Coles Notes, Nineteen Eighty-Four*, Toronto,

1982; Robert Welch (ed.), *York Notes, Nineteen Eighty-Four*, Hong Kong, 1983; *Coles Notes, Notes on George Orwell's Works*, Toronto, 1981.

4 Lionel Trilling, *George Orwell and the Politics of Truth*, reprinted in Raymond Williams (ed.), *George Orwell: A Collection of Critical Essays*, Englewood Cliffs, 1974.

5 A recent instance is D.S. Savage, *The Fatalism of George Orwell*, in Boris Ford (ed.), *The New Pelican Guide to English Literature*, Vol. 8, Harmondsworth, 1983.

6 Discussion of Orwell's failure of stamina in Raymond Williams, *Politics and Letters*, London, 1981, pp. 385-6.

7 Examination questions are taken from a selection drawn from the London Board, Oxford & Cambridge Board, Associated Examining Board, 1950-84, and from a wider sample of Boards over the past decade. Orwell's work appears on each of the Examining Boards in 1984.

8 Oxford & Cambridge Board, A Level, 1971.

9 Robert Welch (ed.), *York Notes, Animal Farm*, p. 8.

10 George Orwell, *The Road to Wigan Pier*, Harmondsworth, 1983, p. 160.

11 The two accounts of Orwell's 'awareness' of the fascism at the heart of socialism in *York Notes, Animal Farm* and *York Notes, Nineteen Eighty-Four* are noticeably similar in argument and phrasing. Across the Study Aids there are similarities of this type, suggesting direct borrowing. This is most apparent where comparison is made between texts on Orwell's work from the same publisher, but it also runs from one Study Aid publication to another. Consensus merges here with something like plagiarism.

12 Oxford & Cambridge Board, 1972. This question is set for a group of related texts: *Gulliver's Travels, News from Nowhere, The Nun's Priest's Tale, Animal Farm*.

13 Robert Wilson (ed.), *Longman Study Text, Animal Farm*, p. xxv.

14 The idea of Orwell as a 'voice in the wilderness', speaking out against Soviet policy, is exaggerated by biographical accounts in the various Study Aids. It fits with the image of the writer as prophet and realist, but not with the facts. See, for example, the account of Anglo-Soviet relations in Angus Calder, *The People's War*, London, 1982.

15 See for example, 'The Structural Study of Myth', in Claude Lévi-Strauss, *Structural Anthropology*, Harmondsworth, 1977, pp. 206-31.

16 Peter Jenkins, '1984', *Guardian*, 28 December 1983.

17 George Orwell, *Politics and the English Language*, in *Inside the Whale and Other Essays*, Harmondsworth, 1982, p. 154.

18 *Nineteen Eighty-Four* has been almost exclusively A Level material up to the present year. In 1984, several Boards have switched the text to O Level.

19 These questions are taken from the London Board, 1972-3.

20 This argument is followed in David Smith and Michael Mosher, *Orwell for Beginners*, London, 1984, pp. 173-4.

21 London Examiners' Report, 1972, p. 79.

22 George Orwell, *Why I Write*, in S. Orwell and I. Angus (eds), *The Collected Essays, Journalism and Letters of George Orwell*, Vol. 1, Harmondsworth,

1970, p. 30.

23 Peter Widdowson, 'Hardy in History: A Case Study in the Sociology of Literature', in *Literature and History*, Vol. 9, No.1, Spring 1983.

24 *Coles Notes, Nineteen Eighty-Four*, pp. 7-8.

25 Frank Gloversmith, 'Changing Things: Orwell and Auden', in Frank Gloversmith (ed.), *Class, Culture and Social Change: A New View of the 1930s*, Bury St Edmunds, 1980, p. 120.

Alaric Jacob

Sharing Orwell's 'Joys' – But Not His Fears

George Orwell had few close friends and I was never one of them, yet I have felt close to him for much of my life because we shared the same schooling and faced the same dilemmas in early manhood when it seemed that the sun would never set on the British Empire in whose tentacles we were both entangled.

I did not envy Orwell his success because it was clear to me from the very first when we were taught by the same teachers at St Cyprian's School, Eastbourne, that Orwell's level of ability would always have been beyond my reach. Much as I admire the best of the essays and the two novels which display him as a worthy successor to his mentor, 'George Gissing – *Keep the Aspidistra Flying* and *Coming Up for Air* – I cannot admire Orwell's work as a whole because I find it flawed by those defects of character which he detected in himself, and which he proclaimed to the world as though challenging his admirers to go away and find someone else to enthuse about. The overriding defect, however, was one of which he was unaware. His dominant aim, as he said, was 'to make political writing into an art'. In this, after years of struggling to purify his style, he ultimately succeeded. But just as it is possible to admire the art of Machiavelli while refusing to enter the political blind alley into which the reader is artfully directed, so one may admire the clarity and simplicity of Orwell's style and yet stand aghast before some of the tortuous conclusions that he reaches. The truth is that Orwell lacked political judgment to a quite astonishing degree.

Notwithstanding his rebellious beginnings in Burma, the days of Bohemian struggle in Paris and his gallant expedition to Spain, he was not a widely travelled man. Russia and America were unknown to him. He was at heart an Edwardian Little Englander, basically uninterested in the life-styles of other peoples, so it is hardly surprising that his politics were often naïve. His lifelong, unrequited love affair with the English working class also contributed to a lack of balance as did his six wretched, friendless years at St Cyprian's School. Those six years and the six months that he spent fighting in the Spanish Civil War marked him for life. The first turned him into a drop-out, the first of the 'angry young men'. The second experience contributed to his early death.

Orwell, or Eric Blair, as he then was, had preceded me at St Cyprian's School and there can be no doubt about the considerable impression he made there, for soon after I entered the school I was encouraged, as it were, to understudy him. The headmaster and his wife, Mr and Mrs Vaughan Wilkes – 'Sambo' and 'Flip' as they were known to succeeding generations – were looking for high fliers who would bring credit to the school by winning scholarships to Eton. When 'Flip', the real driving force at the school, picked out Orwell and Cyril Connolly as the cleverest boys of their generation she proved to be an astute talent-spotter. At that time scholarship boys started Latin at eight and Greek at ten (science was scarcely taught at all). The burden of two dead languages lay heavily on most young shoulders, including mine, but when Flip discovered that my History, English and French were as good as Orwell's she concluded that Sambo would be able to drum a sufficiency of Classics into me to bring me up to Orwell's exceptional overall standards. So I was set down as a potential Eton Colleger. But Flip over-estimated me. Orwell won not just one scholarship but two – Wellington as well as Eton – while I proved to be weak in Latin and utterly resistant to Greek, and finally went to King's School, Canterbury without winning a place there as a King's Scholar.

Superficially, Orwell and I came from the same stable, our fathers having served for years in India, but as Orwell soon discovered, the standards which the Wilkeses had imposed on their school did not in fact permit us to be assessed on equal terms. Over thirty years later Orwell was to write in his celebrated polemic *Such, Such Were the Joys* that St Cyprian's was an expensive and snobbish establishment where the children of aristocratic or rich families were fawned upon, while boys from modest homes such as his own were treated as 'underlings', to be bullied and humiliated by Flip and beaten by Sambo for every minor fault. Orwell could not have gone to St Cyprian's at all had he not been accepted at half-fees, for the full fees were £180 a year and his father was at that time about to retire from an undistinguished post in the Opium Department in India on a pension of £438 a year. After August 1914, however, Orwell senior joined the Army at sixty years of age as a second lieutenant while his wife did war work in London: this eased the family's finances and might well have caused their son to take pride in their patriotism. But contemporaries at Eton say that Orwell never referred to this honourable service by either parent; on the contrary, he is said to have spoken of them in disparaging terms. Charles Dickens blamed his parents for sending him to the blacking factory, but he did not allow the experience to darken his whole life. Dickens could never have penned an indictment so harsh and unforgiving as *Such, Such Were the Joys*.

In my experience, money snobbery was not the dominant influence at St Cyprian's, as Orwell maintained. You did not have to be rich to be accepted. Service to the Empire was well regarded, especially if undertaken in romantic places such as the North West Frontier, Cairo, Constantinople or in the tents of the desert Arab. Orwell's father had married an attractive woman much younger than himself, as my father had done, but he had eked out a dull existence in minor postings. He had no legacy of scholarship or adventure to pass on to his son; rather it was his wife's memories of her colourful girlhood in Rangoon that inclined Orwell to begin his career in the Imperial Police in Burma. The Opium Department and the Burma Police were both services low in esteem, and it is arguable that if Orwell had not been so shattered by experiences at prep school which convinced him that he would always be a failure he might have rebelled against a career which offered no greater satisfaction than his father's had done. But the five years he was to spend in Burma only added

imperial guilt to the sense of social and personal inadequacy
that had plagued him since childhood.

Escaping from British imperialism at last, he wrote that he
carried hatred of oppression to extraordinary lengths ...

> Failure seemed to me to be the only virtue. Every suspicion of
> self-advancement, even to 'succeed' in life to the extent of making
> a few hundreds a year, seemed to me spiritually ugly, a species of
> bullying.

So he set foot upon the lonely road that led to *Down and Out in
Paris and London*.

In *Such, Such Were the Joys* Orwell depicts himself as an
unattractive, cowardly little boy. If he was cowardly, then so
was I. In the weeks before I went to St Cyprian's I cried myself
to sleep night after night. It is, of course, a monstrosity to send
a child to boarding school at the age of eight (my younger
brother followed me there when only six because my mother
had joined my father overseas). Ours was a happy home, so
long as one parent remained available. I feared to leave it
because I had read *Tom Brown's Schooldays* and did not want to
be beaten or roasted on a fire. On the other hand I had been
taught that those who served the British Empire must submit
to a stern apprenticeship before they would be worthy to
exercise dominion over palm and pine. My father had not told
me this because I hardly knew him; like my grandfather,
Colonel George Augustus and *his* forebear, the celebrated
cavalry general who had created Jacob's Horse, equipped the
regiment with a revolutionary rifle of his own design which
enabled it to play a large part in the conquest of Sind and had
then founded the city of Jacobabad, my father had rarely been
seen in England since he left it as a lieutenant in the British
Army. His career developed in the Political Service and later as
the acknowledged expert on south-west Arabia and a leading
Arabist of his day. My mother was of Danish birth but she had
been educated in Edinburgh before joining her parents in
Arabia where they ran a medical mission.

Having looked upon the British Empire when it was red, my
mother had never been sober about it since. She really believed
that the concomitants of Empire – the public schools, the

ancient universities, Sandhurst and the Staff College – were to
be cherished and that the thousand supermen who ran India
and the even smaller nucleus that dominated Arabia, Egypt
and the Sudan were – and she never tired of saying it – *the salt of
the earth*. Consequently I went to prep school fearing the worst
and entered public school in a state of shock when I found that
my mother had slipped an illuminated copy of Kipling's *If* into
my tuck box. Yet, having perhaps inherited a little of my
father's gift for Oriental diplomacy, I found myself able to
cope with St Cyprian's with less stress than I had anticipated.
Not that I was free from *angst*. I developed a stammer from my
childhood friend, Kim Philby. Singing lessons eventually freed
me from this disability, but Kim must have found his affliction
a tremendous help in his subsequent career. To have time to
think and think again under interrogation – what spy could ask
for more?

I benefited from certain refinements of snobbery which
Orwell had overlooked. The fact that my kinsman Claud
commanded an army corps on the Western Front had not
escaped the notice of Sambo, who encouraged us to stick
Union Jack pins into maps of the front. Claud went on to
become a field marshal. Claud's brother contributed
unwittingly to my prestige when he unloaded part of his stamp
collection upon me at school: envelopes addressed to
Major-General le Grand Jacob CB CMG CIE CBE DSO can
have done me no harm among certain sons of hard-faced men
who did no more than do well out of the war. On his first, and
last, visit to the school my father appeared in colonel's uniform
bearing, if I remember aright, pale blue tabs the same colour
as his Star of India. He was also an *Officier* of the Legion of
Honour, and looked it. Asked what his precise contribution to
the war effort was I replied: 'He looks after the Arabs.' And so
he did. First from that forbidding house beneath the clock
tower at Steamer Point in Aden where he was attended by 20
servants, and then at the Arab Bureau in Cairo where his
friends and colleagues were Lawrence of Arabia, Sir Ronald
Storrs and, later, Harry St John Phily, favourite of Ibn Saud
and father of Kim. Kim attended a neighbouring school in
Eastbourne and sometimes stayed with us in the holidays.
Rosemary and Marigold, the daughters of Flip and Sambo,

were to do the same. While Orwell insisted that Sambo never missed an opportunity to remind him that 'You are living on my charity', the fact that my brother and I had also been accepted at reduced fees was never mentioned, much less held against us.

The celebrated opening sentence of *Nineteen Eighty-Four* must be engraved on many a memory: 'It was a bright, cold day in April, and the clocks were striking thirteen.' Scarcely less arresting is the opening of *Such, Such Were the Joys*: 'Soon after I arrived at St Cyprian's (not immediately but after a week or two, just when I seemed to be settling into the routine of school life) I began wetting my bed.'

It was this accident, Orwell maintained, that set in train the systematic persecution and humiliation that Sambo and Flip inflicted upon him over the ensuing six years.

Some critics have concluded that the masochistic horrors of *Nineteen Eighty-Four* were derived directly from *Such, Such Were the Joys*. In August 1946 Orwell began work on *Nineteen Eighty-Four*, and in May 1947 he sent *Such, Such Were the Joys* to his publishers, pointing out that it had been planned as a pendant to Cyril Connolly's own memoir of the school which Connolly had included in *Enemies of Promise* in 1938. Orwell was desperately anxious to complete *Nineteen Eighty-Four* before the tuberculosis which then threatened his life should overwhelm him, so it is likely that the school memoir had been produced in earlier years. Whatever the precise date of its composition, the memoir is the most astonishing document to have been penned by a mature man thirty years after the events described.

'Whoever writes about his own childhood must beware of exaggeration and self-pity,' Orwell began and then, disregarding his own advice, added:

> I do not claim that I was a martyr or that St Cyprian's was a sort of Dotheboys Hall. But I should be falsifying my own memories if I did not record that they are largely memories of disgust. The overcrowded, underfed, underwashed life that we led *was* disgusting, as I recall it … there was the slimy water of the plunge bath − it was twelve or fifteen feet long, the whole school was supposed to go into it every morning and I doubt whether the

water was changed at all frequently – and the always-damp towels
with their cheesy smell ... the sweaty smell of the changing-room
with its greasy basins ... the row of filthy, dilapidated lavatories
which had no fastening of any kind on the doors, so that whenever
you were sitting there someone was sure to come crashing in. It is
not easy for me to think of my schooldays without seeming to
breathe in a whiff of something cold and evil-smelling – a sort of
compound of sweaty stockings, dirty towels, faecal smells blowing
along corridors, forks with old food between the prongs, neck of
mutton stew and the banging doors of the lavatories and the
echoing chamber pots in the dormitories.

It is true that I am not by nature gregarious, and the WC and
dirty handkerchief side of life is necessarily more obtrusive when
great numbers of human beings are crushed together in a small
space ... boyhood is the age of disgust ... one seems always to be
walking the tightrope over a cesspool.

I knew that Orwell had always hated the school, for older
boys who had entered with him had told me so. But I think it
was only after reading these lines that the respect and
admiration I had felt for Orwell over many years finally
crumbled. Boyhood as the age of disgust? For me it had been
an age of friendships, of excitement on the cricket fields and in
school plays, of singing to a receptive audience at concerts, of
having a sonnet printed in the school magazine, of winning the
Townsend Warner History Prize.

In another passage Orwell quite rightly concludes that 'Boys
are Erewhonians; they think that misfortune is disgraceful and
must be concealed at all costs.' But why, with all his talents,
had Orwell succumbed to misfortune in so craven a manner?
He had never complained to his parents but had bottled up the
hatreds and resentments for thirty years until they burst forth
in a document which he admitted was too libellous to be
published until all those involved in it were dead. Including, as
it happened, himself.

'Poor creature!' I thought, 'what a needless misery you
inflicted on yourself! What a grey, unloved and unloving life
you led, and how pitiful the manner of your early death, barely
conscious of the worldwide fame you had earned and too ill to
be able to enjoy the fruits of it.'

Yet I had to admit that my pity for him was darkly tinged with contempt.

The gravamen of Orwell's charge against Sambo and Flip was that they took advantage of his half-fee status to treat him with calculated cruelty and contempt. He knew he ought to be grateful to them because they were going to make it possible for him to go to one of the great public schools which his parents could not otherwise have afforded. But he could feel no gratitude, any more than he could feel love for the father who had handed him over to their care.

> I knew very well that I disliked my own father whom I had rarely seen before I was eight and who appeared to me simply as a gruff-voiced elderly man for ever saying 'Don't!'

From the start Sambo impressed on him that if he failed to win a scholarship he would have to leave school at fourteen and 'become a little office boy at forty pounds a year.' And he quotes Flip as saying:

> It isn't awfully decent of you to behave like this, is it? Idling your time away week after week. You know your people aren't rich, don't you? You know they can't afford the same things as other boys' parents.

According to the Wilkeses' standards, he says:

> ... I was damned. I had no money, I was weak, I was ugly, I was unpopular, I had a chronic cough, I was cowardly, I smelt. This picture, I should add, was not altogether fanciful. I was an unattractive boy. St Cyprian's soon made me so ...

He concludes:

> I have never been back to St Cyprian's ... for years I loathed its very name so deeply that I could not view it with enough detachment to see the significance of the things that happened to me there ... Except upon dire necessity I would not have set foot in Eastbourne. I even conceived a prejudice against Sussex, as the county that contained St Cyprian's ... Now, however, the place is

out of my system for good ... I have not even enough animosity left to make me hope that Flip and Sambo are dead or that the story of the school being burnt down was true.

Was it indeed burnt down by a vengeful pupil, as I too have heard? What is certainly true is that cabbages now grow on the ground where the main building stood. Not a stone of it remains.

* * *

It was precisely at this point in my narrative that I turned aside for a moment to refresh my memory of St Cyprian's by looking through an album of photographs I had taken with my Vest Pocket Kodak more than sixty years before. There on the St Cyprian's playing field stood Anthony Mildmay, Eddie O'Brien and Rory Macleod, my friends of those distant days. Interspersed among the pictures were one or two essays that my mother must have kept. One of them had doubtless appeared in *The Red Circle*, the family magazine I used to run in the holidays but had never taken back to school for fear of ridicule. As I read again for the first time what I had written at the age of twelve I winced to contemplate how justified that fear had been. The piece had evidently been fair-copied for submission to some local newspaper, for the adhesive edge of a stamp for the return of the manuscript still adhered to the paper. It was entitled *My First Day at School*, by 'A Schoolboy'. I feel compelled to quote from it because it demands to be set alongside *Such, Such Were the Joys*:

It was a cab of the four-wheeler variety that brought me there. I shall always remember it. It was painted a rusty black relieved with stripes that had once been green. It rumbled peacefully along the loose gravel and lurched into final somnolence at a red brick porch. A maid servant opened the door and announced that Mrs W. would be pleased to receive Mrs J. in the drawing room. Would Madam kindly step this way?

My mother departed and I was in due course submitted to the tender mercies of the Headmaster's daughter M —, aged six and three-quarters – with special emphasis on the three-quarters,

please! This lady addressed me in tones of compassion and having
wrung from me my name, age, social standing and past history,
conducted me through a maze of white-washed passages and
proceeded to tell me where I must keep my coat, hat and shoes.
My guide then took me into 'the Dinin'-room' to have 'Somfin' to
eat.' I selected a particularly sticky variety of Bath bun and took a
large bite from it. What was my surprise on looking up from this
task, to see my hostess staring at me in blank astonishment –
'What awfu' cheek!' she gasped. 'It's a Sixth Form bun and you've
eat it all up: what will the Sixth say when they arrive?'

As I had no idea what *they* would say I discreetly held my tongue
and tried to look penitent. Presently a plump person in white –
whom I afterwards discovered to be the Matron – entered the
room followed by a convoy of boys. 'Hallo, young man' said the
plump person, 'when did you arrive?' 'At half past five.' 'Hum,
you're an early bedder, so you'd better be on your way. Miss M —
will show you your dormitory.'

M — and I departed, followed by envious glances from the
boys. I lost no time in unpacking and getting into bed. I was just
falling asleep when a sticky little hand was thrust into mine.
'You're er ... rather nice' said a voice, 'so you'd better hold onto
these.' Next morning I awoke to find myself stuck fast to the
sheets. I had lain on top of several Bath buns.

Impossible to believe that Orwell could ever have put his
name to such a composition, anticipating as it does that
winsome style of writing which was to be popularised a few
years later by Godfrey Winn and Beverley Nichols. I would
have denied authorship myself if irrefutable evidence to the
contrary was not lying before me as I write. I have no
recollection today that such an incident ever happened, but I
do not think I invented it. Marigold Wilkes was real enough,
and if she is alive today, the Bath buns may have stuck in her
consciousness as firmly as they seem to have done in mine. In
any event, here surely is confirmation of Orwell's *Erewhon*
theory; here is a boy using a frivolous anecdote as a means of
concealing the real pain of going to school. It is a practice that
some boys carry forward into adult life. George Orwell,
emphatically, was not one of them.

Did Orwell tell the truth about St Cyprian's? It is not the

truth which his contemporaries or those who followed soon after have attested to – not the truth as experienced by Cyril Connolly, Cecil Beaton or by 'Milksop Mildmay' as we called him, a child quite as sickly as Orwell who, on becoming a peer, astonished us all by riding in the Grand National. Even Gavin Maxwell, the author who lived and wrote like a hermit in the Highlands of Scotland after being removed from the school by an indulgent mother because he hated it so deeply, even Maxwell did not allow his adult life to be ruined by it. When E.D. O'Brien, who built a successful career in conservative journalism and public relations, was writing his memoirs ten years ago he wrote, as 'probably your oldest friend', to tell me how much pleasure he was deriving from writing about St Cyprian's and 'that damnable woman Flip – how I loathed the place!' But he felt obliged to add that the education provided there was a good one.

The truth as I saw it was that the Wilkes family, for all their faults, were not monsters and that the education they offered was, within the cramped ethos of that time, admirable. What was it in Orwell's make-up which made him claim that this rather absurd little school had darkened his whole life?

I shall not make myself popular among those latter-day admirers who have described Orwell as 'almost a saint' by venturing to compare my life style with his but, after all, their Mozart is secure upon his pedestal; Salieri still lives though no one is obliged to take him seriously.

Orwell had to face a lifetime of wretched health while I have scarcely known a day's illness. His temperament was depressive, mine was sanguine; he hated sports, I enjoyed being in the first eleven at cricket and in the shooting eight. I was no more 'happy' than he was, but I did not expect to find happiness in any school. Institutional life was never to my taste. I left public school as soon as I possibly could and went to France to study and write. I had a rage to live, a passion to try everything once. I was determined to live in America and then in Russia in order to test for myself the extremes of contemporary society in the days before Hitler tipped the balance towards war. For me the ideal life was that of the free-ranging foreign correspondent, and I was fortunate to be able to lead that life for thirteen years before the restraints of that famous 'pram in the hall' – Cyril Connolly's chief 'enemy of promise' – closed in upon me.

After coasting gently through Eton, earning no laurels but making no enemies, Orwell went tamely to Burma at the age of nineteen for lack of anything better to do. I could not understand how anyone of even moderate intelligence could have taken so retrograde a step. My father had left India to make a new career in Arabia, partly because he felt our family had been in India long enough, and partly because, even before the 1914 war, it was clear to him that India must soon have self-rule. He also disliked the second-rate men in first-rate jobs who already predominated there. Nothing would have induced me to go to India; I had been there and in Arabia as a child, and wanted no part of either world. I had no wish to rule subject peoples. I would rather make a thin living in the arts at home than strive towards a knighthood in some imperial outpost.

So Orwell and I came to be in complete agreement about how we were going to live. But what a very long time it took him to reach that point. He was, in truth, a very slow developer. Even after his Burmese days and his apprenticeship in Paris, some of the English friends who tried to encourage his free-lance writing doubted his capacity to succeed. Ruth Pitter, a family friend who was to win the Queen's Prize for Poetry and become a Companion of Literature, has said that his early writings were so inept that they made her laugh. She did not believe that he had it in him to make a living as an author, let alone to become a master of English prose.

The woman who played Ruth Pitter's part in my early life was Margot Asquith. She was sixty-four and I nineteen when we met, but even before that I had made an impertinent beginning as a writer. My first play was produced at Plymouth Repertory Theatre when I was seventeen. My second followed it on the same stage soon after my eighteenth birthday. Its very title, *The Compleat Cynic: a piece of persiflage in one act* would be enough to wring derisive laughter from any aspiring playwright today, and yet the memory of an audience laughing at some of the lines I had written became a consolation to me in the theatrical disappointments that soon followed. Margot Asquith perceived that I needed a creative sedative rather than encouragement. 'I am sorry you have done a novel so young' she wrote just

before Methuen published my first novel when I was
twenty-one. 'Better to wait till one is thirty but on the other
hand don't leave it too late or one may perpetrate an *Octavia*'
(her own solitary fiction which the critics assassinated.)

So it was that Margot's influence upon me came to be as
strong as Benjamin Jowett's had been on her own youth. She
could not have shown me a finer friendship had I been one of
the great men of her youth instead of a youth of vague promise
and negligible achievement. It was much more fun to go to a
ball with Margot and dance with her all evening than to
frequent young women; in dancing as in conversation, Margot
outclassed any débutante I ever met. At her luncheon table in
Bedford Square one might meet editors with jobs to offer as
well as Edwardians who had already made their appearance in
the history books. Here was education at its most persuasive –
practical as well as entertaining. By now I had acquired the
basic skills of journalism on a newspaper in Plymouth and
thought myself ready for Fleet Street . My eye was on Reuters
where one needed German as well as French to qualify. Margot
saw to it that I met the Reuters chief at her house before I
applied for the job, and when I got it she had the delicacy to
suggest that she had played no part in my success. So I became
diplomatic correspondent at the age of twenty-one and went to
Washington as Reuters correspondent soon after.

At this time my political consciousness went no further than
to inspire a play in which the hero was a communist. Having
written it, I realised that I knew nothing whatever about
socialism, so I borrowed *Capital* from a friend and, much to my
surprise, read it. This stood me in good stead when the hunger
marchers arrived in London like a series of living illustrations
to Marx's work. I felt an immediate rapport with them though
I could hardly understand them when they spoke. From then
on I knew where I stood. I felt that Marx was ninety per cent
right and I have never deviated from that position.

Orwell declared that he cared nothing for politics as a young
man and did not call himself a socialist till he was thirty-three,
in 1936.

That was the year he went to Spain.

*   *   *

When Orwell arrived in Barcelona he was enchanted by what he found there. In the opening chapter of *Homage to Catalonia* he wrote:

> It was the first time I had ever been in a town where the working class was in the saddle. Practically every building of any size had been seized by the workers and was draped in red flags ... almost every church had been gutted and its images burnt. Churches here and there were being systematically demolished by workmen. Servility and even ceremonial speech had disappeared. Everyone called everyone else 'comrade'. In outward appearance this was a town in which wealthy classes had practically ceased to exist. I believed that things were as they appeared, that this was really a workers' state and that the entire bourgeoisie had either fled, been killed or voluntarily come over to the workers' side. I did not realise that great numbers of them were simply lying low and disguising themselves as proletarians for the time being.

Nevertheless Orwell was intoxicated by the prevailing sense of freedom. He had come as a journalist with a group from the Independent Labour Party but he soon determined to fight, not merely to observe. His first thought was to join the International Brigade in Madrid, which was Communist-controlled, but he was persuaded to join the local militia that had been armed by the party nearest to the ILP – the POUM, or *Partido Obrero de Unificacion Marxista*, a group which favoured Trotsky's line in opposition to Stalin – that is, world revolution as opposed to revolution in one country.

When Orwell got to the front he was dismayed to find that the militia spent much of their time in political argument. He used to urge them for God's sake to stop their disputation and concentrate on beating Franco, for if Franco were to win neither Lenin nor Trotsky nor even Attlee would count in Spain – it would be death and destruction for all of them. This was the line of the Spanish Communist Party: first win the war and then decide your form of government and at first Orwell found this reasonable. But, when the POUM began to resist the government's plan to train a regular army with an officer corps and a general staff in order to make better use of the arms which the Russians were supplying, Orwell changed his mind. The POUM wanted to fight on as an independent force; even though their arms were primitive they preferred not to give them up in exchange for modern weapons for they believed the liberal government in Madrid was secretly hostile to any form of socialism and would retain the capitalist system even if it won the war. The POUM argued that in any event the government would betray the Catalan revolution in a bid to buy the goodwill of Britain and France, who were enforcing a policy of non-intervention. Orwell conceded that the Communists were at that time the largest and most popular force in Spain and that the POUM, who never numbered more than 30,000 and who had no more than 8,000 men and boys at the front, could not prevail against them. He knew that the POUM leader Andrés Nin had once been Trotsky's private secretary but believed it was unfair to brand the whole POUM movement as a Trotskyite splinter group which posed a threat to national unity. And so he accepted the revolutionary stance of the POUM *à l'outrance*.

This is how Orwell defined it:

> Bourgeois democracy is only another name for capitalism and so is fascism; to fight against fascism on behalf of democracy is to fight against one form of capitalism on behalf of a second which is liable to turn into the first at any moment. The only real alternative to capitalism is workers' control. If you set up any lesser goal than this you will either hand the victory to Franco or, at best, let in fascism by the back door. Meanwhile the workers must cling to every scrap they have won; if they yield anything to the semi-bourgeois governments they can depend on being cheated. The workers' militias and police forces must be preserved in their present form and every effort to 'bourgeoisify' them must be resisted. If the workers do not control the armed forces, the armed forces will control the workers. The war and the revolution are inseparable.

At the time I used to feel guilty about holding a well-paid job as Reuters' correspondent in Washington while Orwell was risking his life in the front line (he nearly lost it when he was shot through the neck by a sniper), and I used to have arguments with American friends as to whether I ought not to resign and join the International Brigade. Most of them urged me to wait for the much bigger war we were certain was coming. Still, I felt that Orwell could have given me the right answers to innumerable questions if only I could have put them to him. But when Orwell published his considered testimony in *Homage to Catalonia* two years later I was amazed that anyone so experienced and intelligent could have misread the situation so completely. The gist of his argument was that the Spanish Republic had been betrayed not by Britain, France or the United States, who by refusing all aid were ensuring Franco's victory, but by Russia – the only country which was in fact sending help. Had I been in contact then I would have put the case against him thus:

'You used your experience in Spain in an entirely subjective way, without thought for the wider issues. It was wildly romantic of you to suppose that the 30,000 men of POUM could ever have produced a Marxist revolution in Spain while fighting Franco at the same time. They would have produced an isolated Trotskyite republic that would soon have been overthrown. The Western Powers would have seen to that – even if it meant siding with Hitler and Mussolini to do it. Set up a Communist régime in Spain and you justify Franco's case up to the hilt and invite the rest of Europe to join his glorious anti-Bolshevik crusade! You say the Soviet Union has betrayed the Spanish working class by calling for a Popular Front rather than a Communist state. I say that in this particular the Soviet Union is entirely right. Even if Franco is defeated it will be only one battle in a much bigger war. How do you think we can ever deal with Hitler without a Popular Front to confront him with the danger of a war on two fronts – Britain and France on one side and the Red Army on the other.'

But of course what Orwell called 'the Popular Front baloney' was the last thing he wanted. In a letter to Geoffrey Gorer after his return from Spain he wrote: 'I do not see how one can oppose fascism except by working for the overthrow of capitalism, starting, of course, in one's own country.' He predicted that a form of fascism would be imposed on Britain as soon as war against Nazi Germany began, and that Communists and Labourites who should have struggled to stop a war between two rival imperialist systems would meekly side with their own conservative government.

His Spanish experience had caused him to lose hope of any improvement in the human condition and his last two books were the fruit of accumulated despair. Three years before he died from tuberculosis he was to write: 'A socialist today is in the position of a doctor treating an all but hopeless case. As a doctor it is his duty to keep the patient alive and therefore to assume that the patient has at least a chance of recovery. But as a scientist it is his duty to face the facts and admit that the patient will probably die.'

Orwell began to write *Animal Farm* in November 1943 and finished it in February 1944. By July of that year it had been rejected by Gollancz, Jonathan Cape and Faber on political grounds. Orwell then took it to Secker and Warburg, and Fredric Warburg tells us in his memoirs what happened next:

> I realised at once that I had received a gift more precious than rubies – a masterpiece. Some of my staff, however, did not want to publish the book. Was it right, they thought, to publish this bitter satirical attack on our great ally the USSR when its armies were rolling back the German forces and while the UK and USA had established a mere bridgehead on the Channel coast? My wife, who is partly Russian, threatened that if I published the book she would leave me. She thought it an outrage that after the immense sufferings of the Russian people who had after all done most of the fighting since 1941, they should be attacked in this way.

Warburg says he himself was worried and he reveals a curious aspect of his thinking at this time.

> I was obsessed by one thought. The German armies were falling back but their will to resist was not broken. Suppose that Stalin made a second deal with Hitler and made peace, or even turned round against the West, the two totalitarian states against the democracies? It seemed almost plausible to me.

To me – in my post as a war correspondent on the Eastern Front – it would have seemed absolutely inconceivable. And today it still seems incredible that a man of German-Jewish origin could envisage an alliance between the men who had been slaughtering six million of his own people, and an even larger number of Russians, and the army which was engaged in liberating the murder camps. However, Warburg decided to take the risk. And just ten days before the book came out the Americans dropped the atomic bomb on Hiroshima.

Warburg's comment on this coincidence is also worth recording:

> The technical breakthrough that had made the bomb possible had taken just 5 years – about the same time Orwell had required to conceive, work out and write *Animal Farm*. Though the A-bomb was dropped on Japan it was considered as a warning to the Soviet Union. A-bomb and A-Farm thus had the same target – the Soviet Union. Each contained a threat to its existence. Orwell, of course, had not foreseen the atomic bomb but he had foreseen that the world had become one in which such weapons could be produced. As early as 1937 he had proclaimed that 'progress is a swindle' ... at the same time he had concluded that the Soviet Union was the most dangerous threat to liberal values the world had ever seen, and it was against the Soviet Union that his book was aimed. Since 1936 he had concentrated his effort to atack and if possible to destroy the myth of Soviet Communism which between 1936 and 1946 had deluded millions of working people and fatally infected the minds of the left intellectuals who dominated the arts at that period.

This portentous analysis demonstrates, to my mind, that if Orwell's political balance was unstable, his publisher's judgment was downright silly. Orwell can never have anticipated the enormous commercial success of *Animal Farm*. He had conceived it out of his lifelong admiration for Swift – a satire within the framework of a children's story aimed at the politically sophisticated, not a mass readership. Thus it is likely that only a minority of the millions who came to read *Animal Farm* fully appreciated its author's intentions. Equally, the book was misused for political purposes in a manner which Orwell might have foreseen had his own political antennae been more sensitive than they were. I recall that my first wife, Iris Morley, was just as disquieted by it as Warburg's wife had been. She had come to Russia with me in an Arctic convoy to act as correspondent of the *Observer*, to which Orwell also contributed.

'If Ivor Brown asks me to meet that man when I get home I shall refuse' she said. I found a degree of wit, even a certain charm in *Animal Farm* which the earlier books had lacked. I would have accepted such an invitation if only to suggest that if Orwell had experienced the anguish of Russia at war as we had done he might have felt compelled to write something very different from *Animal Farm*.

Nineteen Eighty-Four is an entirely different matter. When Warburg first read it he summarised his feelings about the book for circulation among his staff.

> This is among the most terrifying books I have ever read. Orwell has no hope, or at least he allows his reader no tiny flickering candlelight of hope. Here is a study of pessimism unrelieved ... I take it to be a deliberate and sadistic attack on socialism and socialist parties generally. It seems to indicate a final breach between Orwell and socialism, not the socialism of equality and human brotherhood which Orwell clearly no longer expects from socialist parties, but the socialism of Marxism and managerial revolution. It is worth a cool million votes to the Conservative Party; it is imaginable that it might have a preface by Winston Churchill after whom its hero is named. *Nineteen Eighty-Four should be published as soon as possible* ... It is a great book but I pray I may be spared from reading another like it for years to come ...

In his biography of Orwell, published by Secker and Warburg in 1980, Bernard Crick writes that Orwell was 'at best incautious, at worst foolish' in not realising that *Nineteen Eighty-Four* could be read as an anti-socialist tract and used as such by reactionaries all over the world. Had he forgotten what had happened to *Animal Farm*? At this time, of course, Orwell was a dying man, too weak to write a statement clarifying his intentions: he dictated some notes to Warburg who turned them into a press release. But it was too late to undo the damage that had already been done.

Warburg published 25,000 copies of *Nineteen Eighty-Four* on my birthday, in June 1949. Someone gave it to me as a present and I read it at once. Three months later he published *Scenes from a Bourgeois Life*, an autobiographical book of mine with a print-run, I believe, of 3,000. The irony of our respective situations seemed to me to have been underwritten by the Gods. Apart from one or two reviews that characterised *Nineteen Eighty-Four* as a crude anti-communist polemic, the literary establishment as a whole greeted it as a profound work, destined to become a classic. My book was calculated to present socialism with a smiling face yet I cannot complain that the critics were unfair to me; perhaps they gave Warburg the credit for having balanced his books so evenly. While the *Daily Worker*'s massive notice of my *Bourgeois Life* sent the faithful scurrying to Collet's Bookshop, the conservative press produced quite a run at Hatchard's by presenting me as a naughty yet entertaining iconoclast. 'Scene after glittering scene flashes into life' was how *Time and Tide* put it.

A veritable shower of gold descended upon Orwell from vast sales in America and from translation rights all over the world; so much so that he had to be turned into a limited company to safeguard the future of his estate.

Not for anything would I have been in Orwell's shoes nor he, of course, in mine. He was a heavyweight (size 12 in boots); I a lightweight (size 8 shoes).

For me *Nineteen Eighty-Four* is one of the most disgusting books ever written – a book smelling of fear, hatred, lies and self-disgust by comparison with which the works of the Marquis de Sade are no more than the bad dreams of a sick mind. Only a very sick man could have written it, and six months after it appeared Orwell was dead. Apologists for *Nineteen Eighty-Four* maintain that it is not only a prophecy of what is bound to happen if socialism is misdirected, but an attack on fascism and Nazism as well. We know that neither Hitler nor Mussolini abolished the capitalist system; on the contrary, private wealth continued to accumulate. But in *Nineteen Eighty-Four* Ingsoc has triumphed, the old system of private enterprise has gone for ever, Big Brother rules over a squalid, poverty-stricken society in which only the Party bosses retain some semblance of what had once been the good life. Ingsoc is in fact no more than a projection of the kind of régime which extreme anti-Communists have always envisaged as existing in the USSR since 1917 and which anyone who has lived in that country, as I have done, knows to be a travesty of the truth. Despite all the stupidities, errors and crimes that have been committed in the name of Marx it is absurd to suggest that the millions who live in the Communist world are universally downtrodden and depressed. Aspiration, ambition, love and the pursuit of happiness are as common in Moscow as they are in Manchester.

The history of socialism in England is a history of betrayal. The Labour Chancellor of the Exchequer who observed in recent days that 'Socialism is a word I haven't used for many years' typifies generations of working-class politicians who, beginning as revolutionaries who never bothered to read Marx, ended up in the House of Lords. But a socialist of Orwell's presumed integrity must be judged by higher standards. To write a book like *Nineteen Eighty-Four* is to present a gift of inestimable value to those who hate socialism and who would wish, as Churchill once did, to 'strangle it at birth'. In the thirty years and more since Orwell died several generations have been indoctrinated with the idea that socialism leads inexorably to the horrors described in that book. This is a lie but it is widely believed, and the man who launched it is the same wretched little boy who was so unhappy at St Cyprian's School.

Orwell's basic defect is that although he produced convincing reasons for hating the world he knew, he was quite unable to put forward any ideas for the future happiness of mankind – save for a sentimental vision of rural working life before the 1914 war from which most real workers have been only too eager to escape. Many have moved gratefully into the lower-middle class and have voted in their millions for one of their own kind – a woman more attractive yet more ruthless than Flip who believes in hanging and takes pride in being resolute enough to press the nuclear button.

Had Orwell lived, he might have come to detest the generality of readers who now compete to do him honour. One recalls that Alexander Solzhenitsyn first came to light – thanks to Khrushchev – in the role of an honest Marxist who wished to see Communism with a human face. But Solzhenitsyn has since revealed himself not only as an opponent of Stalin's misrule – as Khrushchev first thought –

but of Lenin, Marx, Engels and all the founding fathers of socialism – even poor old Oliver Cromwell. Like Tolstoy in old age, Solzhenitsyn seems to aspire to be the saviour of the entire Western world. Orwell owed his rise to fame not to fellow socialists but to the conservative establishment in Britain and America who seized upon his last two books with delight. Forty years ago they first heard Orwell's voice telling them just what they wanted to hear, and they were overjoyed. In their eyes, here was a truly honest socialist who had come to hate socialism – not just Russian socialism but socialism of any kind. Because Orwell concentrated on the dangers that are certainly inherent in socialism, rather than the benefits such a form of government can bring, it was possible to read him in this light. And of course, from *Animal Farm* onward, the time was absolutely ripe.

President Truman proclaimed his doctrine and began to set up bases in Turkey, at Russia's back door, in 1947. The conference of the Big Four was meeting in Moscow at the time, trying to reach agreement on the future of Germany. I was coming to the end of a four-year stint as Beaverbrook's correspondent in Russia, and I well recall the disastrous effect Truman's speech had on its meetings. Within a week the conference curled up and died. John Foster Dulles was also there. Secure in the knowledge that America alone possessed the bomb, he laid it down in a private talk with me that Communism must not only be contained, as Truman had stated, but ultimately destroyed. When I asked him if I had heard him aright he said: 'Well, they must be pushed back. Out of Europe and back to the Urals.'

I should have reminded Dulles that this was what Hitler had just failed to do when he shot himself in a Berlin bunker. Instead, I distanced myself forthwith from the nuclear evangelist.

Perhaps it is as well that Orwell died when he did, at the height of his achievement. I don't think he would have enjoyed hearing the pundits say that *Animal Farm* and *Nineteen Eighty-Four* were worth several divisions to the 'free world' at the height of the Cold War. And in 1984 he would scarcely be enjoying a happy old age.

Unable to cherish his memory, yet unable to get him out of

my mind. I have written a book about Orwell and his
contemporaries which, like *Such, Such Were the Joys*, will
probably not be published until all of us are dead.

Bill Alexander

George Orwell and Spain

Every school student taking O or A Level examinations in modern history is told to read George Orwell's *Homage to Catalonia* in order to gain an understanding of the Spanish War of 1936-1939. This is as useful as studying the Second World War from the story of a small group of soldiers in some quiet corner, far from the main fronts of El Alamein, Stalingrad or Normandy. Even Hugh Thomas, no champion of the Spanish Republic, has said that *Homage to Catalonia* is a better book about war itself than about the Spanish war.

Orwell went to Spain largely ignorant of the background, situation and the forces involved. He admits 'when I came to Spain I was not only uninterested in the political situation but unaware of it.' Unlike many European intellectuals he had not understood the essential clash between liberty and fascism. Hitler's brutal destruction of democracy in Germany and even Mosley's violence against opponents in Britain in 1934 must have passed him by. Crick, his biographer, could write that before March 1936, when Orwell saw Mosley's blackshirts beating up questioners at a Barnsley meeting, 'there is no indication before this incident of any great concern in Orwell with the nature and spread of fascism.' Orwell himself wrote in April 1936: 'I would like to know whether Mosley is sincere in what he says or if he is deliberately bamboozling the people.' This a couple of weeks after the brutal treatment of anti-fascists at a blackshirt rally at the Albert Hall had provoked a storm of public protest.

The Spanish Popular Front government, formed after the

elections in 1936, won a substantial majority of parliamentary seats but only just over half of the popular vote. The government drawn from Republican groups began to implement a limited programme of social and liberal reforms. This was too much for the strongly entrenched reactionary forces of Spanish society – landowners, church hierarchy and army officers. Led by the top Generals, a military uprising against the Republican Government, planned and prepared well beforehand, took place on 18 July 1936.

The rebels took with them most of the Army, the paramilitary Civil Guards and most of the personnel of the civil service and organs of government. The loyalty of those not openly joining the revolt was open to question. Decisively, the rebels were assured of help before and immediately after the rising from Hitler's Germany and Mussolini's Italy – the two openly fascist powers of Western Europe.

Military coups and *pronunciamentos* were no new feature in Spain. The generals were confident they would win a quick, easy victory. It was not to be. The people – workers, peasants and middle classes – fought back with incredible *élan*, and in spite of heavy losses, they captured barracks and took weapons in many towns and localities. After the first days five out of the seven main cities were in the hands of the government. But General Queipo de Llano, taking over Seville by bluff, massacred the workers and then poured in the trained and disciplined troops of the Army of Africa through the airport in planes provided by Hitler. Zaragoza was an anarchist stronghold, but the workers were tricked into passivity, giving the rebels control of this key communication centre between the South and North. If the government had exercised a firm united command, workers and loyal forces could have taken these centres and the Generals been defeated.

But the government delayed for the few critical days before releasing arms to the workers. The people, without central leadership at this stage, did not realise the need for offensive action. The Madrileños, helped by loyal army elements, defeated the rebels in the city and moved out spontaneously to defend the passes through the Guadarrama mountains, but did not push on. The victorious workers of Barcelona drove in columns consolidating loyalist control of Catalonia and most of Aragon, but when they met firmer resistance, almost at the gates of Zaragoza and Huesca, halted their advance. Though their arms were limited a planned concentration of forces and weapons could have taken both towns. As it was, John Cornford, a Cambridge student who joined the POUM militia in early August, complained of boredom and inactivity in front line positions just outside Huesca. Later the group of Independent Labour Party (ILP) volunteers, including George Orwell, sat in roughly the same positions outside Huesca from January to June 1937 and then returned home to Britain.

Another reason which brought the advances into Aragon to an end was the dominant political outlook among the workers. The CNT, led and inspired by anarchists, and the POUM, a breakaway group from the Communist Party of Spain, though wanting to defeat the fascists, believed that a revolution should be made. Having defeated and driven the enemy from their own immediate area they concentrated on building a revolutionary society.

The people of the Extremadura, Andalucia and Madrid had no such opportunity for speculation. Their harsh reality was the rapid advance northwards of Franco's Army of Africa, supported in all ways by Hitler, aiming to capture Madrid and link up with the fascist-held areas of Navarre and the North. There was little scope for thinking of the form of society in the future – the one task was to stop and defeat the fascists. The bodies of the butchered peasants, workers and progressive people, the screams of the raped women and orphaned children, were the political arguments that the defeat of Franco and the foreign invaders claimed absolute and complete priority. Though always ill-armed, often in confusion and with weak leadership, the workers' militias fought with tenacity. They knew that if the fascists reached Madrid its capture would mean the defeat of the Republic, the end of any hopes of a socialist revolution. Franco was stopped in the streets of Madrid. Meanwhile, the Aragon front was dormant.

Progressive and anti-fascist people throughout the world watched Spain. Would it be yet another country falling to fascism? Would Hitler and Mussolini, using their front man Franco, put out the fresh lights of freedom in Spain? Could the dictators be allowed to send trained units of their forces to help fascism while the Spanish people struggled alone?

At first spontaneously and then in an organised way, men and women from all over the world made their way to help the Spanish people. Most joined the International Brigades, which were formed officially in Albacete on 12 October 1936. The first hastily formed Brigades went to Madrid and joined the bloody fighting, stopping Franco's forces which had got into the city itself.

A few hundred foreign anti-fascists joined the CNT and POUM-influenced units, based on Barcelona. They went to the fronts in Aragon, outside Zaragoza and Huesca.

In Britain the Communist Party largely organised and influenced the 2,300 volunteers who joined the International Brigades. The ILP recruited the forty-odd volunteers who served with the POUM and anarchist units in Aragon.

There were important differences between the two organisations in their approach to the Spanish struggle. Fenner Brockway, leader and theoretician of the ILP, accepted the views of the leaders of POUM that the need was to prepare Soviets of workers and peasants to take control in the crisis; that the Popular Front agreement tied the working class to a non-socialist government 'putting class struggle into storage' and that the demand for a unified military command took the initiative from the workers. Even late in the war, when the fascists had made great advances and the Republic faced defeat, Brockway was still speculating that if the socialist revolution was to take place after the fascists were defeated the forces to carry out the socialist revolution must be prepared and stimulated to seize the opportunity when it arrived. (It must be said that Brockway in his autobiography *Towards Tomorrow* (1977) recognises the weakness of his attitude then.)

Harry Pollitt, the General Secretary of the Communist Party, urged constantly that the immediate issue was to defeat fascism and, calling for help for the Spanish people, said 'they are defending democracy, not only for themselves but for all people.' He stressed that the overriding task, the only path which could lead to any future, was unity in struggle to defeat fascism.

This difference in estimate, reflecting the differences inside Spain, dictated the fighting and fortunes of the two groups of volunteers from Britain – those in the ILP groups and those in the British Battalion of the International Brigade.

Progressive people everywhere in Europe expressed their support and desire to help. They had seen the persecution of writers and artists because of their views on race, the burning of the books by the Nazis. They were concerned that the 'lights of freedom' would go out in yet another country. Felicia Browne, an artist graduate of the Slade School, joined the militia in the first days and was killed on 25 August 1936. Writers such as Ralph Bates, Ralph Fox and Charles Donnelly, and students like John Cornford, Bernard Knox, Sam Lesser and James Albrighton went to fight. Sylvia Townsend Warner and Valentine Acland saw the plight of the wounded and then campaigned in Britain for Medical Aid. Sir Richard Rees, Julian Bell and the Boulting brothers drove ambulances. Others like Stephen Spender, W.H. Auden and Edgell Rickword visited Republican Spain and wrote about the struggle.

This was the atmosphere in which George Orwell decided, in December 1936, to go to Spain to write or to fight. Orwell, under his real name Eric Blair, went to see Pollitt at the Communist Party's London headquarters to ask his help in getting to Spain. Pollitt refused to help Orwell by using the organisation of the International Brigades. He may have done so because he knew that Blair had served in the imperialist police force in Burma, and Ralph Fox and Dave Springhall, Political Commissars in Spain, had been stressing that all volunteers must have firm anti-fascist convictions. Pollitt then had a close relationship with Victor Gollancz, the publisher, and may have heard of the contents of Orwell's manuscript *The Road to Wigan Pier*. (When this did appear as a Left Book Club choice Pollitt wrote a scathingly bitter denunciation.)

So Orwell went along to the ILP who were preparing to send volunteers to Spain and secured their help.

It is interesting to speculate what would have happened if Orwell had been allowed to join the British Battalion of the International Brigade. In the intense political life and arduous fighting his physical bravery might have been steeled and tempered into steadfast courage, his basic misanthropy replaced by comradeship and trust in humanity, his political ignorance and naïvety turned into understanding, so giving him the purpose and cause he looked for, without success, all his life. If this had happened, who could the establishment have found to provide a best-seller to obscure and denigrate the real issues in the struggle against fascism?

At this time Orwell was not a member of the ILP, indeed he did not become a member until much later, in June 1938. In Barcelona he got in touch with John McNair, the ILP political representative and, as Orwell writes in *Homage to Catalonia*, 'I had come to Spain with some notion of writing newspaper articles but I joined the militia almost immediately because at that time and in that atmosphere it seemed the only conceivable thing to do.' McNair, possibly concerned that a well-known recruit should go off to join the International Brigade, wasted no time in attaching Orwell to a POUM unit. His value there, despite his knowledge of the rifle mechanism, must have been doubtful. Cornford months earlier had found himself in a similar unit of mainly Catalan-speaking POUMistas and, expressing his frustration at their inactivity, joined the International Brigade. After a short period with one other British volunteer in a unit of POUM militia, Orwell joined the group of about 30 volunteers who, organised by the ILP, had travelled out together from Britain, although only a few were actual members of the ILP. Some of the group thought they were joining the International Brigades and indeed in April no less than nine said they wished to join the British Battalion. The group joined the 29th Division under political control of POUM.

In July 1936, at the start of the fighting, all the political parties and trade unions organised their own militia groups and units. But the disasters and fascist advances soon brought the realisation of the need for an organised army and a unified command. On the central and southern fronts, the places of heavy fighting, this was achieved, with some difficulty. But on the quiet Aragon front the POUM and CNT kept largely aloof from reorganisation and unified command, retaining their political control under new titles. The influence of the POUM was declining and they could only muster 6-8,000 men. Their 29th Division with Orwell and the ILP group among them sat on the mountains often far from the fascist lines. In Orwell's own words 'I saw very little fighting. Nobody bothered about the enemy.'

At this time the fascists, having been beaten in their attempts to capture Madrid, were concentrating to take the coal, iron and engineering centres of Asturias and the Basque provinces. Pressure on their flanks from the Aragon front would have made this more difficult. Orwell complains that action was impossible because of the lack of rifles and artillery, but, because of the 'Non Intervention' agreement, this was the general lot of all Republican forces.

Whatever arms the government was able to obtain naturally went to the active fronts. But Orwell himself describes what could have been done in his account of the one offensive raid his group made. George Kopp, the Company Commander, was a Russian brought up in Belgium with no previous military experience. He describes, in a page-long story in the ILP paper *New Leader*, how in a raid by 15 men, and with only one casualty, they captured 2,000 rounds of ammunition and some bombs and 'their action compelled 20 lorries carrying 1,000 troops to be sent from the Alasso front.' Kopp's precise knowledge of the troop movements is very open to question, but the story shows that aggressive action would have weakened the fascist concentration on the North. As it was, the same day the ILP group left the front to go on leave to Barcelona the Nazi planes bombed and obliterated Guernica.

Brockway, the *New Leader* and Orwell stress that the ILP group were entitled to go on leave – being allowed five days leave for every month at the front. This certainly did not apply to any other unit in the Republican Army, since it would have meant that one sixth of the army were on leave at any one time – while the fascists were pressing on many fronts. The British Battalion of the International Brigades, despite losing two-thirds of its strength in three days' fighting at Jarama and spending five months in the front line trenches, had only six days out of the line, and then only three miles behind the front.

Barcelona and Catalonia had maintained a quite separate identity from the Popular Front government – partly because of the CNT's anarchist philosophy and partly because of Catalan nationalist separatism. The anarchists did not accept that the fascists could only be defeated by unified, organised effort and that without their defeat any talk of revolutionary change was futile dreaming.

The government and the growing majority of the Spanish people understood that fascism must be defeated before anything and this needed centralised effort in the military, industrial and political fields.

This difference in the fundamental analysis of the conduct of the war led to tension and difficulties. The leaders of the two main trade unions in Barcelona, the UGT and CNT, agreed not to hold a May Day demonstration for fear of clashes. But the POUM Bulletin of 1 May exhorted the workers 'to begin the struggle for working class power' and *La Battalla*, the POUM newspaper, urged vigilance 'with arms at the ready'.

The government ordered the surrender of all the arms which had been held back in Barcelona in the hands of the political parties. On 3 May they took steps to control the Central Telephone Exchange – still held by CNT. Then elements of CNT (their leaders were generally opposed) and the POUM took to the streets with arms they had hidden, and fighting began. The government used its armed police forces and brought in Assault Guards from Valencia. The fighting lasted four days, with casualties, until the government established control. Though Orwell says no POUM units left the front, Broué and Terminé, French historians in general sympathetic to the POUM position, say that on 5 May groups from the 29th (POUM) Division and from the 23rd (CNT) Division left the front, concentrated on Barbastro (20 miles from the front) to march on Barcelona but did not proceed beyond Binefar (30 miles from the front).

Orwell and the ILP group were caught up in this difficult, complex situation. Negrín, who became Socialist Prime Minister after the May events in Barcelona, became friendly with Orwell in London in the 1940s. He wrote:

> He [Orwell] came to the chaotic front of Aragon under the tutelage of a group *possibly* [Negrín's italics] infiltrated by German agents (read what he says about Germans moving freely from one side to the other and what the Nazis officially stated after the war about their activities on our side) but *certainly* [Negrín's italics] controlled by elements very allergic, not only to Stalinism (this was

more often than not a pure pretext) but to anything that meant a united and supreme direction of the struggle under a common discipline.

(Negrín's little-known relationship with Orwell is discussed by Herbert L. Matthews in an article in the New York magazine *The Nation*, 27 December 1952.)

Only a very few of the group were old members of the ILP, understanding and supporting the political position of POUM. Hugh O'Donnell, a British Communist working in the Foreigners Department of the PSUC (United Socialist Party of Catalonia) met Orwell (Eric Blair) and a number of the ILP group when they arrived in Barcelona on 30 April. He wrote to Pollitt in London that many of the group were discontented and frustrated with being in the POUM unit and he listed nine men, including George Orwell, who said they wanted to join the British Battalion in the International Brigades. O'Donnell wrote: 'the leading personality and most respected man in the contingent at present is Eric Blair. He has little political understanding and said he is not interested in party politics and came to Spain as an anti-fascist to fight fascism. As a result of his experience at the front he has grown to dislike the POUM and is now awaiting his discharge from the POUM.' Orwell himself bears this out in a letter to Frank Jellinck in 1938, after writing *Homage to Catalonia* – 'I've given a more sympathetic picture of the POUM line than I actually felt, because I always told them that they were wrong and refused to join the party.'

Yet Orwell went voluntarily to the POUM headquarters when the fighting began on 3 May. He was given a rifle from their store and helped to guard the building, though he did not fire his weapon and went down to a hotel for meals. Most of the ILP group kept away from the events, staying indoors in their hotels; some then made their own way back to Britain, and others joined non-POUM Spanish units.

Orwell explains his action thus: 'When I see an actual flesh and blood worker in conflict with his natural enemy, the policeman, I do not have to ask which side I am on.' Strange reasoning given his own past, and when one recalls he had not taken part in the unemployed and anti-fascist demonstrations in Britain, the targets of much police brutality. Even McNair saw the fighting was opening the way to the fascists. Perhaps the clue to Orwell's behaviour may be found in the comment by Sir Richard Rees, his friend and literary executor, on Orwell's account of life on the Aragon front – 'written almost in the style of a schoolboy's letters, it was not bad fun in a way.' Orwell himself wrote 'it was not bad fun wandering about the dark valleys with the stray bullets flying overhead like red shanks whistling.'

Orwell had no understanding of the world-wide significance of the struggle in Spain, he knew little of the national efforts of the Popular Front government to achieve a united front against fascism, he had never seen the Republican flag, he did not agree with the actions of the POUM – he took the rifle in the role of an outsider, a journalist looking for different experiences to figure in a future book.

When the fighting was over, with the CNT leaders convincing those who were still fighting of the folly of their action, only *La Batalla* urged the continuation of the fighting and spoke of 'the glorious days'. On 10 May Orwell and what was left of the ILP group returned to their front. Wally Tapsell, a political leader of the British volunteers, had gone from the International Brigade Base in Albacete to establish contact with the group and persuade them to join the British Battalion, but McNair would not let him have discussions with them.

Again of this POUM-held sector Orwell says 'there was not much happening at the front', though at this time 4,000 Basque children were being organised in Bilbao to be sent to safety in Britain, while Franco's concentrated forces smashed the last defences of the Basque country. Ten days later Orwell was hit in the throat by a bullet and after treatment in several hospitals arrived at a POUM convalescent home.

After the May events in Barcelona the Popular Front government took steps against the POUM. Its paper was suppressed, many of its leaders arrested, and its military units disbanded. Most of the ILP group had already gone home to Britain. At the end of June Orwell, his wife, McNair and Cottman decided that they might be arrested and left Spain.

Orwell went to his home and began the actual writing of *Homage to Catalonia*, though he had been thinking about the book in Spain. Warburg (of Secker and Warburg – the eventual publishers) says that Orwell saw him in December 1936 saying 'I want to go to Spain and have a look at the fighting ... write a book about it. Good chaps these Spaniards, can't let them down.'

Bob Edwards, leader of the ILP group at the front, wrote about Orwell's attitude to the war: 'I got the impression that he was allowing his needs as a writer to override his duty as a soldier. He was wanting, I thought, as many experiences as possible as background material for the book he was writing.' On 9 May 1937, almost before the fighting was over in Barcelona, Orwell wrote to Gollancz, 'I hope I shall have a chance to tell the truth about what I have seen. I hope to have a book ready for you about the beginning of next year.' Gollancz refused to publish it, but *Homage to Catalonia* appeared in 1938 and today, in 1984, it has appeared in twenty reprints.

How does Orwell himself appear from his own writing of his life as a soldier? There is a strong sense of remoteness and detachment from his comrades-in-arms – both in the ILP group and the Spaniards and other nationalities in his company. He appears as a loner. This characteristic is in reality confirmed by the fantasised, romanticised account – both in his book and in his near-doggerel poem – of his very brief encounter with an Italian volunteer in the Barcelona barracks.

The conditions of muck and filth in the shallow trenches, expressive of primitive life in most of Spain, are scathingly described. There is no account of efforts to change conditions and so, by example, help to break Spain from its primitive, backward past. He states that the floor of his unit cookhouse was deep in wasted food. It must have been unique among all the Army cookhouses. The shortage of food was general – mess tins and utensils were scraped clean by the ever hungry soldiers.

His aloofness from the common spirit of Popular Front Spain is strikingly exposed in his cynical dismissal of the fact that wounded soldiers demanded to return to the front. It happened! Without this spirit the Republican forces, outnumbered and outgunned, could not have fought on for eighteen more months after Orwell had gone home. Resistance to Franco would not have persisted despite forty years of terror and repression following his victory.

Although Orwell admits that he saw very little fighting, was in a remote, dormant sector of the front and hurried out his book without time to study the military lessons of the fighting on the Madrid, Málaga or Basque fronts, he has no hesitation in pronouncing on military matters. In an Olympian, chauvinist way he says, 'The Spaniards are good at many things but not at making war.' But the Spanish people, despite most of the regular army going over to Franco, deprived of weapons, held back not only the Spanish fascists but large military units of German and Italian forces for thirty-two months. Far longer than the French and Belgian forces did in 1940!

He pronounced that 'the anarchist militia, in spite of their indiscipline, were notoriously the best fighters among the pure Spanish forces.' The reality was that their behaviour in battle, because of their philosophy, was unpredictable – brave advances negated by unnecessary retreats. Durruti's column of 3,500 avowed anarchists from Barcelona went to Madrid in the crucial battles for its defence – at times they fought as fiercely as anyone, but at others left open vital sectors in the Casa del Campo, thus allowing the fascists to get a foothold in the city. Indeed it was only when the anarchist soldiers, after experience in battle, recognised the need for unified leadership, organisation and discipline and so changed their philosophy that they became dependable units in the Popular Army.

The fundamental reason for Orwell's attitude to the war – on top of his British upper-class arrogance and overriding personal objective to write a book – was his lack of understanding of anti-fascist feeling. He had visited, with an eye to a future book, the down-and-outs in London. Commissioned to write a book, he had briefly visited the distressed industrial areas of the North of England. But there was no sense of identification with the men and women caught in the capitalist crisis – no sense that 'there but for my family background go I.' The horrors of fascism in Italy and Germany do not appear to have made him angry, emotionally concerned to do something. This lack of deep feeling, almost one of neutrality, shows itself throughout his writing. The man Orwell refuses to shoot at because he had his trousers down might have fired machine guns to butcher 4,000 in the Badajoz bullring. The same man would certainly have tried to kill Orwell when he had fastened his belt. Orwell feels no anger at the man who wounds him – indeed wishes to congratulate him on his good shooting. He is certainly not concerned at his own absence from the battle line. Orwell saw the war as a game, material for a book.

After a brief two months in the North of England Orwell wasted little time before writing *The Road to Wigan Pier*. But he used his description of conditions there to attack those drawn towards socialism and communism as a caricature composite figure of 'fruit juice drinker, nudist, sandal wearer, sex maniac, Quaker, Nature cure quack, pacifist and feminist.' A description ill-fitted to his guides, leaders of the National Unemployed Workers' Movement, one of whom, Tommy Degnan, was to become a tough fighter in the International Brigades and a leader of the Yorkshire miners. No! Orwell had qualities as an observer but his conclusions have little relation to what he had seen.

So retiring from the Spanish War, admitting that he knew little before he went and saw little there, again he wasted no time in studying the complex situation before expounding his opinions. It is true that after the ILP group went home the *New Leader* largely ignored the Spanish war, but the *News Chronicle, Daily Worker* and Tory newspapers all carried reports showing the tenacity and determination of the People's Army. But Orwell used his skill as a writer to mask his prejudices and ignorance.

Throughout his writing his sheltered life-style coupled with his ignorance of the realities of Spanish life led him to many pronouncements hostile to the people. 'The latrine in the Barcelona barracks did its necessary bit towards puncturing my own illusions about the Spanish civil war.' He was familiar with water closets in his middle-class English surroundings, but they were unknown outside the bigger Spanish towns. His recurring thought was 'the detail of our lives was just as sordid and degrading as it could be in prison let alone in a bourgeois army.' Life in the Republican Army was hard, often very hard. There were times of danger and diarrhoea when men had to relieve themselves in the slit trenches. But the soldiers, coming from mainly peasant backgrounds, tried to keep clean, learnt to read, wrote home, sang and discussed, thus showing that the fuller life they were fighting for was beginning in the trenches. In another of his cynical, oft-quoted pronouncements Orwell says: 'a soldier anywhere near the front line is usually too hungry or frightened or cold or above all too tired to bother about the political origins of the war.' Orwell, despite his very limited experience, had not bothered to acquaint himself with the behaviour of the men of the Lister, Modesto, Campesino and other Spanish units who showed outstanding fighting qualities because 'they knew what they were fighting for and loved what they knew.'

If Orwell was sincere and honest with himself he must have been aware of his limitaions and his temerity in writing *Homage to Catalonia*. When he met Negrín on a number of occasions in 1940 he did not tell him that he had fought in Spain and written *Homage to Catalonia*. Negrín did not know of Orwell's book at the time, and wrote of Orwell: 'he was very eager to enquire about policies, internal and external in line with conduct of the war. I have the impression that Orwell was satisfied with my explanations given to him without reserve.' Orwell's silence about his experiences in Spain and his failure, given this unique opportunity, to check his views and conclusions can only bring into question his honesty. But there is no sign in Orwell's essay 'Looking Back on the Spanish War', written in 1943, that he was willing to modify his written opinions and admit that he had pronounced without understanding.

Many other writers on the Spanish War have expanded on the difficulties, confusion, muddle and frequent incompetence in the Republican front and rear. But the great merit of Orwell's writing in the eyes of the establishment is his contention that the revolution was cynically betrayed, and that the Popular Front collapsed into warring factions. Orwell is used to distract attention from the real lessons of the struggle – though it must be said that young people, despite the obfuscating influence of Orwell's book, still want to learn what really happened.

Fascism in Italy and Germany had appeared invincible, almost inevitable as a stage in social development. Mosley, the

Daily Mail and his supporters in Britain were confident that democracy and the working-class movements would be broken. Spain and its defenders destroyed such ideas when they held in check the fascist war machines for nearly three years. Orwell sneered at the Popular Front slogan 'It is better to die on your feet than to live on your knees' but it entered the consciousness of the democratic armies in the Second World War, and it was the philosophy of the resistance fighters throughout occupied Europe.

The German, Italian and Austrian democratic movements were defeated by fascism because they could not agree to sink their differences and did not accept that the defeat of the fascist menace took priority over all else. From 1934 the Spanish people understood and worked for united action against reaction. The Popular Front pact of January 1936 was an electoral agreement, but the bitter experiences of the war brought the political groupings together as they saw that reaction threatened them all. This meant changes in political ideas. The anarchist philosophy crumpled and retreated when faced with better armed and organised fascist units. The communist and socialist ideas – organisation and priority to defeat fascism – were proved right in practice and gained ground. The Communist Party, in particular, gained influence because the Soviet Union was the only power to give active help to the government, and because the Communists had shown in policies and by personal example the ways to victory.

When Orwell left the front for Barcelona he deplored the fact that civilian clothes had replaced the uniforms seen in the city in January. True, for the Spanish people the red scarves and the euphoria of the early days had been replaced by the grim, sober realisation that the defeat of fascism was going to be very difficult. Orwell did not understand or even know about the general organisation and training going on outside the towns to form a Popular Army. He did not understand the general demand by all groups in the government that Catalonia and Aragon should also end romantic, adventurist talk and inactivity, get industry working for the war and the men organised into effective military units.

The POUM slogan 'The war and the revolution are inseparable' had already been shown as hollow phrase-mongering – an

attitude which threatened both the war effort and the prospect
of any revolution. Those sectors where the POUM and some
anarchist elements held influence, far from being on the
offensive in fighting the fascists, were stagnant. As Orwell put it
'We didn't worry much about the enemy.' Far from winning
more support for revolutionary change, there was growing
opposition by small farmers and land workers to the
'libertarian' experiments imposed by POUM and anarchists in
much of Aragon.

Orwell, in his version of the Barcelona events and his
pronouncements on the Spanish scene, directs his anger at the
Communists and the Soviet Union, saying that 'the one thing
for which the Communists were working was not to postpone a
Spanish revolution till a more suitable time but to make sure it
never happened.' Orwell had had little contact with
Communists. There were certainly none at that time in the ILP
group, he could have read very little of their policies and
attitudes (the ILP group complained that they only received
the *New Leader*), and the statements by Spanish Communists
like Pasionaria, Lister and Modesto were ignored in *La Batalla*.

The Spanish government which was taking steps to bring
Aragon and Catalonia into the war effort had only two
Communist Ministers; it was far from being Communist, as
even Crick, Orwell's biographer, continued to suggest in a
recent television programme. Prieto, a right-wing socialist and
certainly no crypto-communist, had, from the War Council,
initiated the military moves to end the chaos in Barcelona. The
two anarchist Ministers in the government, García Oliver and
Frederica Montseny, appealed to the anarchists to stop
fighting. There was general popular condemnation throughout
all Republican Spain of those who were undermining the
defeat of fascism.

Orwell's views of the possibility of a revolution in Spain in
1936 and 1937 were naïve in the extreme. The conditions and
forces to make a revolution did not exist. The dictators had
shown their determination to defeat the Popular Front even
before the Generals revolted. The USA, Britain and even the
Popular Front government in France helped the fascists and
hindered the Republic, especially by depriving them of their
right to buy arms. The German and Italian workers were held

in subjection, while in Britain the TUC had gone alone with 'Non Intervention' until September 1937. There could be very little support from outside for a revolution in Spain. By November 1936 the fascists had conquered nearly half Spain and had a foothold inside Madrid, being checked only by bloody battles. Even the Barcelona Regional Committee of the CNT said on 4 May – while Orwell was guarding the POUM headquarters with a rifle – that 'It is fascism which must be defeated.'

The Soviet Union had become very popular in Spain because it was were the only power to fight in the London 'Non Intervention' Committee and the League of Nations for the legal right of the Republic to buy arms. Their words were backed by supplies of arms and food. In the early days they sent a few pilots, tank crews and military instructors and advisers to help the Republican Army. According to Soviet sources only about 2,000 military men went to Spain and there were never more than 600 to 800 there at one time. The delivery of Soviet material was very difficult and hazardous; their ships were attacked by the Germans and Italians in the Mediterranean and the French government blocked supplies by land. Chamberlain was manoeuvring to isolate the Soviet Union diplomatically while encouraging the fascists. The Soviet Union had every reason – morally and politically – to work for the victory of the Republican government. But they did not have the power and influence either to start a revolution or equally to delay one.

Orwell's political estimation of the position in Spain and of the Barcelona May events have small foundations in reality. His position as an outsider is confirmed in his description of England as he retired from the Spanish struggle – 'all sleeping the deep, deep sleep of England'. His London-bound train may have passed another carrying British volunteers to help the Spanish people fight on for another two years. In the poor streets of Wigan and Barnsley unemployed men and women were collecting food and medical supplies. In Stepney and Cheetham anti-fascists were resisting Mosley's blackshirts. In meetings, organisations and demonstrations the people were exposing Chamberlain's sell-out and appeasement and demanding real opposition to the fascist powers and their preparation for war. In England the people were understanding the depth of Pasionaria's appeal: 'Stop the Bombs on Madrid and Barcelona or they may fall on London and Paris tomorrow.'

Orwell had not learnt the true lessons of Spain.

Robert Stradling

Orwell and the Spanish Civil War: A Historical Critique

The object of this essay is to examine George Orwell's writings on the Spanish Civil War from the standpoint of the professional historian and that of the student of History. The texts which form the subject of this exercise – Orwell's Spanish *curriculum vitae* – comprise a full-scale book, *Homage to Catalonia*, four discrete articles of varying length, and reviews of eleven books on Spain which appeared in the three years following his return from service in the Republican forces.[1] It is thus a sufficiently large and variegated body of work upon which to base an appraisal of Orwell's contribution to our knowledge of the Civil War, and an evaluation of his role in forming subsequent opinion about its central issues.

It might be noted at the outset that Orwell's own judgement of work on this subject other than his own was distinctly unfavourable:

> The immediately striking thing about the Spanish War books, at any rate those written in English, is their shocking dullness and badness. But what is more significant is that almost all of them ... are written from a political angle, by cocksure partisans telling you what to think.[2]

Some years later, he commented *à propos* of *Homage* itself, that it was 'a frankly political book, but in the main it is written with a certain detachment'; adding that 'I did try very hard in it to tell the whole truth.'[3] In this, as in so many other places,

Orwell invites (nay, challenges) the reader to approach his writings with the tools of historical criticism. How 'certain' was the detachment, how 'whole' the truth? When we ask such questions historians know in advance that no absolutely satisfying answer is obtainable. The results of investigation can only be more or less adequate or inadequate, and this has to suffice for working purposes.

Not long ago the present writer prepared an undergraduate teaching option on the history of Spain in the 1930s, automatically including *Homage* in the reading list. Leaving aside the subliminal implications of this act, the conscious reasons were quite straightforward. In the English-reading world *Homage* is by far the most familiar contemporary account of the Spanish War, and was also written by a participant. Unlike hundreds of others of its species it is easily and cheaply available. Its form and style are surpassingly lucid and approachable, the narrative dramatic, the analysis strong and sharp, the argument (in every sense) perfectly transparent. It seemed likely that no other book would so well present the student with the physical and political realities of the war, or expose so clearly the arcane ideological atmosphere of the struggle, all within the authentic context of the universal issues of the 1930s. Further, Orwell was so open about his own fallibility, especially in matters of detail, that it may be considered, *prima facie*, that even where it was less than utterly reliable, *Homage* rather enhanced than diminished our understanding. Thus the book seemed both good History and an extremely useful document.

Shortly before *Homage to Catalonia* was published, Orwell wrote to a friend that he and his publisher had given it this title because they could not think of anything better.[4] It is impossible to tell whether (if true) this was merely disingenuous, or intellectually bankrupt. It certainly made no sense commercially, since such a title could hardly be regarded, in 1938, as a good selling point. At any rate it is a bizarre fact concerning one of the most famous books of the age, and points up the absurd fact that it's not about the ostensible subject at all. How would the innocent eye or ear react to the semiotics of the title 'Homage to Catalonia'? Your average *habitué* of Hampstead might imagine it to describe a piano piece by a musical son of Catalonia – Albéniz or Granados, say – incorporating the rhythm of the national dance, the *Sardana*. A more specifically academic mind would probably envisage a *festschrift* of some kind, presenting essays on the folklore, literature and history of the Catalan people. Surely a book with such a title should address itself in part to the suggested subject, or even (since 'Catalonia' is more intensified than otherwise by the word 'Homage') place it at the centre of its cogitations?

In fact 'Catalonia' is about as meaningful a guide to the contents of this book as 'Wigan Pier' is to those of his previous one. 'I'm afraid I must tell you', replied Orwell to an enquiry during a BBC broadcast, 'that Wigan Pier does not exist.'[5] Similarly, Catalonia has no observable existence in Orwell's book about the Spanish War. It displays awareness of no aspect of the history of the country, nor of its culture and society, either *sui generis* or in the context of Spain as a whole. Although he does refer to Catalan, only two words of the language appear in the text, and one of them is persistently mis-spelled.[6] In no other way does Orwell distinguish between the Catalans and other Spaniards. This is not surprising in itself, because he spent only two of his six months in Spain inside Catalonia's borders. Most of the Spaniards he met, whether at the front, or behind the lines in the villages, were Aragonese. Moreover, the Catalan language was then not widely spoken amongst the working class of Barcelona, and during the war their organisations were actively discouraging its use.[7] Of course Orwell does devote some of the most memorable sections of his book to Barcelona, and aspects of its topography and daily life are mentioned *en passant*. But the Catalan capital is for his purposes any large industrial city in the world where the revolution of the proletariat happens to be taking place. The city is essentially a site of socialist struggle, and only accidentally Barcelona. And even here, nothing is said about Barcelona antedating the moment – six months before Orwell's arrival – of the defeat of the military uprising. In short, anyone who turns to *Homage to Catalonia* in the hope of being informed about its apparent subject is totally wasting his or her time.

The evidence (as we shall see) strongly suggests that Orwell did no background reading on matters Iberian before he went to Spain. None of his writings on the war indicate that he learned anything subsequently about Spain which he regarded as relevant. The events he describes and analyzes therefore take place in an almost complete historical and cultural vacuum. As usual, Orwell composed his book in a terrific hurry – about five months of the second half of 1937 – but whilst he was doing so he read and reviewed E. Allison Peers' book *Catalonia Infelix*, the first modern scholarly study of Catalonia to appear in English.[8] This contained a graphic account of the anarchist terror, along with scathing condemnation of the Catalan revolutionaries in general. Peers' conclusions, agonizing enough for a man who was a sincere friend of Catalonia's nationalist aspirations, were of the 'better Franco than Durruti' variety. For Orwell, who was at this point more attracted to the anarchist than to the POUMist cause, this was sufficient to reject everything about Peers' book, except for one useful anti-Communist quotation which he quietly expropriated.[9]

It is a remarkable paradox that Catalonia owes its very existence in the consciousness of nine out of ten people in the non-Hispanic world to the title-page of a book in which it has no tangible existence. This is the strange kind of publicity which the autonomous government of Catalonia celebrated in February 1984, when they and Barcelona's two Universities sponsored an international conference, which might have been titled 'Homenatge a George Orwell'. During this prolonged act of gratitude, the High Priest of Orwelliana, Professor Bernard Crick, solemnly attended a Catalan rock opera based on *Animal Farm*![10]

What is true of Catalonia is only slightly less so of Spain as a whole. Orwell was remarkably ignorant of all things Iberian in terms of 'background', either regarding it as unimportant, or (more probably) being unable to spare the time to find out. As Crick says, he 'seems to have had very little idea *where* he was';[11] at the front his mind was fully occupied with physical comfort (or rather the lack of it) and survival. In the few moments when he was not mentally exhausted, he investigated and reported his immediate surroundings, but in the manner – so often encountered in his work – of the almost painfully guileless naïf. For the academic, Orwell's epistemological innocence, which he rather proclaimed than disguised, can cause embarrassment and irritation. If Foucault's theory that knowledge-systems are the fundamental medium of social conditioning and the exercise of power has validity, then Orwell is what he wanted to be, one of the most nearly independent of writers. Because he represents that comparatively rare thing in Western society, the untutored intellectual (despite, or perhaps because of, his Eton education) he has achieved something of the status of the Holy Man. It is interesting that in the 1950s both Stephen Spender and Lionel Trilling saw the Orwell of *Homage* as a uniquely virgin soldier in the army of truth.[12] Strange as it may seem to the lay reader, such apparently striking references are of little help to the historian, any more (as can be readily observed elsewhere in this volume) than to the modern philosopher and literary critic. Let us leave aside his disdain for all the obvious sources of study in his subject, with the *possible* exception of the POUM newspaper, *La Batalla*. It seems likely that Orwell understood spoken Spanish (or rather, Castilian) badly – if at all – and there is an element of doubt concerning his ability to read it with any real fluency. At times, of course, he is quite frank about this, referring several times in *Homage* to difficulties with the language, and admitting that his spoken Castilian was 'villainous'. Elsewhere, however, he is more ambiguous, allowing the impression that for practical purposes he was an able conversationalist. Let us explore some instances.

During his sentry-duty on the cinema rooftop, at the height of the May Events in Barcelona, he reports an elaborate conversation with a Civil Guard opposite his position. This individual was stationed over fifty yards from Orwell, on the other side of the Rambla (the city's main boulevard), and the exchange seems to have taken place above the crackle of small arms fire.[14]

In his attempt to save his unit commander, Georges Kopp, from a government prison, Orwell claims he went to the War Department HQ and explained a very complex and delicate situation to the duty officer. If (on his own part) occasionally lapsing into French, he understood the technical queries of his interlocutor, and actually obtained the specific document he was seeking.[15] Even those who speak Spanish like a native will readily appreciate the nature of this achievement.

In the course of his 'Notes on the Spanish Militia' (?1939), Orwell explained his position of minor responsibility within the English contingent of his POUM company by the unambiguous assertion that 'so far as the English were concerned it was simply a question of choosing among the few men who spoke Spanish.'[16]

Finally, and most remarkably, as he was lying on the ground, moments after the sniper's bullet had passed through his throat, Orwell claims not only to have been conscious, but conscious enough to have heard and understood every word of what an excited Spanish comrade was saying.[17]

These incidents (among others) give rise to suspicion concerning Orwell's honesty and consistency. Such doubt must be placed alongside his lack of information about Spain, in our assessment of his capacity to understand and interpret what he observed. It seems to receive corroboration from those occasional passages in *Homage* where original Spanish phrases and snatches of conversation crop up. Given the author's description of it as 'a frankly political book', these passages must be regarded as more than an attempt to give *Homage* an artistic verisimilitude in the same manner as the Spanish writings of Ernest Hemingway. They must in addition, and unavoidably, be seen as laying claim to a specific *qualification* for comment. Yet, under examination, these passages often fail to sustain such a claim to a sufficient degree.[18] In a specialist study of Orwell's 'road to Catalonia', it is asserted (without supporting evidence) that he had in 1936 'a non-political reading knowledge of Spanish'.[19] No other work on Orwell that I have seen takes this matter as sufficiently important even to merit mention, far less discussion, yet it seems fundamental in conditioning our acceptance of many things described and commented upon in *Homage*. It seems fair, therefore, to remark that as a *study of the history* of the Spanish Civil War, *Homage to Catalonia* is of questionable value. Not only did its author fail to carry out basic research, he was not qualified to perform it in the first place.

Did Orwell intend his book as a work of History? The question is otiose, since there can be little doubt that thousands – wholly or partly – have always perceived and received it as such. In any case, even when clearly accessible, the 'intentions' of the author, although not irrelevant, are not definitive either. Despite his statement that books of the genre to which *Homage* obviously (*inter alia*) belongs – eyewitness accounts or memoirs – have a useful life of about six months, he evidently did not see his own work as ephemeral, and later came to suspect that it might be perennial.[20] As a piece of 'inside' documentary reportage and commentary, *Homage* shares characteristics with two of its author's earlier works, *Down and Out in Paris and London* and *The Road to Wigan Pier*. Is it, therefore, to be classed as a work of 'superior' journalism? Most Orwell experts – including his biographer, Bernard Crick – contradict his own (repeated) insistence that he went to Spain to write, and not, necessarily, to fight; but their reasons for so doing are by no means convincing.[21] In later years, he was obliged to join the NUJ in order to earn a living, but his suspicion of journalists as a professional species was hardened into contempt by his Spanish experience. If there is one category of humanity which emerges from *Homage* with less credit than Soviet agents and international capitalists, it is surely the Fleet Street hack. For many years thereafter, Orwell excoriated journalists as a gang who deal *exclusively* in fraud and swindle, who are disciples of Satan, in the sense of the Devil's alleged fatherhood of lies. If we may interpret his aim 'to make political writings into an art',[22] it seems likely that he looked upon *Homage* as an artistic document of the historic reality of the Spanish War, akin in significant respects to the outstanding memoirs of the Western Front (which he knew well), but also – *mutatis mutandis* – to the poetry of the Spanish Civil War and to Picasso's *Guernica*.

Orwell was an emphatically non-academic writer. But this does not invalidate the academic's task of exploring the potential taxonomic locations of a book like *Homage*: herein, after all, lies one key to the plurality of meaning in a text. Highly relevant here is Orwell's own attitude to history as the thing to which he wished to contribute his 'artistic document'. His time in Spain gave him an intense awareness of the necessity of history, which he saw as inseparable from artistic freedom. But his perception of history differed markedly from that of the student of the academic discipline of 'History', in a manner not dissimilar to that in which his appreciation of literature – as exhibited in his critical essays – differs from that usually inculcated into students of 'English literature'. In his wartime articles, such as 'Inside the Whale', 'The Lion and the Unicorn', and (above all) 'Looking Back on the Spanish War', he stated and re-stated a passionate belief in the hermeneutic role of historical perspective, and the pristine inviolability of the recorded past. One of the most chilling of the horrors of *Nineteen Eighty-Four* – one of two novels in which Orwell's central character is a writer – is the professional delight taken by the slave-journalist Winston Smith in his constant and thorough rape of something which his other self knows to be the most precious of humanity's resources – the 'historical truth'. Thus, in an essay composed whilst in the throes of gestating his last book ('Why I Write') he included as one of the four factors of his inspiration, 'Historical Impulse. Desire to see things as they are, to find out true facts and store them up for the use of posterity.'[23]

All this gives rise to considerable problems for the historian, who must be on guard against being seduced by Orwell's blatant respect for the subject. First, because for Orwell, history is 'the present as seen from the future', and not 'the past as seen from the present'. In the quotation just given from 'Inside the Whale' – perhaps unknowingly – he transposed Ranke's famous principle of historical writing (*wie es eigentlich gewesen*) from the past to the present tense. His concept of history, therefore, was the dim sense of the 'historian of the future' to which the articulate layman and many politicians often give rhetorical voice. In the first critical appraisal of Orwell to appear, Tom Hopkinson rightly pointed out that 'he was without any historical perspective. He saw the world of his day with peculiar intensity because he saw very little of its past.'[24] Second, it will be apparent that Orwell's chief concern was with the concrete, atomic 'facts' of history, which, preserved and guarded against interference, will inevitably yield a harvest of literal and universal truth. Leaving aside the historian's profound reservations on this assumption, it is more important to note the serious contradictions it suggests in Orwell's method of writing in *Homage*. He felt himself (it is commonly agreed) free to interfere with the chronology and the detail of his Spanish experiences in the interests of aesthetic balance and artistic emphasis. It follows that *by Orwell's own standards*, 'art' is not in harmony with 'history' but, on the contrary, in conflict with it. This inconsistency is so salient and creates such an audible discord in Orwell's intellectual principles, that it is difficult to believe that he never recognised it.

We have seen how unimpressed Orwell was with the literature of the Spanish War. It was not simply an aesthetic judgement. He was filled with horror and foreboding at the promiscuous distortion, manipulation, suppression, and invention of reality; untruths which were disseminated in the interests of established power-systems, and thus oppression. Not only was 'the truth' itself being thus annihilated. In addition the course of the war and of the revolution, and with them the aspirations and lives of Spaniards – perhaps as a prelude to those of all humanity – were being literally dictated by the written and broadcast word. It is necessary to bear in mind that, as a man of the 1930s, Orwell's reaction to all this was *necessarily* more emotional (and more moral) than our present, culture-conscious 'detachment'. He reached maturity in the first age of mass-communication and mass-reception, the first generation of near-universal literacy in Great Britain. Most families by the mid-1930s had access to a radio receiver and a cinema screen which completed the preconditions for the first era of overt and ubiquitous propaganda.[25] Yet again, it is not difficult to detect a contradiction at the core of Orwell's attitude to this question. The conjunction of the media-maturation of this decade with his own suffering, persecution, and near-death in Spain, gave Orwell a missionary sense of truth and 'socialism', which was as all-pervading as it was self-righteous. 'Every line of serious work that I have written since 1936 has been written ... *against* totalitarianism and *for* democratic socialism, as I understand it.'[26] In other words, he was a self-confessed propagandist, indistinguishable in one respect from the outstanding victim of his onslaught (in *Homage*) against left-journalists, 'Frank Pitcairn'.[27] All the same, it is ultimately to his credit that Orwell deplored the use of history as a tool of power, and that we find this salutary – if unoriginal – message inscribed in all his Spanish writings.

In general comment by historians on these texts has been
appreciative. Most commentators at least accept that they
provide reliable, (thus essential) material for the history of the
Spanish War. The outstanding exception, however, is the
author of the most widely-utilised comprehensive account of
the war in any language, Hugh Thomas.[28] In all editions of this
work to date, a dismissive footnote on *Homage* has been
included; and the year following its first appearance, Thomas
published a longer notice in the *New Statesman*.[29] The latter is
intended as a demolition job on a competitor, but in practice
the charge completely fails to go off. Thomas admits that
Homage is 'the best' of over 3,000 contemporary effusions on
the subject, yet asserts that it 'is very misleading about the
Spanish Civil War'! Having neglected to illustrate this
contention, Thomas goes on to state that 'the book is simply an
account of Orwell's experiences, written almost in diary form';
adding the observation that 'since he (Orwell) got on very well
with the POUM at the front he assumed that the POUM's
policy behind the lines was correct.' None of these statements
is valid. *Homage* is by no means a straightforward account of its
author's experiences. Two of the longest chapters – about a
quarter of the whole – are devoted to political analysis and
polemic, and much of the remainder is punctuated by
commentary passages. Though the fundamental structure is
narrative, it is pretty far removed from diary form. Moreover,
Orwell insists that he resisted the POUM arguments about
war-policy with which he was pressured at the front, finding
those of the Communists far more convincing. (This claim is
sustained by others.)[30] In May 1937, during the days
immediately preceding the Barcelona 'events', he made
strenuous efforts to transfer from the POUM militia into the
Communist-run International Brigades.[31] He later, on several
occasions, stated or implied the admission that, despite the
means utilised to achieve them, PCE/PSUC policies were alone
capable of winning the war for the Republic. Given the status
of his own book, and his other *dicta* on the subject, it seems
necesary to conclude that Hugh Thomas is so mistaken in his
assessment of *Homage* that one suspects he had either never
read it, or had just spent a good lunch-time at his club (or
both), when he wrote his *New Statesman* review.

Several Catalan historians have commended the value of Orwell's account in the years since the lifting of censorship in Spain. (Some of these, it is true, are declared POUMistas, like Alba, and Coll and Pané.)[32] In a recent study of Barcelona, Joan Villaroya states that Orwell 'has synthesised marvellously, and in a lucid and economical way', the atmosphere in the first European city to come under repeated aerial bombardment.[33] One of the most distinguished historians of Republican Spain, if with reservations, writes of the 'vivid and sympathetic account' of the May events given in *Homage*.[34] Finally, the classic description of revolutionary Barcelona, encountered early in the book, is given its place in the first selection of documentary readings on the Civil War made for use by students, which recently appeared.[35]

Though not overwhelming, this consensus is justified, for much of Orwell's detail can be corroborated from other sources. Nevertheless, when he *did* make a mistake, he was often inclined to be both persistent and dogmatic in his error. A few examples must suffice.

In his essay on the Spanish militias, Orwell wrote that 'a lot of harm was done by the lies published in the left-wing papers to the effect that the fascists were using explosive bullets. So far as I know there is no such thing as an explosive bullet, and certainly the fascists weren't using them.'[36] In fact the Nationalists *were* using explosive bullets during the time that Orwell was in Spain, though probably not on the Aragon front. Jason Gurney, who arrived on the Jarama battlefield within days of Orwell's arrival at Huesca, had his right hand destroyed by such a bullet at much the same time as the latter received his injury.[37] The memoirs of the mercenary fighter-pilot Oloff de Wet, and those of the American Communist Ralph Bates, also confirm the frequent use of this weapon on the Madrid front at this period.[38] Here, Orwell is merely the victim of his own prejudice against the 'left-wing papers'.

In *Homage* itself there is a fascinating trail of confusion concerning the distinction between the two corps of paramilitary police, the Civil Guard and the Assault Guard. The 'May Events' in Barcelona – four days of street fighting between the government forces and the pro-revolutionary organisations, which formed the crisis of intra-Republican politics – were sparked off, according to *Homage*, by the Civil Guard.[39] In fact the provocative attack upon the anarchist-held Telephone Exchange was made by the Assault Guards. When Orwell's friend, Geoffrey Gorer, reviewed the book, he evidently sent him a pre-publication copy of the notice, since the former went to some lengths to make a pedantically insistent correction:

> You say the fighting in Barcelona was started by the Assault Guards. Actually it was the Civil Guards. There weren't any Assault Guards there (in Barcelona) then, and there is a difference, because the Civil Guards are the old Spanish gendarmerie dating from the early nineteenth century … the Assault Guards are a new formation (and) pro-Republican.[40]

When Gorer's review appeared, it contained the somewhat arkward correction '*It would seem as though* the starting point of the fighting was the attempt of the *re-instated gendarmerie*, the Civil Guards … to take the Telephone Building'.[41]

Before his death, Orwell himself corrected this error in his private papers, claiming to have been misled by the fact that the *Barcelona* Assault Guards wore a different uniform from those sent in later by the *Valencia*-based Republican government to maintain order.[42] When Secker and Warburg published a collection of extracts of contemporary Civil War writings in 1963, they changed the guard at the Telefónica to make Orwell's account consistent with other eyewitness reports it contained, whilst oddly leaving the Civil Guard on duty in the book itself.[43] Orwell had quickly and uncritically picked up the traditional working-class hatred of the Civil Guard, to the extent that he neglected to mention that they had – in a highly emotional event – sided with the people against the military in Barcelona in July 1936.[44] After this, they were kept on a short leash by the anarchist rulers of the city, though pressure for their disbandment was resisted. By May 1937, it was the Assault Guard (*Guardia de Asalto*) who had fully replaced the older body as the chief object of proletarian suspicion. The *Asaltos* were mainly loyal members of the PSUC, the United Catalan Socialist Party, dominated by Communists. Their vendetta with the anarchists originated from the notorious affair of Casas Veijas (1933) when the *Asaltos* had massacred CNT prisoners in Andalusia.[45] If the Generalitat, or its Communist members, *did* want to provoke a showdown in May (and the case is not proven) the *Asaltos* were the obvious instrument.

With one exception, writers on the May Events in Barcelona do not follow Orwell's ascription.[46] It is further clear from such sources that contrary to his assertion the Civil Guard did not take part in other attacks (since none took place) on anarchist strongholds, and that the *Guardia* unit holed up in the Cafe Moka, next door to the POUM offices, were also *Asaltos*, not *Civiles*.[47] Thus the 'Civil Guard' who was Orwell's partner in the conversation earlier discussed (if he ever existed) was not a Civil Guard at all. It seems probably, therefore, that Orwell had never set eyes on a Civil Guard, the police body he writes about so much, and with so much affected distaste, in *Homage*. The uniform of these men is so distinctive – as will have been universally appreciated since the abortive *golpe* of Colonel Tejero received worldwide television coverage in February 1981 – as to be quite unmistakble. Orwell's whole approach to this matter is redolent of the apostate policeman, 'the natural enemy of the working class', who in attempting a complete transference of his allegiance to the other side, has succeeded in preserving a certain myopia.

During the *Sucesos de Mayo*, the revolutionary parties were accused by the PSUC of hoarding weapons in Barcelona which officially should have been sent to the front. This was an important item in Communist propaganda against their rivals, and helped to justify the later suppression of the 'Trotskyist' POUM on the grounds that they were preparing a *coup* and thus (by logical extension) were *effectively* fascists. In *Homage*, whilst admitting this charge as regards the CNT, Orwell denies it on behalf of the POUM on the basis of his own observation within the latter's HQ.[48] Whatever Orwell saw – and we must remember that he had refused to join the party, and very recently had been in contact with the Barcelona agents of the International Brigades – the fact seems established that Andreu Nin's organisation, like all others, kept large quantities of arms in store against a day of reckoning. A recent article on the Catalan militias which concludes thus, also argues that the need to defend sectarian interests in Barcelona was a major reason for weapon-starvation at the front, and therefore for the failure of loyalist operations in the Aragon theatre of war.[49] Morreres also confirms that POUM units in Aragon temporarily abandoned the line in May, intending to march to the relief of their comrades in the Catalan capital (an intention they did not, in the event, pursue). Once again, Orwell is unusually emphatic in denying this incident, which he alleges he specifically verified by inquiry when he returned to his unit after the May Events.[50] (Presumably, even his English comrades were prepared to deceive him on this point.) Orwell, in a striking passage about the 1930s, was later to write that atrocities took place even though establishment worthies (like Lord Halifax) and rightist newspapers (like the *Daily Telegraph*) said they took place – in other words, that something can be true even though it is also propaganda.[51] He did not always retain a full enough awareness of this principle; but what directly political writer ever did?

Attention must be drawn to a further example, which may be regarded as something of a darker shade than a mere mistake. In his essay 'Inside the Whale' (1940), Orwell attacked W.H. Auden in a famous remark about the latter's poem 'Spain'. If not in so many words, he accused Auden of espousing – in the phrase 'the necessary murder' – the maxim of 'the end justifies the means', lumping him by implication with Stalinist executioners. It is astonishing that Auden was cowed by this into disavowing his poem, for surely the construction that Orwell placed upon it was deliberately and crudely literal. Moreover, he underlined his moral condemnation by the claim 'it so happens that I have seen the bodies of numbers of murdered men – I don't mean killed in battle, I mean murdered. Therefore I have some conception of what murder means ...'[52] In the circumstances it seems reasonable to enquire, when and where did Orwell have this experience? There is no other reference to it in his published work, nor is Crick's biography forthcoming on the point.[53] Given the context in which he was writing on this occasion, the reader is obviously intended to assume that the incident took place in Spain. But who were the victims and who the assassins? If the latter were Communists or fascists he would certainly have reported it at some place in his Spanish writings. If the anarchists or the POUM then he was guilty of suppressing a part of 'the whole truth' harmful to the interests of his own side. The alternative explanation, that he invented this story to gain a moral advantage over the hapless Auden, although even more damaging to Orwell's reputation, seems nevertheless the more likely. He had, and was not slow to display (even after becoming friendly with Spender) a prejudice against 'the pansy poets of the left'; and was himself, of course, a palpably failed poet.[54] If this explanation is correct – and proceedings cannot be conclusive – then his act was all the more dishonest because Orwell, unlike Auden, *had actually* espoused the principle that 'the end justifies the means'. In *Homage*, and elsewhere, he stated unequivocally that he wished to see Franco defeated 'by any means whatever',[55] which may be held to cancel out everything he ever wrote about the ethical dimension of the Spanish War, and which in *Nineteen Eighty-Four* he reasserted *a fortiori* as the fundamentally self-annihilating principle of political consciousness. Victory resides only in becoming like the enemy, coming to love the enemy, becoming the enemy.

Finally, we may turn from Orwell's treatment of an individual to his treatment of a people.

> During the first year of the war the entire British public is thought to have subscribed to various 'aid Spain' funds about a quarter of a million pounds – probably less than half of what they spend in a single week in going to the pictures ... To the British working class the massacre of their comrades in Vienna, Berlin, Madrid, or wherever it might be seemed less interesting and less important than yesterday's football match.[56]

It is not difficult to appreciate that, for many, such insensitive remarks – even from a man who volunteered, and came close to death – are impossible to understand or forgive. Hywel Francis has described, in perfectly unsentimental terms, the sacrifices for Spain made in the poverty-stricken communities of South Wales. This example was by no means unique.[67]

On the broad level of overall interpretation of the Spanish War, Orwell's writings are seriously limited by his exiguous treatment of the Nationalist side. Little more than a page of

Homage, with a couple more pages in 'Looking Back', are devoted (if that is the right word) to the Francoist movement. Where not utterly dismissive, Orwell's comments are essentially speculative, since he knew very little about the enemy. He had no ideas on what caused millions to fight against the Republic beyond what he tamely accepted from the left-wing sources that he distrusted on almost every other matter. As Douglas Woodruff, reviewer of *Homage* in the Catholic magazine *The Tablet* acutely (if predictably) pointed out, 'it is curious that a man who tells us that for a year or two past the international prestige of fascism had been haunting him like a nightmare, should not display more intellectual curiosity.'[58] The *movimiento* is (to Orwell) simply a horde of drones and coolies driven to destroy the workers by the bosses – whether capitalist, landowner, army officer or priest makes no difference – and supplied and paid for by international fascism. There could be no altruism or idealism on the other side, indeed nothing that was not inspired by vested interest and regimented by power. In this sense, despite its determined onslaught upon the Communists, perhaps in part because of it, *Homage* remains a classic contribution to the vaguely 'liberal' myth of the Spanish War; a myth now so hegemonic that remorse over Franco's victory is part of the guilt-complex of the western intellectual, a stock-in-trade of a whole ethical culture.

Throughout these texts, Orwell invariably refers to the enemy as 'fascist' yet makes no mention of José Antonio and the Falange, nor indeed of any other figure or party amongst the rebels apart from Franco – an interesting tribute to the success of the *caudillo*'s political tactics. But the fact that currently many scholars of Politics and History – including some Soviet writers – acknowledge that fascism was an authentic and popular revolutionary movement, a heresy, or perhaps simply a variant of Marxism, is more or less irrelevant.[59] For the Franco movement was not fascist in any strict, or even meaningful sense, however it was perceived from a European power/ideology standpoint. The nationalist rebels were a hugely heterogenous collection of malcontent elements, welded together by army and church, in pursuit of reactionary objectives in which the interests of the two latter forces were paramount. Franco cynically exploited the dangerous ideas and the useful accidentals of fascism – above all to attract foreign support – with the full intention of suppressing them after victory, a feature closely analagous to the Republican government's view of the anarchists. In spite of his facile usage of the current leftist vocabulary, and some other ideas about the war that a historian would regard as eccentric, Orwell perceived clearly enough that Francoism was a phenomenon of the nineteenth century, not of the twentieth. With equal acuteness, he foresaw that, whichever side won the war, the ensuing régime 'would have to be a dictatorship *of some kind of fascism*'; but that, Spain being Spain, this 'fascism' would be considerably less totalitarian, and more humanely inefficient, than the Italian, German, or Soviet models.[60] Rarely can a political idealist's disillusion – the very Iberian *desengaño* – have been so complete, for Orwell came to realise not only that he had not been fighting *for* socialist revolution, (rather, bourgeois democracy) but also not even *against* fascism, (rather a pseudo-fascist reaction). Nonetheless on many central issues his intelligence did not let him down, neither did he fail to manifest some elemental understanding of Spain and its history.

In his direct treatment of the political and ideological issues of the war – if again by his own admission – Orwell operated constantly on superficial knowledge and subjective experience. To his own satisfaction, at least, sincere emotional commitment and common sense compensated for vulgar pragmatism on the one hand and fancy theory on the other. Perhaps he made a virtue of necessity, for previous to Spain his ignorance was so profound that he was obliged thereafter to subsist as a writer on what he picked up as he went along. His innocence of Marxism-Leninism affected his judgement of all parties of the Spanish War, and since he was unaware of modern socialist dialectic and its tropes he was unable to examine them via a critical comparison with empirical reality. All the same, his particular works, for the most part, contain a textual consistency of view and argument: that is to say, where doubt, ambiguity or plurality *do* exist the author is usually conscious of it. By contrast, it is well known that he was capable of mercurial, and sometimes radical, shifts of opinion from one piece of writing to the next. It is historical practice (and would be a reasonable procedure for any critic) to approach this phenomenon diachronically rather than synchronically.

Orwell joined the ILP – the British group equivalent and affiliated to the POUM – in June 1938.[61] For about a year before and after this date, some thirty months in all, he generally followed the Trotskyist line, if more faithfully on matters not directly related to Spain than otherwise. His earliest Spanish essay, 'Spilling the Spanish Beans' (June 1937) represents the most uniformly bitter anti-Communist polemic he ever wrote. He argues here that the purpose of the Republican government's formation of the Popular Army (*Ejército Popular*) in 1936-7 was not to win the war, but to suppress revolution. The Communists, to the fore in its organisation and command, were agents of capitalist reaction, *ergo* 'fascists'.[62] These charges were no less (if no more) absurd than those forwarded by the Cominternists against the POUM. Thereafter, as can be seen from *Homage*, the red mist cleared a little from Orwell's eyes. By October, during the composition of *Homage*, he was able to display an almost irenic detachment. A book-review appeared in which he characterised two authors as 'Trotksyists', pointing out that 'their prejudice is against the official Communist Party to which they are not always entirely fair.'[63] By the end of 1938, he actually admitted that in his book he had 'given a more sympathetic account of the POUM "line" than I actually felt ... I always felt they were wrong.'[64] Yet all this time, and down to the eve of the Hitler war, he continually subscribed in print to the Trotskyist-pacifist view of the coming European conflict, acting explicitly as a party propagandist. There is more than a hint here of an Orwell who was schizoid, or perhaps simply a charlatan. For he was not merely a somewhat wayward comrade but a disloyal one. In the middle of his honeymoon with the ILP he had a secret affair with the more orthodox socialist mistress, thus turning Warburton's famous maxim on its head. Early in 1939 he wrote a little-known article on Spain, probably on commission, for the WEA magazine *The Highway*.[65] The occasion was a special issue designed (in the words of its editor, W.E. Williams), 'to reveal the vitality and the potentialities of democracy, to hearten the timid and confound the Fifth Column.'[66]

At this time, as all his other public and private writings illustrate, Orwell could hardly find adjectives strong enough to convey his suspicion of democracy in general and his disgust over the Spanish example in particular. In response to this commission he was nevertheless capable of a piece of official labourist optimism. The essay praises the Spanish Republic's preservation of 'both the forms and the spirit of democracy', passing lightly over its 'internal power struggles'. It asserts, clean contrary to *Homage*, that 'any government which triumphs over Franco will be of liberal tendency', and in several other matters spiritlessly retails the Popular Front-liberal line on the Spanish War. A generous extract is necessary to impart the full utopian and paternalist flavour of this perplexing article. The war, claims Orwell,

> was acting as an educational force ... If men were suffering, they were also learning. Scores of thousands of ordinary people had been forced into positions of responsibility which a few months earlier they would never have dreamed of. Hundreds of thousands of people found themselves thinking with an intensity which would hardly have been possible in normal times, about economic theories and political principles. Words like fascism, communicism, democracy, socialism, Trotskyism, anarchism, which for the mass of human beings are nothing but words, were being eagerly discussed and thought out by men who only yesterday had been illiterate peasants. There was a huge intellectual ferment, a sudden expansion of consciousness. It must be set down to the credit side of the war ...

It has only been possible here to prise open slightly the lid of the Pandora's Box of experience, ideas, and reflections which are Orwell's Spanish writings. They are by turns real and phoney, convincing and naïve, perceptive and plain silly. Perhaps the best summation of him was that made by the last leader of the Second Republic, Juan Negrín, who met him in London in 1940. He seemed to the Spaniard

> decent and righteous, biased by a too rigid puritanical frame,

gifted with a candour bordering on naïvety, highly critical but blindly credulous, morbidly individualistic ... and so supremely honest and self-denying that he would not hesitate to change his mind once he perceived himself to be wrong.[67]

Orwell carried honesty as a badge, more self-consciously and prominently than almost any other English writer. He continually seeks to confront the reader unavoidably, and often embarrassingly, with his emblem, like someone who displays prominent evidence of a radical inclination on his or her person at a social gathering. In *Homage*, perhaps unusually, he clearly intended his ubiquitous self-awareness of fallibility to be an incontrovertible index of his veracity. To the historian, this often works on one level. To be reminded of the writer's prejudices, exhorted to accept his statements only provisionally, and to check them against other evidence, is somehow disarming and comforting.[68] For the student, too, Orwell's translucent approach is a refreshing change from the complex certitudes of so many scholarly works. To remove *Homage* from the bibliography of the Spanish War therefore might be discouraging to discourse in a subject which, in any case incapable of objective certainty, ought to thrive on permissiveness and plurality. At the same time, students must be invited – if the Orwellian style may be adopted for a moment – to consider that he may be wrong even where he says he may be wrong. 'Honest George' was a writer, not a bookmaker, but he is no more to be regarded as the horse's mouth.

Notes

1 *Homage to Catalonia* was first published by Secker and Warburg in 1938. I have used the Penguin edition of 1966, referred to almost throughout as '*Homage*'. This also contains the article 'Looking Back on the Spanish War' (1943), which is cited in this compilation. Orwell's relevant reviews appear *passim* between pp. 309 & 453 of S. Orwell and I. Angus (eds.), *The Collected Essays, Journalism and Letters of George Orwell*, Vol.1, Harmondsworth, 1970, referred to hereafter as '*CEJL*'. Full references to the three other articles appear below.

2 'Inside the Whale' (1940), *CEJL*, Vol. 1, p. 549.

3 'Why I Write' (1946), ibid. p. 29.

4 Letter to J. Common (5 February 1938), ibid. p. 330.

5 'Your Questions Answered' (2 December 1943), ibid. p. 296.

6 Orwell writes 'Generalite' for 'Generalitat' – the Catalan word for the autonomous government – throughout *Homage*. When in hiding from the police in Barcelona, he says he daubted '*Visca* POUM!' on the walls – his own adumbration of 'Down With Big Brother!', *Homage*, p. 215.

7 R. Fraser, *Blood of Spain: An Oral History of the Spanish Civil War*, London, 1979. p. 532.

8 London, 1937 (reprinted, 1970).

9 *Homage*, p. 51. Cf. Peers, op.cit., pp. 290-91.

10 B. Crick, 'Homage to Catalonia and the British Council', *Times Higher Educational Supplement*, 24 February 1984, p. 12.

11 Ibid.

12 J. Meyers (ed.), *George Orwell: The Critical Heritage*, London, 1975, pp. 134-37 (for Spender); L. Trilling, 'George Orwell and the Politics of Truth', in R. Williams (ed.), *George Orwell: A Collection of Critical Essays*, Englewood Cliffs, 1974, pp. 62-79.

13 *Homage*, pp. 14 & 210. It ought to be said that Orwell's account of the May Events in Barcelona is close enough to that given by *La Batalla* to suggest that he may have had some kind of access to it. See the extracts from the editions of 4 and 13 May 1937, printed in F. Díaz-Plaja (ed.), *La Guerre Española en sus Documentos*, Barcelona, 1974, pp. 306-07 & 318-19.

14 *Homage*, p. 128.

15 Ibid., pp. 209-12.

16 *CEJL*, Vol. 1, p. 355.

17 *Homage*, p. 178.

18 Orwell (as the above Catalan example in n.6 illustrates) seems to have often spelled as he heard. He did not realise, therefore, that the letter H is not pronounced in Castilian (*Homage*, p. 38, several examples) and that the letter P is never doubled (ibid., p. 14). He transforms a widely used four-letter word – which he is unlikely to have seen in print – into a five-letter Italianate hybrid (ibid., p. 97). As often as not he gets his accents wrong, and never uses the inverted preliminary interrogation and exclamation marks characteristic of written Castilian.

19 P. Stansky and W. Abrahams, *Orwell: The Transformation*, London, 1979, p. 189. Neither this, nor any other major Orwell source indicates any encounter with Spanish before 1936.

20 See below, n.42.

21 B. Crick, *George Orwell: A Life*, Harmondsworth, 1982, pp. 308 & 317. Stansky and Abrahams are equivocal on the point, op.cit., p. 176. Cf. *Homage*, p. 8, and (especially) 'Notes on the Spanish Militias' (?1939) *CEJL*, Vol. 1, pp. 351-52.

22 'Why I Write', *CEJL*, Vol. 1, p. 28.

23 Ibid., p. 26.

24 T. Hopkinson, *George Orwell*, London, 1953 (reprinted 1977), p. 7.

25 For the role of British Newsreels in the Civil War, see A. Aldgate, *Cinema and History*, London, 1979.

124 *Inside the Myth*

26 As for n. 22 above.
27 Claud Cockburn. See *Homage*, pp. 158-59.
28 H. Thomas, *The Spanish Civil War*, London, 1961.
29 Reprinted in Meyers, op.cit., pp. 150-51.
30 *Homage*, pp. 57, 62 & 66. Stansky and Abrahams, op.cit., p. 201 (evidence of P. Blackstein).
31 Ibid., p. 207; *Homage*, p. 113; B. Alexander, *British Volunteers for Liberty. Spain, 1936-39*, London, 1982, p. 108.
32 V. Alba, *Catalonia: A Profile*, London, 1975, p. 150; J. Coll and J. Pané, *Josep Rovira: una vida al servei de Catalunya*, Barcelona, 1978, pp. 128-41.
33 J. Villaroya i Font, *Els Bombardeigs de Barcelona durant la guerra civil, 1936-39*, Montserrat, 1981, pp. 36-7.
34 G. Jackson, *The Spanish Republic and the Civil War, 1931-39*, Princeton, 1967, p. 370.
35 H. Browne, *Spain's Civil War*, London, 1983, pp. 102-03.
36 *CEJL*, Vol. 1, p. 253.
37 J. Gurney, *Crusade in Spain*, London, 1974, pp. 167-68.
38 R. Payne (ed.), *The Civil War in Spain, 1936-39,* London, 1963, pp. 163 & 350.
39 *Homage*, pp. 117-18, 144, 156 *et seq.*
40 Letter to G. Gorer (18 April 1938), *CEJL*, Vol. 1, p. 349.
41 G. Gorer's *Time and Tide* review (30 April 1939) as reprinted in Meyers, op.cit., p. 122. (The emphases in the quotation are mine.)
42 Orwell's own '*errata in Homage to Catalonia*'. I owe this information to Professor P. Davison, who kindly provided me with a photocopy of the material from the Orwell Archive in University College, London.
43 R. Payne, op.cit., pp. 235 & 238-46.
44 The footnote in *Homage* (p. 152) which draws attention to the fact that 'at the outbreak of war the Civil Guards had everywhere sided with the stronger party', whilst omitting to specify Barcelona, rather strengthens this point than otherwise.
45 Thomas, op.cit., Harmondsworth, 1965, p. 93; Jackson, op.cit., pp. 101-02.
46 The exception, interestingly enough, is Thomas, the only specialist scholar actively to denigrate Orwell's historical reliability (loc. cit., p. 544, and p. 654 in the 1977 edition). Several others, it is true, carefully refrain from specification. See Jackson, op.cit., p. 369 for the correct version.
47 Crick, *A Life*, p. 332.
48 *Homage*, pp. 151 & 159-60.
49 J. Morreres i Boix, 'Las Milicias Populares en Cataluña, 1936-37', *Historia 16*, No. 55 (1980), pp. 27-38.
50 *Homage*, pp. 155-56.
51 'Looking Back on the Spanish War', ibid., p. 230.
52 'Inside the Whale', *CEJL*, Vol. 1, p. 566.
53 Crick (*A Life*, pp. 313 and 615) deals with the Auden incident in some detail, but records no opinion on the issue of this inquiry.
54 Ibid p. 244.

55 *Homage*, p. 69.
56 Ibid pp. 68 & ('Looking Back') 239.
57 H. Francis, *Miners Against Fascism: Wales and the Spanish Civil War*, London, 1984, esp. pp. 119ff.
58 Meyers, op.cit., p. 133.
59 See, for example, A. Beichman's survey of recent work on fascism, *Times Literary Supplement*, 19 February 1982, p. 180.
60 *Homage*, pp. 48 & 173.
61 *CEJL*, Vol. 1, p. 373.
62 Ibid., pp. 301-9. For the PCE view of the Popular Army, see E. Lister, *Memorias de un Luchador* Vol. 1, Madrid, 1977, pp. 119-61. For the Catalan view, V. Guarner, *L'aixecament militar a Catalunya i la guerra civil (1936-1939)*, Montserrat, 1975.
63 Ibid., p. 231. For evidence that Orwell was sympathetic to the anarchists during the composition of *Homage*, see also pp. 323 & 325.
64 'Caesarean Section in Spain', *The Highway*, March 1939, pp. 145-47. This piece has escaped notice in any of the literature on Orwell, or on the Spanish War, that I have seen, save for J. García Durán, *Bibliografía de la Guerra Española*, Montevideo, 1964, p. 401. In the Introduction to their 'complete' Orwell, (*CEJL*, Vol. 1, p. 15) Sonia Orwell and Ian Angus claim to have included 'anything that he (Orwell) would have considered as an essay', but not everything which 'is purely ephemeral'. The actual contents of the collection suggest that this article qualified for inclusion by these criteria. The conclusion must be either that it was unknown to the editors or that it was suppressed as inimical to Orwell's reputation. I am given to understand that it will appear in the forthcoming *definitive* complete Orwell to be edited by Professor Davison for Secker and Warburg.
65 Editorial, *The Highway*, loc. cit., p. 127.
67 Meyers, op.cit., p. 149.
68 In six pages of *Homage*, for example, (144-149) there are no fewer than nine *different* expressions of uncertainty!

Beatrix Campbell

Orwell – Paterfamilias or Big Brother?

If we are to measure George Orwell's success in the durability of his two later novels, *Animal Farm* and *Nineteen Eighty-Four* then what we need to examine is his projection of Big Brother – the modern authoritarian state.

Big Brother has become *the* metaphor for the modern state, and, although its success is formidable, since the term has become part of our political vocabulary, it is also a problem. Orwell's state is not just a spectre of secrecy and surveillance, because the whole thesis also depends on a notion of absolute power which depends on the condition of mass powerlessness. In this context it is significant that Orwell feels comfortable in the temperate climes of English capitalism before the Second World War, only decades after the working class had won the franchise and before it was a major power in the land.

It is post-revolutionary power which inflames his nightmare of the future state – his critique of the modern state is unmistakably directed against the socialist state. But Orwell's equally nightmarish vision of absolute powerlessness derives not from some future defeat, but his own feelings about the working class who were his contemporaries. The horrors of *Animal Farm* and *Nineteen Eighty-Four* extend not only to the misuse of state power, but to the failure of politics itself. That failure derives from Orwell's big-brotherly view of the working class.

I want to argue, as Raymond Williams has in his excellent book *Orwell*, that the problem with Orwell is his represent-ation, or rather misrepresentation, of the working class. More than that, there is also a problem in the way that masculinity, femininity and the family feature in his representations of class.

While Orwell's invincible edifice of the state may seem modern, his view of the working class isn't – it's the quaint, old-fashioned chronicle of a self-confessed snob. Despite his wish to invest his revolutionary optimism in the people, what he feels for the common people edges on contempt. Actually, he thinks they're dead common. He may *think* the working class is the revolutionary class, but he doesn't *feel* it.

Nowhere in Orwell do the working class *make* history. And in his quest for an authentic English socialism it is not the working class, but a sort of hybrid southern suburban species which becomes the revolutionary class – not because of its capacity to struggle, but because in some way it fits Orwell's notion of quintessential Englishness.

Throughout *Nineteen Eighty-Four* the off-stage appearances of the working class are remarkably resonant of *The Road to Wigan Pier*. The power of the state in *Nineteen Eighty-Four* seems perpetually stabilised in its very instability – but the instability is only a chimera. There is no real challenge to the state from its own people, and particularly not from the proles.

George Orwell's life and times with the proletariat began with *The Road to Wigan Pier* when, in keeping with a long tradition of English literature, the quest for the 'state of the nation', he set off on an expedition into the natural habitat of the working class. The tradition itself depends on a relation of otherness to this class. In the first place, normally such journeys could only be undertaken by people with the time and money to make them, in other words with resources not possessed by the working class itself. But more importantly, that relationship always inscribes the author in a relation of exclusion from the working class. The odd thing is that this quest for Englishness necessitates the discovery of that working class, as if it were hidden and mysterious. And of course, coming from Orwell's class position, that is exactly what they were. And remained. In *The Road to Wigan Pier*, Orwell depended on the activists for his access to the working class. But as Williams shows, Orwell insists on a separation between the working class and its activist intelligentsia. He cannot conceive of the working class itself as a *thinking* class with its own history, with a history of making itself. The result is the representation of a class which is thoughtless and leaderless, a class in its natural state.

Again, as Williams shows, Orwell's omission of working-class activists and organisations leaves him with the slate clean for his own observations. What Orwell brings to his journey is primarily himself, an observer who takes no counsel, an author with all the arrogance of innocence. Insofar as he is concerned with working-class politics as an organised force, he represents it as showing a flair for organisation but not for thinking. This separation is achieved because Orwell kidnaps working-class thinkers out of their class: 'I think, therefore I am' apparently doesn't apply to the proles; to think is to become middle class. It is this which enables us to track a continuity between *Wigan Pier* and *Nineteen Eighty-Four*. It is as if the documentary material of *Wigan Pier* provided him with his source material for *Nineteen Eighty-Four*: the proles are the same in both.

In *Wigan Pier*, Orwell seeks to sum up the working class in the archetypal proletarian group – the miners. For all that his description of miners' labour and their poverty is sympathetic, it is hardly radical. How does he describe these archetypal proletarians, and why did he single out the miners?

Orwell's graphic description of the work of miners facilitates his representation of workers as elemental creatures, work-horses. Williams reminds us that this is how they appear in *Animal Farm*, and so it is again in *Nineteen Eighty-Four*. As I have argued in *Wigan Pier Revisited*, I think Orwell's choice of miners is significant. As the mysogynist he is, it is not surprising that he has chosen the most masculinised profession.

Undoubtedly, his celebration of the miners was in part an attempt to restore them to a respected place in the ranks of the working class. He challenges the denigration of miners as noble savages because they are dirty by describing the conditions of their work and their bathless homes, and by establishing trenchantly the necessity of their work. For it is coal, he says, that makes the world go round. And at the same time he, too, casts them in the role of noble savages by his panegyric on their physique. He loves their lean, supple, black bodies. And so his celebration of the miners is both an

affectionate discovery of their heroism *and* their masculinity –
their work is a *man*ful struggle down there in the dark and
dangerous abdomen of the earth. It is of course essentially
physical work, and what Orwell is not concerned with is the
history of that masculinisation of the work of miners. Mining is
only men's work because women were banned from the work of
hewing coal in the nineteenth-century struggle to expel women
from hard physical labour. The feminisation of women
demanded that expulsion. But that feminisation had an
answering echo in the masculinisation of men. This is important
for several reasons. The selection of the miners in this way as the
most exotic martyrs of the working class is itself part of the
process of masculinising the history of the working class.

Orwell visited Wigan in the 1930s when it was still one of the
outposts of women's work in the mines. After the expulsion of
women from the underground in 1842, there were campaigns
throughout the late nineteenth century to purge women from
the pit top, where it was believed by some that they were
de-sexed by their strength. The campaign failed in Wigan,
where women were only finally pushed off the pit top in the
1950s after nationalisation and a deal between the National
Coal Board and the National Union of Mineworkers. Wigan was
famous for its 'pit brow lasses'. Not as you'd know from *The
Road to Wigan Pier*.

Wigan was also as much a cotton town as it was a coal town.
Indeed, it is significant that Orwell spent a substantial part of his
journey in Lancashire around the cotton belt, towns which
employed women in the mills, towns which where the crucible
of the English industrial revolution, towns were working-class
history cannot be written other than as the struggles between
men *and women* and capital. Not as you'd know that from *The
Road to Wigan Pier* either.

So, women do not appear as protagonists in Orwell's working
class. And neither does capital. And what we are left with is a
sense of a class which suffers, but not of a class which struggles.
And certainly not a class which wins. It's a class summed up in
the anthem of the washerwomen in *Nineteen Eighty-Four*:

They sye that time 'eals all things,
They sye you can always forget;

But the smiles an' the tears acrorss the years
They twist my 'eart strings yet!

True to the tradition of such representations of the working
class, the imagery contains pathos, isolation, inertia, defeat: it
incites pity and philanthropy rather than protest and politics.
The washerwoman in *Nineteen Eighty-Four* has her parallel in
Wigan Pier in a solitary image of an exhausted, but noble,
woman, poking a stick down a drain. Both figures are used by
Orwell to gather and focus his fondness for these poor people.
But they are silent women, even when they are singing. They
are sad, but above all they are solitary. And Orwell is about to
entrench them in their solitude: in *Wigan Pier* he sees her as he
is on his way, leaving town. In *Nineteen Eighty-Four* he discovers
his affection for his washerwoman just before Winston is about
to be arrested. The isolation of these figures in their
proletarian landscape is about to be completed in both cases
by the observer's departure. The only feelings we can be left
with are grief and impotence.

Among the middle class and the upper class, women are
targets of his acidic class contempt, expressed in the same vein
as the mother-in-law joke. It's the 'Brighton ladies' and rich
women lolling around in Rolls Royces whom he can't abide,
presumably because they are the quintessence of the idle rich.
They're an easy target, of course, given their unstated but
enforced idleness as women.

It is women whom he identifies as the fifth column of the
upper classes. In *Wigan Pier* Orwell briefly considers the lack of
political solidarity among the middle class, not as a function of
its dominance – for the upper classes are organised in a web of
political associations of which there is no account in Orwell –
but as an expression of women's backwardness.

You cannot have an effective trade union of middle-class workers
because in times of strikes almost every middle-class wife would be
egging her husband on to blackleg and get the other fellow's job.

The unity of the working class, on the other hand, is
assumed and cemented in the unity of the family, 'the fact that
the working class combine and the middle class don't is

probably due to their different conceptions of the family.'
Orwell is clearly innocent of the tension within working-class
households in precisely the case of that litmus test of intra-class
solidarity, the strike.

The history of the working class is, however, a minefield of
negotiated settlements between men and women, not least in
the classic case of the strike. Men's strikes have always carried
the proverbial risk of the complaining wife who was never
consulted – it is classically represented in *Salt of the Earth*, an
American film of a Mexican-American miners' strike in which
the women's communal demands were never given political
priority by their men. The men's strike is lived by women as an
economic hardship that they were never consulted about. But
when the women propose taking over the picket line after the
coalowners take out an injunction against the striking miners,
the men balk; the men vote against it, but the women – having
first fought for their right to vote – all vote for it. The women's
tenacity becomes the source of the strike's survival, demanded
from them initially as individuals and yet opposed when it
takes the form of a collective intervention. Individual
solidarity, of course, is always in the service of the men.
Collective action among the women always carries the threat of
an organised power beyond the men's control. Orwell's
observations about class loyalty between the genders are just
another example of his unsubstantiated sentiments.

Take a look at the gender breakdown in voting patterns. The
gender gap is dramatic within the working class. It is among
middle and upper-class voters that there is a remarkable
political symmetry. The fact is that the upper class is united
across gender and class in ways that the working class isn't. It is
conventional wisdom that the reason for this is that the labour
movement and the Labour Party have faced women with a
contradiction: it demands their class solidarity while it
sanctions their sexual subordination.

Part of the problem is that Orwell's eye never comes to rest
on the culture of women, their concerns, their history, their
movements. He only holds women to the filter of his own
desire – or distaste. We've already seen how he makes women
the bearers of his own class hatred. In his avowedly political
work the snarling innuendo he reserves for his 'Brighton

ladies' and 'birth control' fanatics is rarely directed towards the figures of *real* power in capitalist societies – the judges, the parliamentarians and the capitalists. In fact, you are left with a sense of a society run, not only by the national family's old buffers, but of a society run by a febrile femininity, an army of doddering dowagers.

The point is that given his own centrality, and that of masculinity in Orwell's work, women are congratulated only when they stick to their men. The sexual filter surrounds all his female personae.

In *Nineteen Eighty-Four* we have working-class women represented by poor Mrs Parsons and a prole washerwoman. Mrs Parsons is a 'woman with a lined face and wispy hair, fiddling helplessly with the waste pipe', an infuriating person, always in the slough of a housewife's ruinous mess. And then there is the washerwoman whom Winston discovers during his fugitive flights into proletaria. He only begins to reflect on her with any respect when he inexplicably discovers the revolutionary potential of the proles. Her 'indefatigable voice' sings on, as she endlessly hangs out her washing. He watches her 'solid, contourless body, like a block of granite', quietly admiring 'her thick arms reaching up for the line, her powerful mare-like buttocks protruded.' She's as strong as a horse, an image which has echoes in *Animal Farm*, where as Raymond Williams reminds us, 'the speed of his figurative transition from animals to the proletariat is interesting – showing as it does a residue of thinking of the poor as animals: powerful but stupid.'

As Orwell's Winston watches the 'over-ripe turnip' of a washerwoman reach for the line 'it struck him for the first time that she was beautiful.' Her 'rasping red skin, bore the same relation to the body of a girl as the rose-hip to the rose. Why should the fruit be held inferior to the flower?'

So we start with the strong but stupid work-horse and move to a vision of a woman in labour: both as she labours solitarily and stoically, and as a symbol of fertility. As Winston muses on how he and his lover Julia will never bear children he reflects on this washerwoman-mother: 'The woman down there had no mind, she had only strong arms, a warm heart and a fertile belly.' Just like Orwell's panegyric on the miners, all brawn and no brain, this quintessential proletarian woman is all belly and no brain. She has no culture and no consciousness worth contemplating.

His image of this woman echoes his more poetic representation of the miners as the archetypal proletarians, but there is more: her labour is solitary. Like the miners, her labour is elemental, basic: it is a fundamental, natural force. There is in these accounts no representation of subtlety, of craft and the consciousness associated with workers' combination. This representation of heroic manual labour is consonant with his celebration of her biology. It is only a short step from this to his formation of Julia's rebellion. Julia is Winston's sleeping partner in sedition. Her rebellion is essentially sexual. She's promiscuous, she's had hundreds of men and her subversion is sealed in an equation between corruption and sexuality. 'I hate purity, I hate goodness! I don't want any virtue to exist anywhere,' shouts Julia. That's the extent of her opposition to totalitarian puritanism. 'I'm corrupt to the bones.' Winston loves that, not merely her capacity for love, 'but the animal instinct, the simple undifferentiated desire: that was the force that would tear the party to pieces.'

In a curiously sexual politics, he counterposes Julia's revolutionary rapaciousness with his former wife Katherine's puritanism. Her party loyalty is expressed in her frigidity. Julia's delicious revolt is consummated in her illicit collection of make-up: throwing off the uniform of the party she dons the mantle of feminity.

But of course, the consequences of this reduction of Julia to her corrupt biology are to render her rebellion as something seething below the threshold of political consciousness. It is spontaneous only, and only so because it is only sexual. She's not interested in politics as such, even though she'll lay down her life for her revolt. When Winston finally gets his hands on Goldstein's bible of dissidence, he tells her urgently that they must read the forbidden text together. What does she do? She tells him to read it to her. And when he does? She falls asleep.

Women are akin to the proletarian man in Orwell's work, they are rendered natural rather than skilful, almost infantile in their unconsciousness rather than alert and organised. This

facilitates the elision between work and politics – the workers
work in their natural state and they have their social existence
still in a kind of natural state. The working class is
pre-conscious, tasteless and mindless, child-like in its quest for
immediate gratification. Yet for some reason, which Orwell
never explains, the working class is the material of revolution.
Perhaps because of some quasi-religious notion that the meek
shall inherit the earth. The people store in their hearts, muscles
and bellies the power to change the world. All body but no
brain – and yet without the collective brain of politics, the
Machiavellian 'prince' of the party, how is their strength to
turn into consciousness? This is perhaps the greatest lacuna in
Orwell's work: Williams declares that 'in a profound way, both
the consciousness of the workers and the possibility of
authentic revolution are denied.' There is no sensitivity to the
repertoire of tactics and strategies which the working-class
movement, despite its many weaknesses, has deployed. The
very absence of the problem of ideology and consciousness
produces an assumed leap from brute strength to the power of
the *will*.

That leaves him without anything to say about working-class
politics as such, and its metamorphosis into revolutionary
culture – you are always left with the feeling of contempt for
'the masses' and for the left intelligentsia. A thinking worker is
never allowed to remain a member of the working class. It
leaves him with insuperable contradictions – the workers are
the revolutionary class and yet they aren't. Thinking workers
are part of the intelligentsia and therefore irrelevant. It's as if,
like so many members of his class, he can't forgive the
working-class thinkers for their capacity to think. For all that
Orwell in *Wigan Pier* owns up to the partiality of his class
perceptions, he never shares the privilege of *thought* with his
new class allies.

If the working class are the material of revolution, they are
never the makers of revolution, despite his rhetoric. And so he
compromises. Slumped in his own contradictions, he gives the
middle class the ticket. They've been elbowed out of their
revolutionary credentials by pansy intellectuals on the one
hand and by their rough neighbours on the council estates on
the other. They become the radical Englishness, WASPs to the

last, moderate in all things. Not surprisingly, Orwell's revolutionary transition is a remarkably banal, anglo-saxon prospectus. Looking now at his Six Point Programme in *The Lion and the Unicorn*, it is hard to see how it really differs from militant social democracy. English socialism, he says, will nationalise, it will equalise incomes, it will have its own catchy tune, it will leave the Christians alone, it will be sensible. What his programme doesn't have, however, is any sense of *struggle*. The working class have created programmes like these, of course, but in Orwell's scenario they haven't produced his. At least, though, it would 'give the working class something to fight for.' He excludes the working class from history and fails to give it any place in the revolutionary cast, other than the supporting role, the proverbial extras.

In *Wigan Pier*, having exploited the services of the movement's activists, Orwell thanks them with:

> The English working class do not show much capacity for leadership, but they have a wonderful talent for organisation. The whole trade union movement testifies to this; so too the excellent working men's clubs – really a sort of glorified co-operative pub, and splendidly organised …

Elsewhere in *Wigan Pier* Orwell muses on the contradictions in English culture, between its polite respectability and its boozy, bawdy post-card culture. It all works towards an image of working-class men at play, training pigeons, swearing and gambling. Orwell thus summarises the working-class culture of 'the warm-hearted, unthinking socialist, the typical working class socialist' in a kind of bar talk. It produces a vision of the future, he says, 'of present-day society with the worst abuses left out, and with interest centring on the same things as at present – family life, the pub, football and local politics.'

The roots are already in *Wigan Pier* for Winston's shocking discovery of and disappointment in – the proles in *Nineteen Eighty-Four* when he sees a clutch of men peering at a newspaper, talking earnestly. Something must be up, thinks Winston. But no, they're only looking for the lottery results.

Orwell anchors his own anti-economism in a critique in *The Lion and the Unicorn* of the trade-union politics which dominate

English Labourism. In this he was hardly original, as socialists and Marxists have always been pre-occupied by this English disease. But in Orwell, anti-economism is associated with a sense of the working class as not only myopic but degenerate. Just as Orwell finds no point of resistance rooted in the working class itself in *Wigan Pier*, so is there none in *Nineteen Eighty-Four*.

There is more to say about the problem of economism, however. For Orwell is not alone in stumbling across it only to be mystified by it. As he eloquently suggests, for the working class men's movement, socialism is capitalism with the worst abuses left out. I have to confess that Orwell's own political prospectus, outlined in *The Lion and the Unicorn*, seems barely any different. What neither he, nor the men's movement on the left seem to have registered is that this problem of economism may be associated with the masculinisation of working-class politics, its reduction to a men's movement. Orwell is a participant in this because he, too, writes women out of working-class history and politics. It isn't because working men are thick that they're economistic, as Orwell seems to suggest, but it may be that the historic settlement between capital and the men's labour movement over the role of women reinforces economic individualism and defuses the *social* dimensions of socialist struggle. Certainly, that economic individualism is associated with the economic subordination of women, and not surprisingly it produces a politics which evacuates the terrain of private life, on the one hand, and issues outside the parameter of the wage contract on the other.

Orwell argues for a cultural revolution as the necessary ignition to political revolution in England, and his great virtue is his attempt to anchor that vision in the continuity of commonsense culture. But far from that taking him towards the culture of those constituencies marginalised in the hierarchy of WASP socialism, he seeks to radicalise those components of consensus claimed by the right – the steadfast pillars of family and patriotism.

As Williams shows, Orwell's starting point is his quest to belong, a quest which leads him towards an attempt to produce a unity called England and Englishness. His metaphor for nationhood is the family, the collectivity in which all know their place in relation to each other, in which all are intelligible to each other. In the family, as in the nation, we all share the same concerns, the same interests and the same language. It is in the working-class family, above all, that we all come home to rest:

> you breathe a warm, decent, deeply human atmosphere which is not easy to find elsewhere ... His home life seems to fall more naturally into a sane and comely shape. I have often been struck by the easy completeness, the perfect symmetry, as it were, of a working class interior at its best ...

It hangs together, he suggests, as a middle class family does, 'but the relationship is far less tyrannical.'

It is only in the context of feminist politics that the critique of the family clarifies it as a site of contradiction between men and women, as a settlement, always negotiated between unequals. Orwell's suggestive symmetry is exactly the simmering, seething volcano which has always, explicitly or implicitly, fuelled movements for women's economic, social and sexual independence. Feminism falsified the Orwellian romance with the proletarian family as an institution. It is not that feminism seeks to damn the strong bonds and loves lived within the family, but rather the *conditions* in which men and women negotiate their encounter with each other, their children and the rest of the world, based as they are on the principle of dominance and subordination. If, for feminism, that institution is challenged, then whither Orwell's appeal to patriotism?

Britain, however, was, and now is more than ever before, a richly cosmopolitan society. Orwell's 'patriotism' is an appeal to just one of those 'families', the English working class. In the aftermath of the family outing to the Falklands there is no guarantee that this patriotism would have a progressive hue.

There is an easy equation in his social democratic programme between *giving* the workers something to fight for and his sentimental construction of nationhood within the parameters of the family. His thesis of progressive patriotism works because his view of the nation is that of the family, an essentially unified whole, speaking the same language, united by kin, not divided by class. Because the socialist family would have the right people in control, the working class would presumably remain as they are – the children.

Deirdre Beddoe

Hindrances and Help-Meets: Women in the Writings of George Orwell

This essay examines Orwell's portrayal of women in his writings. The structure which I have adopted is firstly to scrutinise his fictional female characters, as portrayed in his five novels, and secondly to look at the women – where they can be found – in his documentary works. This division into fiction and fact is parallelled by another division, i.e. the separation of women along class lines: middle-class women are to be found almost exclusively in his fiction and working-class women, with a few exceptions, in his documentary writing.

Before turning to Orwell's representation of women, a few points need to be clearly stated. Firstly, a pervasive anti-feminism is evident in Orwell's writing. In 1934 he wrote to a friend, Brenda Salkeld,

> I had lunch yesterday with Dr Ede. He is a bit of a feminist and thinks that if a woman was brought up exactly like a man she would be able to throw a stone, construct a syllogism, keep a secret etc. He tells me that my anti-feminist views are probably due to Sadism! I have never read the Marquis de Sade's novels – they are unfortunately very hard to get hold of.[1]

Brenda Salkeld, a friend of Orwell from Southwold days, described his attitude to women in general very succinctly. 'He didn't really like women', she said in a Third Programme broadcast in 1960.[2]

But one does not need other people to testify to Orwell's anti-feminism and to his contempt for women: he does a splendid job quite unaided. He cannot mention feminism and the women's suffrage movement without scorn. Writing of the period following the First World War he states,

England was full of half baked antinomian opinions. Pacifism, internationalism, humanitarianism of all kinds, feminism, free love, divorce reform, atheism, birth control – things like these were getting a better hearing than they would get in normal times.[3]

Writing on socialism, he expressed his fear that it was a refuge for every 'fruit juice drinker, nudist, sandal wearer, sex maniac, Quaker, Nature-Cure quack, pacifist and feminist in England'.

Secondly, Orwell was not only anti-feminist but he was totally blind to the role women were and are forced to play in the order of things. His prejudice severely hampered his analysis of capitalism and its workings. He saw capitalism as the exploitation of a male working class by a male ruling class. Women were just men's wives – middle-class nags and working-class housekeepers, to be judged simply as good or bad in keeping a 'decent' home. He failed to see how capitalism manipulated both men and women, middle class and working class, alike. He seems to have been totally unaware of the integral role played by the family unit in capitalist production, i.e. male bread-winner with dependent wife (who serviced the male bread-winner and produced the next generation of workers) and dependent children. He was unaware too – or chose to ignore – the role women played in the waged work-force, either as poorly paid workers who could depress wages or as a reserve army of labour, to be brought in and out of the work-force to suit the changing needs of capitalism.

In short, Orwell as an Eton-educated, middle-class man, had little or no understanding of the role and predicament of women in the society in which he lived. His fiction presents us with a series of nagging middle-class wives whom he saw as a brake on the radicalism of their husbands: 'you cannot have an effective trade union of middle-class workers, because in times of strikes almost every middle-class wife would be egging her husband on to blackleg and get the other fellow's job.'[5] While there may be an element of truth in this, Orwell did not see the reasons for it, i.e. the dependency of middle-class wives, lack of employment opportunities for women, the operation of marriage-bars in many professions. His non-fiction ignores women workers and judges working-class wives by their abilities as home-makers. Orwell's awareness of class divisions in society went alongside his lack of understanding of gender divisions, and is summed up in his discussion of women's magazines. He was perceptively aware that these magazines project a fantasy of 'pretending to be richer than you are' for the bored factory-girl or worn-out mother of five, but totally unaware of how these magazines reinforced gender divisions in society and promoted the dominant female stereotype of the interwar years – the housewife.[6]

George Orwell's female fictional characters contain within their ranks some of the most obnoxious portrayals of women in English fiction. I have in mind particularly the grasping, husband-seeking, 'low-brow' Elizabeth of *Burmese Days* (1935), who is prepared, when something better comes in sight, to pass her erstwhile beau lying wounded on the ground 'as though he had been a dead dog',[7] and finally to throw him over because he is tainted with scandal and a birthmark. Hilda Bowling in *Coming Up For Air* (1939) is similarly depicted as a totally appalling character. She is the nagging wife who ties down that potential free spirit, George Bowling, by pestering him with household cares and bills.

By contrast, Orwell's remaining female characters are much more attractive. Dorothy Hare, the title character of *A Clergyman's Daughter* (1935) and Orwell's only female protagonist, is a pathetic drudge whose life is rendered miserable by her service to others and by the tyranny of her selfish clergyman father. One can at least feel sympathy for Dorothy in her plight as unpaid curate, and excitement for her too when a blow to the head brings about amnesia and a total change in her lifestyle. But Dorothy simply does not have it in her to attain happiness and freedom, and the novel ends with her returning to the pathetic role of middle-class spinster living in her father's rectory. If Elizabeth and Hilda are stereotypical portrayals of dreadful middle-class women, Dorothy is merely pathetic.

Rosemary, the leading woman character in *Keep the Aspidistra Flying* (1936) is quite the 'nicest' of all Orwell's female characters. She is cheerful, outgoing and smart: she rescues the whining Gordom Comstock from the abyss of poverty by marrying him and making an honest man of him. She is, however, the witting ally of money and of capitalism, against which Gordon has declared unremitting war – the sort of intellectual conflict a woman could not possibly understand.

Finally, there is the youthful, lithe Julia of *Nineteen Eighty-Four* (1949), Winston Smith's ally in the fight against Big Brother and totalitarianism; but whereas Winston's fight against the system is inspired by a desire for intellectual freedom, Julia goes along with him for illicit sex, black-market coffee and finally for love of Winston. In short, this is a list of stereotypes – with the possible exception of Rosemary.

Some general rules underpin Orwell's female characters. They can be summarized roughly as follows. Women like money and tying men down; women are incapable of intellectual pursuits and enthusiasms; women are either young and attractive and hunting for husbands, or they are nagging unattractive wives; sporty women and women's rights campaigners are particularly unappealing types. Orwell's methodology is to portray a particular individual woman and attribute a set of characteristics to her: from her he is then prepared to generalize about *all* women. In order to demonstrate Orwell's jaundiced and unsympathetic view of middle-class women, I shall look firstly at the main female characters in a little more detail and then, briefly, at the subsidiary characters.

Elizabeth, the central female figure in *Burmese Days*, is an obnoxious character. She is depicted as a young woman who, after the death of her feckless, pseudo-artistic mother and after several years hard grind in poorly paid jobs in Paris, joins her only remaining relatives, the Lackersteens, in Burma. During her girlhood Elizabeth had been led to expect better from life. During the period of her father's short-lived prosperity she had attended for two terms a girls' boarding school. 'Oh the joy, the unforgettable joy of those two terms! Four of the girls at the school were "the Honourable ..." ' Orwell, who on other occasions takes swipes at the bad influence of girls' schools upon their inmates, remarks that this short interlude had firmly fixed Elizabeth's character. 'There is a short period in everyone's life when his (*sic*) character is fixed forever, with Elizabeth it was those two terms during which she rubbed shoulders with the rich.' Her schooling had taught her two general principles, i.e. all that is good or 'lovely' in life is synonymous with the expensive and all that is bad, or in her words, 'beastly', is the cheap. There was only one way in which Elizabeth might attain the money to enjoy the 'lovely' things of life and shun the 'beastly', and that was through marriage. To this end, encouraged by her aunt, Mrs Lackersteen, she sets out to find herself a husband from amongst the small European community of Kyauktada in upper Burma.

The central theme of the novel is the relationship between Flory, a jaded, disfigured, middle-aged employee in the service of a timber firm and the young, attractive Elizabeth. Flory, in contrast to Elizabeth, is portrayed with a measure of sympathy. He is presented as an intellectual who loves reading, as a man with a true appreciation of Burmese culture, who speaks Burmese and who enjoys the close friendship of the Indian civil surgeon, Dr Veraswami. In the first part of the book, after his initial meeting with Elizabeth, Flory deludes himself that Elizabeth shares his intellectual, cultural and humanitarian interests. In fact, Elizabeth reads only popular fiction, feels ill at ease with and disdainful of natives and has no time for 'highbrow ideas'. 'Real, people, she felt, decent people – people who shot grouse, went to Ascot, yachted at Cowes – were not brainy.' In short, the two main characters totally fail to communicate with each other. At the moment when Flory, who is about to propose to her, talks sincerely of his loneliness in exile, she is not even listening. The only moments in which she has any admiration for him are when he talks about tiger shooting and when he actually shoots a leopard. Elizabeth warms to Flory when he is behaving in an accepted masculine way, which suggests how women's crude expectations of men confine men to boorish activities and desensitize them.

Throughout the rest of the novel Elizabeth behaves quite abominably. She abandons and ignores Flory in favour of an aristocratic young police officer who is temporarily stationed at Kyauktada. Even though Flory at last sees her as she really is – 'silly, snobbish, heartless' – he desires her physically. Men are slaves to their sexuality in Orwell's writing, whilst women manipulate theirs. He is eager to win her back when the upper class policeman deserts her, and she too entertains the thought of returning to Flory because he emerges as the hero of the hour when the Burmese attack the European club house. In the last pages, however, Flory is discredited by the appearance of his erstwhile Burmese mistress at the church service, and Elizabeth once again scorns him. Flory shoots himself and Elizabeth marries the older leader of the white community, which enables her to become a true 'burra memsahib' who terrorizes her servants.

Elizabeth is made to appear especially pernicious because she is portrayed as being representative of all women. When she acts evasively and refuses to talk to him in a straightforward manner, i.e. 'man to man', 'she was going to leave him in the dark, snub him and pretend that nothing had happened; *the natural feminine move*.'[8] Orwell does offer some explanations of Elizabeth's predicament, including her experience of poverty and the need to move from her uncle's bungalow because of his lecherous advances, but he conveys no real understanding of her situation and merely produces a cruel parody of a young middle-class woman.

Dorothy Hare is the title character of *A Clergyman's Daughter*. She is the only female character in Orwell's writings who is the protagonist of a novel, but unfortunately it was a novel of which Orwell was far from proud, describing it variously as 'tripe'[9] and 'bollox'.[10] Despite his low opinion of this work which was written hurriedly when he was very hard up, it is a sympathetic portrayal of one group of middle-class English women, spinsters.

Dorothy is the ascetic, unpaid drudge – daughter of an aristocratic but impecunious clergyman, who leaves all the cares of his parish as well as of his household to Dorothy. For her life is a round of shame-facedly avoiding tradesmen (creditors), of parish visiting, jumble sales and Sunday school pageants. The futility and loneliness of her existence are emphasized as she sits late at night making costumes from glue and brown paper for Charles I and Oliver Cromwell in the forthcoming pageant. Dorothy's sexual anxiety traps her in the lonely world of the spinster. 'If only they (men) would leave you *alone*. For it was not that in other ways she disliked men. On the contrary she liked them better than women.'[11] She is repelled by the bluff neighbour, Warburton, who tries to kiss her and will later propose to her. Sexual anxiety is the block – more than her father – to her escape into marriage.

> Part of Mr Warburton's hold over her was in the fact that he was a man and had the careless good humour and the intellectual largeness that women so seldom have. But why couldn't they leave you *alone*?[12]

A fall from her bicycle, a blow to the head and amnesia remove Dorothy from life at Knype Hill. Unaware of who she is, she tastes life among the London down-and-outs, in the hopfields and finally in the appalling Ringwood House, a private school for girls owned by the grasping Mrs Creevey. Orwell's account of the school, with its useless education for middle-class girls and his description of the exploitation of its staff of spinsters make good reading. Dorothy, even though starved by Mrs Creevey, emerges as an innovative and progressive teacher who is motivated by concern for 'the poor children'. Mrs Creevey, backed by the oafish parents, soon puts a stop to that.

From Dorothy Orwell moved outwards and expands, very sympathetically, upon the loneliness and dejection of middle-class spinsters.

> If you have no family and no home to call your own, you could spend half a lifetime without managing to make a friend. There are women in such places, and especially derelict gentlewomen in ill-paid jobs, who go on for years upon end in almost utter solitude.[13]

The end of the novel comes with Dorothy's return home to her selfish old father and to a bleak future of spinsterdom. It is an unsatisfactory but inevitable ending. Unless Dorothy were to take up with a man she would be doomed. Women in Orwell's fiction are not capable of happiness without men.

Rosemary is the jolly, outgoing, kindly and exceptionally nice girl-friend of the whining, poverty-stricken poet Gordon Comstock in *Keep the Aspidistra Flying*. The main theme of the book is Gordon's war against money and the forces of capitalism. It is a losing battle and he sinks lower and lower into the abyss of poverty, only to be rescued by the fact of Rosemary's pregnancy, which stirs him into marrying her and returning to a reasonably paid job in an advertising agency, the very hub of capitalism. Rosemary has of course eventually trapped him – but it is a trap into which he is willing to fall, despite his earlier rantings against marriage and against women's adulation of the Money-God.

> 'Women! What nonsense they make of all our ideas. Because one can't keep free of women, and every woman makes one pay the same price. 'Chuck away your decency and make more money' – that's what women say. 'Chuck away your decency, suck the blacking off the bosses' boots, and buy me a better fur coat than the woman next door.'[14]

But Rosemary is depicted as a charming character. Her charm lies in the fact that she is *not* like other women. Rosemary is a girl a man, a poet even, can talk to: Rosemary could discuss similes and metaphors. Rosemary is *not* like other women: she doesn't harp on to him to go back to the advertising agency until he is absolutely destitute. In short, Orwell uses Rosemary to point to the faults which exist in all the other middle-class women: a desire for money, security and a total inability to appreciate 'ideas'.

Keep the Aspidistra Flying also contains a portrait of Gordon's spinster sister Julia, who is exploited by a female 'friend' as an under-paid worker in a teashop. It is a sympathetic depiction – as is the description of Dorothy Hare's exploitation at Ringwood House. It is in these depictions of middle-class spinsters that Orwell comes nearest to understanding the plight of women workers; there are no similar depictions of single or married working-class women workers.

Hilda Bowling in *Coming Up For Air* is a crude caricature of a lower middle-class wife. The central character of this novel is George Bowling, a five to ten pound-a-week insurance clerk who decides to 'escape' to his childhood home of Lower Binfield. It is as much a retreat from Hilda as a search for a lost past. Hilda, once young, pretty and a social class above him turns, upon marriage, into a nagging wife, pestering George about bills and spreading gloom in the household; she is totally without joy and without interest – she only attends left-wing meetings because they are free and felt to be vaguely improving. She is the Elizabeth of *Burmese Days* ten to twenty years on, if Elizabeth had stayed in England.

Orwell's portrayal of middle-class women – of sexually attractive young women who turn into old, grim nags – is the convention of the seaside postcard. When Orwell discussed the postcard art of Donald McGill he pointed out the two fundamental conventions of depicting women in postcards,

a. Marriage only benefits the women. Every man is plotting seduction and every woman is plotting marriage. No woman ever remains unmarried voluntarily.

b. Sex-appeal vanishes at about the age of twenty-five. Well-preserved and good-looking people beyond their first youth are never represented. The amorous honeymooning couple reappear as the grim-visaged wife and shapeless, mustachioed, red-nosed husband, no intermediate stage being allowed for.[15]

They are precisely the conventions on which Orwell himself drew.

Julia, Winston's mistress in *Nineteen Eighty-Four*, is distinguished from Orwell's other female characters in that she shows courage. She flouts the minor and then the major rules of this future totalitarian society. It is she who initiates contact with Winston: she has the enterprise and experience to arrange liaisons with him.[16] She is prepared too to follow Winston in joining the Brotherhood, the opposition to Big Brother. But the protests of Winston and Julia against the régime are inspired by totally different motives. Whereas Winston is inspired by intellectual concepts like the integrity of history and the notion of freedom, Julia is only 'a rebel from the waist downwards'. The sexually attractive and sexually active Julia objects to the regime because it stops her having a good time. She is totally incapable of understanding the motives which

drive Winston to revolt. 'Any kind of organized revolt against
the Party, which was bound to be a failure, struck her as stupid.
The clever thing was to break the rules and stay alive all the
same.' When Winston talks to her of the Party and its
doctrines, she invariably falls asleep. Her response to his
reading of Goldstein's subversive text is the same. Julia is as
brainless as Elizabeth Lackersteen or Hilda Bowling.

Orwell's portrayal of the main female characters in his
novels encapsulates his opinions on women. He is contemptuous of women's intellects; he reduces married women
and spinsters to stereotypes and in the portrayal of both he
draws on the conventions of seaside postcards. But it is not
only the main characters who reveal Orwell's outlook.
Subsidiary characters and passers-by who are singled out for
derision are often feminists – for example Elizabeth's feckless
mother in *Burmese Days*;[17] the whole Pankhurst generation in
Keep the Aspidistra Flying;[18] sporty and horsey women in *Burmese
Days*,[19] and *Nineteen Eighty-Four*.[20] Working-class women make
few appearances in the novels – when they do it is as
half-brained readers of Ethel M. Dell[11] (why are we not treated
to equally contemptuous asides on the male readers of Zane
Grey and war novels?) or sluttish landladies.[22] But the
haunting archetypal figure of a working-class woman is the
prole washerwoman of *Nineteen Eighty-Four*, of whom more
anon.

If Orwell's fiction provides the clearest indication of his
attitudes towards middle-class women, it is necessary to turn to
his documentary writing and his journalism to find out his
views about working-class women. The most important work
for this is *The Road to Wigan Pier* (1937), read together with the
diary which lies behind it. Yet in *The Road to Wigan Pier* there
are relatively few references to women. To understand why this
is so it is necessary to understand Orwell's male prejudices.

Orwell's world view was male: all the important things in
life were done or thought about by men – work, politics,
revolution. It was typical of him that in going north he should
have gone to a coal-mining area – coal-mining is a heavy
extractive industry, and in the twentieth century an almost
entirely male preserve. He could just as well have concentrated

on the effects of the Depression and of unemployment in the cotton industry, but women workers predominated there and that would not have accorded with his world view and his concept of the working class as male. By concentrating on Wigan coal he could glory in the male strength of miners with 'noble bodies' and see working-class women only as wives.

Orwell's male arrogance and his selection of what is important, judged only by male standards, make *The Road to Wigan Pier* not only a poor source for the history of women in this period but a positively misleading one. Margery Spring Rice's *Working Class Wives*, originally published in 1939,[26] and numerous other social surveys give far more information.[24]

Given Orwell's prejudices, the areas of discussion which arise from *The Road to Wigan Pier* are most crucially: the working-class family, domestic work, the impact of unemployment upon men and women, waged women workers and women and politics.

Orwell had a great affection for the English working class and in particular for the institution of the working-class family. He approved of male dominance within the family: 'in a working class home it is the man who is the master and not, as in the middle class home, the woman or the baby.'[25] He held an idyllic view of the working class family, provided that the father was in well paid and regular work. He held in his mind a picture of the family sitting around the fireside:

> Especially on winter evenings after tea, when the fire glows in the open range and dances mirrored in the steel fender, when Father, in shirt-sleeves, sits in the rocking chair at one side of the fire reading the racing finals, and Mother sits on the other with her sewing, and the children are happy with a pennorth of mint humbugs, and the dog lolls roasting himself on the rag mat.[26]

(It is noteworthy that Mother is the only one working in this picture!) All this is threatened not only by the mass unemployment of Orwell's present but by visions of a Utopian future in which there will be no manual work and there won't even be as many children – if the birth controllers have their way. This last point is significant. It was made at a time when birth control campaigners were fighting hard to set up clinics throughout Britain. Orwell, who seemed to have regarded birth control as some Mathusian plot to limit the lower orders, shows a lack of understanding of the impact of successive child-bearing on women's lives. He was aware that the number of children in a family was the single most important factor as to whether a home could be kept 'decent' or not, but he retained an image in his mind of the fruitful working-class woman. She is represented clearly by the prole woman in *Nineteen Eighty-Four*. The woman fills her washing line with nappies: she was a woman of fifty 'blown-up to monstrous dimensions by child-bearing, then hardened, roughened by work' – but to Winston (and Orwell) she was beautiful.

Orwell's observations on working-class women in *The Road to Wigan Pier* are concerned almost exclusively with women in the home. He provides us with illustrations of what many of these homes were like. His notes on the cramped and insanitary dwellings in Wigan, Sheffield and Barnsley conjure up the horror of the conditions in which many working-class families lived, and his writing brought this home to a wide public. Women spent even more of their lives in these wretched houses than did men, and as Orwell realized, 'In such places as these a woman is only a poor drudge muddling along among an infinity of jobs.' He records that domestic chores continued to fall exclusively on the woman despite the fact of male unemployment. 'The man is idle from morning to night but the woman is as busy as ever – more so, indeed, because she has to manage with less money.' Even Orwell noted that this practice 'on the face of it seems a little unfair'.[27] Orwell wrote that the women as well as the men believed that housework should be done exclusively by women. 'I believe that they, as well as the men, feel that a man might lose his manhood if, merely because he was out of work, he developed into a "Mary Ann".' The inclusion of this discussion on household chores in *The Road to Wigan Pier* apparently results from an argument which occurred when he was staying with the Searle family in Leeds. Orwell had helped Mrs Searle with the washing-up, and her husband and another man who was present strongly disapproved. Interestingly Mrs Searle seemed only 'doubtful' and had, after all, accepted his help. In the diary he notes that she took the fact that even unemployed men did not help in the house for granted but she 'did not see why it should not be changed'.[28]

Although Orwell takes note of the ceaseless round of chores which women had to do in the home – 'No sooner have you washed one child's face than another is dirty: before you have washed the crocks from one meal the next is due to be cooked' – he displayed little patience with 'bad housekeepers'.

Of course the squalor of these people's houses is sometimes their own fault. Even if you live in a back to back house and have four children and a total income of thirty two and sixpence a week from the PAC, there is no *need* to have unemptied chamber pots standing about in your living room.[29]

He admits however that 'it is equally certain that their circumstances do not encourage self respect', but does not seem to grasp how depressing and demoralizing mass unemployment was for women. There is, he wrote, 'no doubt about the deadening, debilitating effect of unemployment upon everybody, married or single, and *upon men more than upon women*.'[30] A social investigation in the South Wales coalfield in the same period was more perceptive. The Carnegie Foundation report found as follows:

The outstanding fact about many of these homes was that the men in them appeared to have higher standards of personal cleanliness than those reflected by their living conditions. It seemed, very largely, their womenfolk who had lost all pride in personal appearance and the appearance of the home. Men folk were obliged to go out of doors, even if only to the Employment Exchange; this was a reason for washing and dressing up. The women had not this incentive. Their outings extended little beyond the small shops at the corner of the street, and to these they could 'slip-down' without washing. To them there seemed little point in washing the children, as they just got dirty anyway. All this is highly regrettable and, quite apart from unemployment and bad housing conditions, many of the women, even if given the opportunity and money for improved standards, would find it an exceedingly difficult task to break away from their acquired habits. But we must face the fact that to live constantly on a depressed standard of living, where life is a hand-to-mouth existence, is, except for the bravest souls, to experience the bitterness of defeat.[32]

When Orwell wrote about women in *The Road to Wigan Pier*, he wrote about women as wives. In his fiction there are many references to middle-class single working women: there is no corresponding concern shown for working-class women, single or married, who were employed outside the home. The book opens with a reference to the sound of the mill girls' clogs on the cobbled streets, but there is no discussion or further allusion to the conditions of women in the cotton industry. There is likewise only a single reference to women in coal-mining: Orwell mentions that there were a few women still alive who in their youth worked underground.[32] He ignores totally the fact that at the time he was writing there were still women working at the pitbrow – they were still there in the 1950s.[33] Nor does he write of that great army of exploited women, the largest single category of women in waged employment – domestic servants. Orwell simply failed to see the vital role that women both as unpaid home workers and poorly paid waged workers played in the workings of capitalism. He failed to perceive that the unpaid work of the miner's wife was as vital to the mine-owners as to the miners themselves. His whole discussion of socialism in *The Road to Wigan Pier* and elsewhere is devoid of any reference to that key analytical tool, the sexual division of labour.

When Orwell wrote about politics, which for him meant trade-unionism and socialist thought, he wrote about men and he wrote for men. As usual, he ignored women. He seems to have thought women incapable of thinking on a political level. He was genuinely surprised when Mrs Searle, the Sheffield woman who had let him wash up, displayed a 'grasp of the economic situation and also of abstract ideas'; he hastened to add that in this she was unlike most working-class women and that she was scarcely literate.[34] This reference comes from his diary and does not appear in the published text of *The Road to Wigan Pier*. Similarly there is an account in the diary, but not in the book, of his attending a social evening organized by the National Unemployed Workers' Movement (NUWM) to raise money for the defence of Thaelmann, the German Communist leader. His diary notes read,

> About 200 people, preponderantly women, largely members of the Co-op, in one of whose rooms it was held and I suppose for the most part living directly or indirectly on the dole. Round the back a few aged miners sitting looking on benevolently, a lot of very young girls in front. Some dancing to the concertina (many of the girls confessed that they could not dance, which struck one as rather pathetic) and some excruciating singing. I suppose that represented a fair cross-section of the more revolutionary element in Wigan. If so, God help us. Exactly the same sheeplike crowd – gaping girls and shapeless middle aged women dozing over their knitting – that you see everywhere else.[35]

In this account Orwell's overt sexism and contempt for women gushes forth.

In *The Road to Wigan Pier* Orwell omitted any reference to the political activities of women in the North of England. It is precisely this sort of omission which wipes women from our history. For the record, I am impelled to note that Lancashire women cotton operatives had been very active radical suffragists in the years before the First World War, and that they were strong trade unionists.[36] Lancashire women had participated in the National Hunger Marches to London organized by the NUWM,[37] and Lancashire women were active members of the Women's Co-operative Guild, which in the 1930s was campaigning, amongst other things, for contraception, better health care, international peace and for full employment by the reorganization of industry on a co-operative basis.[38]

Orwell altered the record of the past, so far as women are concerned, as efficiently as if he had been in the employ of Minitrue. He was part of a conspiracy of silence.

Notes

1 Letter to Brenda Salkeld, 27 July 1934 in S. Orwell and I. Angus (eds.), *The Collected Essays, Journalism and Letters of George Orwell*, Vol. I,

Harmondsworth, 1971, p. 160, referred to hereafter as '*CEJL*'.

2 B. Salkeld, 'He didn't really like women', A. Coppard and B. Crick (eds.), *Orwell Remembered*, London, 1984, p. 68.

3 G. Orwell, *The Road to Wigan Pier*, Harmondsworth, 1969, p. 121.

4 Ibid., p. 153.

5 Ibid., p. 103.

6 G. Orwell, 'Boys Weeklies', (1940) in *CEJL*, Vol. 1, p. 505.

7 G. Orwell, *Burmese Days*, Harmondsworth, 1983, p. 179.

8 Ibid., p. 184. The italics are mine.

9 Letter to Brenda Salkeld, 7 March 1935 in *CEJL*, Vol. 1, p. 174.

10 Letter to Henry Miller, 26 August 1936; ibid., p. 258.

11 G. Orwell, *A Clergyman's Daughter*, Harmondsworth, 1982, p. 75.

12 Ibid.

13 Ibid., p. 227.

14 G. Orwell, *Keep the Aspidistra Flying*, Harmondsworth, 1975, p. 122.

15 G. Orwell, 'The Art of Donald McGill,' in *CEJL*, Vol. 2, p. 186.

16 G. Orwell, *Nineteen Eighty-Four*, Harmondsworth, 1983, pp. 96-7.

17 Op.cit., p. 85.

18 Op.cit., p. 123.

19 Op.cit., p. 69.

20 Op.cit., pp. 14, 326.

21 *Keep the Aspidistra Flying*, pp. 15-17.

22 Ibid., p. 221.

23 Margery Spring Rice, *Working Class Wives*, London, 1939 (reprinted 1981).

24 See John Stevenson, *Social Conditions in Britain between the Wars*, Harmondsworth, 1977.

25 G. Orwell, *The Road to Wigan Pier*, Harmondsworth, 1969, pp. 72-3.

26 Ibid., p. 104.

27 Ibid., p. 73

28 *CEJL*, Vol. 1, p. 195.

29 *Wigan Pier*, p. 53.

30 Ibid., p. 73. The italics are mine.

31 Carnegie United Kingdom Trust, *Disinherited Youth*, Edinburgh, 1943.

32 *Wigan Pier*, p. 30.

33 For the history of women in the Wigan coalfield and attempts to oust them from the industry see Angela V. John, *By the Sweat of their Brow: Women Workers in Victorian Coalmines*, London, 1980. For the continued employment of women in Wigan mines to the 1950s see B. Campbell, *Wigan Pier Revisited*, London, 1984, pp. 100-1.

34 *CEJL*, Vol. 1, p. 220.

35 Ibid., p. 207.

36 See J. Liddington and J. Norris, *One Hand Tied Behind Us: The Rise of the Women's Suffrage Movement*, London, 1978.

37 See P. Kingsford, *The Hunger Marchers in Britain, 1920-1940*, London, 1982.

38 See Jean Gaffin and David Thoms, *Caring and Sharing: The Centenary History of the Women's Cooperative Guild*, Manchester, 1983.

Stephen Sedley

An Immodest Proposal: 'Animal Farm'

'No, I don't think he was ever a socialist, although he would have described himself as a socialist.' (Fredric Warburg, publisher of *Animal Farm*)[1]

Imaginative literature does not have to justify itself politically. On the contrary, part of its value may be to enhance or modify its readers' political comprehension. Marx's well-known preference for Balzac, a royalist, over Zola, a socialist, makes the point well enough, but it is or ought to be the experience of every socialist that it is not shared assumptions but shared experience that makes good literature a humanising and encouraging force.

Re-reading *Animal Farm* a generation after I first encountered it – as you my reader probably did – on the school curriculum, I am struck by its distance from any of these considerations. It lacks, deliberately, any effort to draw the reader into a convincing fiction, to invite a willing suspension of disbelief. Instead it demands assent to its major premiss that people in their political lives can be equated with domesticated animals, and to its minor premiss that civil society, like a farm, will be run for better or for worse by those who by birth or force inherit power. From these premisses the story and its moral follow; without them there is neither story nor moral.

The book is still required reading in most schools. Its presence on the curriculum does not disturb Sir Keith Joseph, Dr Rhodes Boyson or the *Daily Mail* in their crusade to eradicate political bias from the classroom, but I was interested that my eldest child, a good reader who was given it at the age of thirteen, was bored stiff by it. The reason, it turned out, was that she was too new to political ideas to have any frame of reference for the story: she literally couldn't see what it was about. There was no invitation to enter into the fiction, no common point of departure for reader and writer.

This is certainly not a necessary condition of political allegory or satire: one has to go no farther than Orwell's next major work, *Nineteen Eighty-Four*, to see that. Nor is it a necessary condition of animal fables: our literature is rich in examples. It is an abdication of imaginative art, and one which makes the critical and pedagogic success of *Animal Farm* a sobering example of the substitution of political endorsement for critical appraisal (a vice of which the political right does not have a monopoly).

Orwell's lineage from Swift is frequently spoken of. In background and personality there are similarities, and in some of their writings too, but not in *Animal Farm*. It is not only that Swift has humour as well as passion, which Orwell does not. Swift's satirical method is practically the reverse of Orwell's. Through the picaresque fantasy of *Gulliver's Travels* or the solemn reasoning of *A Modest Proposal* Swift draws the reader down a convincing false trail. The fiction stands, as his contemporaries would have said, on its own bottom. It is only when his readers have passed the point of no return that they realise that they are reading about themselves. But you cannot get into the fiction of *Animal Farm* at all without accepting as your starting point the very thing that Orwell has to prove – that in politics people are no better than animals: their traditional rulers may be feckless but ungovern them and a new tyranny will fill the place of the old. Naturally if you are prepared to accept that conclusion as your premiss, the story follows. You can demonstrate that the earth is flat by a similar process.

The use of animals to make a point about people is as old as art itself. Folk literatures abound in animals which are not only human but superhuman. Through them the human endeavour to understand and control the natural and social environments is expressed and developed. You find it in English folk tradition in the ballad of the *Cutty Wren*, the hedge-king; in

Irish tradition in *Reynardine*, the man-fox; in Scots tradition in the *Grey Selchie*, the man-seal. In modern English literature we have at least two exponents who show up the poverty of Orwell's creativity, Beatrix Potter and Kenneth Grahame. The best of Beatrix Potter's stories are so well made that it is easy to lose critical perspective in evaluating them. It is enough perhaps to observe how meticulously she invests her animals with sufficient human qualities to enable them to be real characters without ceasing to be animals. Mr Jackson is a revolting old toad with a toad's predilections in food, but he mimics human character in ways which wryly enlarge your appreciation of human character. The quiet analogy between the amphibious and the human Mr Jackson neither demands assent to the proposition that there is not much to choose between people and toads nor invites that conclusion. In its small way it is a piece of humane imaginative literature, drawing on the links between human and animal life without straining them.

Perhaps the most indicative contrast is between Potter's and Orwell's versions of the scatter-brained and least rational members of their animal societies – in Potter's books the ducks and rabbits, in Orwell's the sheep. The puddleducks, especially Jemima Puddleduck who nearly gets eaten by the fox in her desire to establish her independence (an interesting parallel with the *Animal Farm* story), are again small mirrors of humanity, pompous and opinionated in proportion to their foolishness. The extended rabbit family is what Beatrix Potter's successors would have regarded as a problem family, delinquents and all, held together by a long-suffering mother. The human presence, Mr McGregor the grumpy old market gardener, is simply another element of risk in their world: they eat his lettuces and, when he can, he eats them.

In Orwell the silliest of the animals are the sheep. They are the essential and unwitting allies of the tyrant pigs, endlessly bleating the slogan 'Four legs good, two legs bad' in any controversy and drowning all serious discussion. They have no reality as characters, but they do represent the British upper class's opinion of the working class: mindless creatures who do what others direct and bleat what others devise. The remaining farm animals, apart from the pigs, are more or less stupid and more or less good natured. The pigs are cunning and evil.

It is in the pigs that the political allegory takes its most precise form. The dream of revolution is dreamt by the old pig Major, who dies before it happens. His manifesto speech to the animals is couched in terms of self-evident absurdity:

> Man is the only real enemy we have. Remove Man from the scene, and the root cause of hunger and overwork is abolished for ever … No argument must lead you astray. Never listen when they tell you that Man and the animals have a common interest, and that the prosperity of the one is the prosperity of the others. It is all lies.[2]

So it is, we are to understand, with civil society: only a fool could talk like this. (The sidelight this passage throws on Orwell's brand of socialism is interesting.)

To Major's Marx, Napoleon plays Stalin and Snowball Trotsky: the allegory becomes a simple set of personal disguises. The brightest of the other animals, the dogs, are finally bribed and bred into a private army at the pigs' service. The rest, from the willing cart-horses to the fecund hens, are put upon endlessly to keep the pigs in idle comfort.

No honest socialist or communist ignores or underrates the structural and political problems and distortions which have characterised the Soviet Union and other states that have taken a similar path. 'More equal than others' is a barb which has stuck painfully in the consciousness of the left, for the existence of a privileged élite in any socialist state is a fundamental contradiction in political terms. For some on the left it argues that Marxism is not the way to socialism; for some, that Marxism has been betrayed; for some, that Marxism has been vindicated by the state's survival. Not one of these viewpoints, nor any variant of them, is explored or enriched by *Animal Farm*. Orwell's argument is pitched at a different level: it is that socialism in whatever form offers the common people no more hope than capitalism; that it will be first betrayed and then held to ransom by those forces which human beings have in common with beasts; and that the inefficient and occasionally benign rule of capitalism, which at least keeps the beasts in check, is a lesser evil. That proposition is Orwell's alpha and his omega.

So it is that the allegories of Soviet history in *Animal Farm* are just that – translations of the fall of Trotsky, the failure of the electrification programme, the enforcement of collectivisation; of a ruling élite looking for scapegoats for its own errors or for other catastrophes. Nothing in the use of an animal society as the vehicle of allegory particularly illuminates or enhances it or the points it seeks to make. It certainly does not make the case against Soviet socialism any more convincing. In fact it appears to confirm the underlying hostility of its opponents to any suggestion that the working class can emancipate itself. It does nothing to cast light on what for any socialist is the real question: what has gone wrong and why? If anything it has tended to fix the left in its own errors by aversion.

Is this essay then a criticism of *Animal Farm* for what it is not, for lacking a stance which was never Orwell's anyway? It would be less than candid to deny that both its assumption that people and animals are alike in their social or political existence, and its use of that assumption to insult the belief that ordinary people can put an end to want and privilege, make *Animal Farm*, to this writer at least, a pretty unattractive book. But that is not what makes it a poor piece of literature.

To take a second contrast from modern animal fiction, *The Wind in the Willows* is redolent of a particular social and political philosophy, all of it growing into and out of a beautifully told tale. Enough has been written about the class microcosm which contains the aristocratic playboy Toad, his yeoman friends Rat, Mole and Badger, and the feared (because unknown) Wild Wooders – the commoners, rogues and vagabonds. One can see and appraise Grahame's thoughts and feelings about class society and the stratum in which alone he feels secure, and one can have one's own views about them and him, without ever falling out with the fiction through which his idyll of contemplation and loyalty is conveyed.

The same is true of the misanthropy with which *Gulliver's Travels* is shot through. More to the point, both stories, because they work as stories, earn a measure of understanding for their authors' viewpoints. They enlarge intellectual as well as emotional horizons. For similar reasons more socialists have probably been made in Britain by *The Ragged Trousered Philanthropists* than by the *Communist Manifesto*.

Between its covers *Animal Farm* offers little that is creative, little that is original. Those who are interested in the links between politics and literature have far more to learn from the circumstances of the book's success. It is an extraordinary fact that it was written in the latter part of the Second World War, when the defeat of Nazism depended upon the Soviet Union's survival and military victory, and published (after three rejections) in the year of Labour's historic electoral victory. It was therefore certainly out of joint with its time, and it was no doubt in keeping with Orwell's penchant for heresy. But it was admirably in line with what rapidly became the political mode of government and press – a virulent and often unreasoning anti-communism. The prophet, to his own surprise, rapidly achieved honour in his own country.

When in 1947 Orwell wrote the preface to a Ukrainian edition of *Animal Farm* he explained that his aim had been to disabuse 'the workers and intelligentsia in a country like England' of their naïve notions about the USSR (his Ukrainian readers were not there). He blamed their naïvety on the relative liberality of English political life:

> Yet one must remember that England is not completely democratic. It is also a capitalist country with great class privileges and (even now, after a war that has tended to equalise everybody) with great differences in wealth. But nevertheless it is a country in which people have lived together for several hundred years without knowing civil war, in which the laws are relatively just and official news and statistics can almost invariably be believed, and, last but not least, in which to hold and to voice minority views does not involve any mortal danger. In such an atmosphere the man in the street has no real understanding of things like concentration camps, mass deportations, arrests without trial, press censorship etc. Everything he reads about a country like the USSR is automatically translated into English terms, and he quite innocently accepts the lies of totalitarian propaganda.[3]

This view of English political life in the mid-1940s does not now simply appear breathtakingly foolish; nor does it simply betray Orwell's socialism as a pose unsupported by analysis, experience or comprehension: it underscores *Animal Farm*'s message that ordinary people are too simple-minded to appreciate about Russia what is appreciated by a man who a page earlier has written:

> I have never visited Russia and my knowledge of it consists only of what can be learned by reading books and newspapers.

He goes on in the preface to explain how, years after Spain, his thoughts were crystallised by seeing a small boy driving a huge cart-horse with a whip:

> It struck me that if only such animals became aware of their strength we should have no power over them, and that men exploit animals in much the same way as the rich exploit the proletariat.
>
> I proceeded to analyse Marx's theory from the animals' point of view. To them it was clear that the concept of a class struggle between humans was pure illusion, since whenever it was necessary to exploit animals, all humans united against them: the true struggle is between animals and humans. From this point of departure, it was not difficult to elaborate the story.

The muddle is remarkable. Where, for instance, does Marx argue that there is a class struggle between members of the ruling class ('a class struggle between humans')? More important, whether the idea that 'the true struggle is between animals and humans' is being attributed to the animals or to Orwell himself, the book begins and ends by debunking it, as of course it asks to be debunked. I have mentioned Major's fatuous early speech to this effect. The book goes on to argue that through revolution a human (that is a capitalist) oppressor will simply be replaced by an animal (that is a proletarian) oppressor. And remember how it ends?

> The creatures outside looked from pig to man, and from man to pig, and from pig to man again; but it was already impossible to say which was which.

If Orwell in his preface is trying to say simply that human beings, however divided among themselves, are united in their exploitation of animals, this is *not* the point of departure of *Animal Farm*. Its point of departure, like its conclusion, is the proposition that human beings and beasts share characteristics of greed and ruthlessness towards their own kind.

Orwell concluded his preface:

> I do not wish to comment on the work; if it does not speak for itself, it is a failure.

He was of course right: but it is an interesting comment on the ideological argument of *Animal Farm* that its author was so unable to give an intelligible account of it.

Notes

1 Fredric Warburg, in a BBC interview in 1970, quoted in A. Coppard and B. Crick (eds.) *Orwell Remembered*, London, 1984, p.194.
2 *Animal Farm*, Harmondsworth, 1982, p.11.
3 S. Orwell and I. Angus (eds.), *The Collected Essays, Journalism and Letters of George Orwell*, Vol. 3, Harmondsworth, 1970, p.458. The original English text is lost. The citations are from the unattributed retranslation from the edition distributed in 1947 by a Ukrainian displaced persons' organisation in Munich.

Lynette Hunter

Stories and Voices in Orwell's Early Narratives

George Orwell has always been a singular figure for speculation within literary criticism. A main thesis of Raymond Williams's influential book *Orwell* was to present the man as a paradox of conflicting attitudes to the duality of dominated and dominator in all situations social, historical and political. Of course this presentation also raises the parallel problems of authority in writing. But rather than look at any of the supposed tensions in an exemplary light, as attempts at stances for dealing with the conflict, much recent criticism has tended to concentrate on the negative aspects of the conflict itself. This odd emphasis on the content of Orwell's writing – one that occurs less often with other writers – may have to do with the continuing relevance of the topics he discussed; but it also appears to have derived from rather ungenerous readings, of the early fictional writing in particular.

Throughout those early works Orwell is learning. The fictions have aspects that he would later come to consider flawed, such as the 'purple passages' that he dismisses in 'Why I Write' (1946).[1] But these novels are by no means polished products of a mature artistry, and the writer is taken to task by critics time and again for poor plots, 'weak' characterisation, and especially for the relationships that exist between writer and character.[2]

Critics have perhaps been too ready to assume that Orwell was just not *aware* of what was going on in his writing, to regard the skills that his documentaries and later fiction evidence almost as fortuitous, and even to devalue those skills by insisting on readings that carry the weaknesses of the early work into the later.[3] I would also suggest that when the early novels are read as product rather than origin, the paradoxes that have led to a widespread condemnation of Orwell become more open, so that their complexities engage rather than estrange.[4]

During the years 1932 to 1935 Orwell wrote four narrative works, all of which explored the possibilities of voice, of the stances of writer, narrator and character. Despite initial appearances, *Down and Out in Paris and London* is not a 'naïve' story, but a study of varied ways of telling and writing in the first person. The same experimentation with voice is found in *Burmese Days*, but within this attempt at a classical naturalistic novel the presentation of voice is far more subtle. *A Clergyman's Daughter*, written immediately after *Burmese Days*, is by comparison an obvious experiment with techniques that often lie outside the naturalistic novel, such as caricature, report and 'stream-of-consciousness'. Rather heavy-handedly, it tries to strip away expected elements and examine what results in terms of writer, narrator and character relationships. Written in 1935, the year before *The Road to Wigan Pier*, *Keep the Aspidistra Flying* shows a far more confident handling of voice, in which the writer is moving toward an interaction with the writing that will inform all his later works and provide much of their enduring appeal.

From the beginning Orwell is obviously fascinated by the tensions that arise between the dominated and the dominator. Not only does this fascination run through the themes of the early novels, but it also informs his handling of stance and therefore the way that the writing is structured. *Down and Out in Paris and London* is ostensibly the work of a narrator who has sat down to 'write what he sees', but learns that this is impossible. Although all the characters tell stories of one kind or another, within the first part of the book an index to the narrator's growing consciousness of the difficulty of writing is found in the character of Charlie, who recounts three very different tales. The first is a first-person, melodramatic account of one of Charlie's sexual forays. Its clichéd semi-pornographic patter, complete with dark alleyways, blood-red furnishings and whimpering girls, is part of the stance of the narrator at the start of the book. He speaks in a patronising tone, counting on assumptions that both he and his magazine-educated readers will presumably find familiar. For example the book begins with a 'typical' French scene of street argument, using scattered French words to authenticate the telling, but it is an event that the narrator thinks needs little explanation and he concludes with a comment that 'It was quite a representative Paris slum.'⁵ The narrator's confidence in the common ground he shares with his readers is further reflected in his preface to Charlie's story itself and the proprietory manner in which he promises to 'give' us Charlie as one of the 'local curiosities, talking'.

Charlie's second story is an anecdote that is recounted in a rather different manner. The narration is explanatory, interspersed with humorous comment and contains a great deal of reported speech. The anecdote provides a view of some of life's little ironies, and reveals much not only about Charlie's life but also about the narrator's changing attitude towards him as a written character. Although criticising the 'peasant girl' that he lives with, it is apparent that Charlie cares enough for her to think of a way for her to get food, asking at one point 'has not every woman something to sell?' Yet the implication of prostitution has been set up specifically so that it can be subverted to indicate character. In the event, what Charlie is referring to is his more innocuous plan to disguise the girl and send her to a kitchen that has been set up for pregnant women. But for Charlie the point of the story is that he can tell of his witty remark that saves the girl from discovery when she is met by someone from the kitchen a year later. Again the unspoken evaluations are clearly there in the rearranged expectations of the reader: Charlie is still with this girl a year later, and while there was no need to protect her he does so anyway. Charlie may be self-glorifying but because of the internal commentary it is now difficult to take his egoism too seriously.

For this second story the narrator moves from the direct speech of the first melodramatic tale to reported speech within direct speech. He is more distanced, no longer claiming to 'give' us Charlie and becoming aware of the impossibility of

exact description. Charlie's final story is narrated entirely in
reported speech, with the narrator emphasising the second-
hand nature of the story by saying 'Charlie told me' and
'Charlie said', and even commenting, 'I should very much like
to have known him'. The story is prefaced with the remark:
'Very likely Charlie was lying as usual, but it was a good story';
and the entire tale may be seen as a formal and conventional
parable beginning with the traditional 'One day ...'. The two
men involved in the tale, Roucolle and an acquaintance,
arrange to buy some cocaine and the police get wind of the
matter. When the police raid their rooms, they pretend that the
cocaine is face powder; but on examination in a laboratory,
the police find that it is indeed face powder and the joke is
turned the other way around. Yet at the end the humour is
undercut. The narrator says, 'Three days later he [Roucolle]
had some kind of stroke, and in a fortnight he was dead – of a
broken heart, Charlie said.'

   The parable concerns being taken in by something that
appears to be the real thing but is not. In this the narrator
makes it clear that in this first part of the book, not only has he
learned about the dangers of observation, but also he is
beginning to recognise the activity of convention and fiction in
expression. The parable is placed immediately following a
chapter of discussion in which the narrator has claimed that
the middle class only hate and fear the working class because
they do not understand them; they allow their prejudices and
assumptions to govern their response rather than actively
examining the situation. Just so: the parable provides, by
analogy, a way of reading the book and involves the writer in
examining his own writing. At the start there the
familiarisation through a bourgeois narrator, which was
followed by naïve attempts at confrontation and alienation
through Charlie's first story and other recounted events, and
which then moved on to a re-familiarisation with the narrator
on a different footing. The 'average' reader, the middle-class
magazine consumer who was led to identify with the initial
voice through vocabulary and received idioms, is here asked to
become distanced and to examine the background of
distorting assumptions. The juxtaposition of social discussion
with fictive parable is being suggested as a more valuable

reading than cliché, melodrama and stereotyping.

Throughout the second part of *Down and Out in Paris and London*, an index to the narrator's awareness of writing is provided in the two types of tramps that he meets: Bozo and Paddy. Here the consciousness of the effect of 'story' is stronger and clearer: there is specific reference to language and literature and the writer is moving the topic directly into the crisis of authorial writing which raises the issues of dominator and dominated. Bozo is articulate, intelligent and interesting. He is one of the few tramps the narrator meets who are neither ashamed nor self-pitying, and the narrator associates this with Bozo's 'gift for phrases. He had managed to keep his brain intact and alert ... he was, as he said, free in his own mind'. Soon after this description comes the narrator's chapter on slang, swearing and insulting. The discussion indicates a curious two-way process in effect, for words sometimes define their users and yet are sometimes defined by them, 'being what public opinion chooses to make them'. Yet in both these cases there is a sense of fixity that Bozo's activity and alertness has little to do with. Where they are seen in action is in the stories that the rest of the tramps, including Paddy, tell to each other on the road.

The tramps have stories about each particular 'spike', about the managers and about individual characters on the road, all of which establish points of reference and contact, put them at their ease and allow them to cope with the various situations they are faced with: the consoling value of their stories is underlined explicitly when the narrator comments, 'The tramps liked the story, of course, but the interesting thing was to see that they had got it all wrong ... The story had been amended, no doubt deliberately ... giving them happy endings which are quite imaginary'. Although they define their stories in this way, every action they perform has a story attached to it as if these fictions are needed to keep them alive, to define them. But it is not the stories themselves that are criticised, it is the way that the tramps use them to maintain their self-pity and shame by accepting their prejudices and assuming that there can be no change in the status quo, in contrast to Bozo's humorous and often deflating stories about himself.

The activity of defining and being defined by raises directly the topic of dominator and dominated. The tramps' stories have a self-deceptive narration like that of the initial narrator of the book, one that creates a circular tautological world. But the narrator develops for himself a stance that moves away from his initial unspoken control by means of a particular class idiom, to the point of consciously situating himself within a class structure through telling the story about his 'educated' accent. He also changes his mode of narration into one that inquires, compares and assesses. He suggests in the latter part of the book that we can learn to evaluate through close attention to language, and he does so by presenting himself as learning to differentiate between ways of narrating and developing new skills to activate responses.

However, the penultimate chapter shows him trying not to dominate by *reporting* rather than *recounting* his experience. He moves to discussion of the issues in terms of statistics and pragmatics without realising that these techniques are unwittingly manipulative. Just because they are no longer 'subjective' or 'abstract', as was the discussion following part one, it certainly doesn't follow that their grounds and assumptions are somehow 'true'. The final chapter indicates the unreliability of this stance by underscoring the second-hand nature of the experience and the narrator's essentially trivial understanding of the issues. The writing suggests that the content of what is said is of less importance than the process of the narrator's understanding.

Down and Out in Paris and London is an uneven fiction, but one that illustrates the movement of all Orwell's writing towards greater interaction between reader and writer. The narrative is uneven particularly because the second half concludes far more ambivalently than the first: as if the first half reveals his conventions and prejudices, and so in the second he attempts his famous 'plain style' for the first time. Yet he concludes by being obviously dissatisfied with the limitations of that same 'plain style', limitations which derive from a lack of explicit stance.

The concerns of *Down and Out in Paris and London* with language and literature as ways of establishing stance, either of interaction or of the isolated tautology of dominator and dominated, are further developed in *Burmese Days* not only as a theme, but also as an aspect of the narrator-and-character relationship.[6] This relationship is presented within a conventional, authorial structure that the writer foregrounds through pointing his ironic comments. From the start the narrator is shown observing and typifying, fixing characters into a prejudice. In the opening scene a Burmese official, U Po Kyin, is presented by an authoritative, ironic voice as a man who sees spiritual life in terms of success, and is surrounded with ludicrous images of food such as 'satin praline' clothes and more ominously, a shape 'swollen with the bodies of his enemies'.[7] Yet the reader is alerted to the difference between narrator and character, because the former thinks in words and the latter in'pictures'. All these details are a translation. The reader reacts more directly to the official's reported speech yet this too is a translation from the Burmese: when he shifts into English he develops 'the base jargon of the Government offices ...' The contrast in communication – within the character and between the character and the narrator – indicates the concern with the elusiveness of language that the writing will pursue.

The authoritative irony that the narrator initially uses asks the reader to make judgments according to unspoken but understood assumptions. Just because the narrator does not have to make these clear, his presentation may appear balanced, and it is all too easy for the reader to forget those underlying assumptions and fall into the trap of accepting the proffered prejudices. The first person that the main character, Flory, meets is Westfield the District Superintendent of Police. Westfield is described with 'his hands in the pockets of his shorts', speaking with a catalogue of boys' magazine epithets: the archetypal sahib, made ludicrous with 'abnormally' thin calves and eyes too far apart. And there is the casual observation that 'Nearly everything he said was intended for a joke', where the word 'intended' indicates the continual failure of his sense of humour. All of this typifies him, makes him into a comic character that many readers would recognise: but in order to recognise that comedy, one has to enter into the conventions on which it is based. One is led to criticise the man (albeit gently), but to do so within the terms of the world he represents.

The analogical point being made is that this is Flory's central dilemma, and awareness of the authoritative irony of the narrator makes it possible for the reader to experience it at first hand. But the narrator also attempts other voices. During an incident where Flory goes off into the jungle to work out his confusions, we discover that he cannot do so effectively in language but only through the direct action of casting off his corrupt life and swimming in a pool. He literally loses his way, and when he returns he has regained his perspective. At the same time the narrator takes on the burden of expression for him in an observing voice. During the experience the narration gradually detaches itself from Flory's frustration and moves into distanced observation of colour, shape and sound. As it does so the reader follows Flory's own gradual detachment, yet the expression of it is strictly the narrator's. When Flory does overtly verbalise he says 'Alone, alone, the bitterness of being alone!'; the melodrama clashing sentimentally with the restraint of the observation. Later the narrator takes on a voice of commentary that re-phrases Flory's melodramatic sigh into a different mode: one that could possibly look at and assess the basic issues and assumptions. He says:

> Since then each year had been lonelier and more bitter than the last. What was at the centre of all his thoughts now, and what poisoned everything was the ever bitterer hatred of the atmosphere of imperialism in which he lived. For as his brain developed – you cannot stop your brain developing, and it is one of the tragedies of the half-educated that they develop late, when they are already committed to some wrong way of life – he had grasped the truth about the English and their Empire.

Because this commenting voice of the narrator can find expression for Flory's predicament the narrator can go on to examine it, to discuss the social and political dimensions, the enclosed worlds of individual and public despotism that are both generated by and yet also maintain the imperial rule in Burma.

While Flory is unable to express himself, he is aware of the need to do so, to discuss and interact in the way that the commenting voice makes possible. His relationship with

Elizabeth Lackersteen is a desperate attempt at communication, but their private worlds can only touch through the mingling of a superficial vocabulary which restricts itself to speaking of the 'beastly' weather. On the occasions that he does break through to her, she rejects his individual world. In doing so she not only undermines the bases for his escape into this world, which have been constructed in isolation and which cannot stand criticism, but also points to its corruption. Flory has always been able to pretend that he lived cleanly and differently in his secret world, away from the compromises of the public sphere. However, it is impossible to exist without some contact with the public, and Elizabeth's presence highlights those moments of conflicting contact, focusing on them as the source of Flory's ambiguity and confusion. But Flory is not completely enclosed. He comes to recognise the corrupting nature of his escape, yet can see no alternative except to conform to the escapes offered by the public.

The split between the melodramatic and the detailed approach that distinguishes Flory from the narrator is similar to that between the initial narrator and the second narrator who is learning, in the earlier work. Turning back one or two years to the short story 'The Spike' one finds an interesting development in narrative technique. The narrator of 'The Spike' over-reacts using melodramatic vocabulary and sentimental description. The governor of a spike is referred to in *Down and Out* as being 'renowned as a tyrant', but in the short story he is 'a devil ... a tartar, a tyrant, a bawling, blasphemous, uncharitable dog'.[8] In the latter story, the tramps 'shuffled in' to the house, which is itself 'gloomy and chilly' as if part of a gothic horror tale. The narrator distinguishes himself from the tramps as a 'gentleman', but in contrast with the same distinction in the longer fiction he does not make it clear that no one usually notices his difference. This gives rise to the generally patronising and condescending air of the short story writer.

Underlining the lack of sympathy or connection between the earlier narrator and the tramps is a clear difference in vocabulary. The language is literary, using similes such as 'looking like the corpse of Lazarus' or the comment that his 'spirit soared far away, in the pure aether of the middle

classes.' This narrator is longwinded and officiously explanatory, using large numbers of adjectives and excessively
complicated constructions. In contrast, the narrator of *Down
and Out* is more concise, straightforward and colloquial. And
whereas the tramps are allowed to tell their stories in the later
version, pointing up their world of self-enclosure, these
anecdotes in the earlier version are merely dismissed as
outrageous.

While 'The Spike' does evidence clear reporting of dialogue
and occasional succinct phrasing, it is written overwhelmingly
as if to ingratiate the writer with his magazine audience. It is a
game, an adventure story, closely paralleling the approach to
the French slum of the initial narrator of the novel. That it has
so much in common with the style of the initial narrator, and
that it also contains scenes identical with those in the second
section of the novel, indicates that the narratorial change in the
latter part of *Down and Out* is purposeful and necessary. But it
also suggests that Flory's similar vocabulary and observation is
unreliable. 'Why I Write' noted that *Burmese Days* probably
came the closest to the early 'purple passage' aims of the
writer, yet it may also be read as self-criticism of those aims. It
conveys the message that melodrama, cliché and the language
of the public are only effective modes of expression in the
short-term. They leave you enclosed, with no way of relating to
what lies outside.

The main technique in *Burmese Days* is a study of language:
of how far the vocabulary and constructions of each character
measure up to or deviate from the officialese, the slang and the
stereotyped expression. Apart from Flory, the only characters
who have specific problems in saying what they mean are Mrs
Lackersteen, Elizabeth's aunt, and Verrall, who for a time
becomes Elizabeth's boyfriend. Mrs Lackersteen's problem
arises from her complete restriction to public language; her
communication becomes a standard that other characters
adapt to their own mode of officialese, but which isolates her
within its barriers. Verrall on the other hand is anarchic; he
uses virtually no public language at all. But whereas Flory's
anarchism simply drives him to suicide because he cannot
realise his individual world within the public, Verrall is a
member of the ruling class. Unlike ordinary members of

society he can live out his fantasies in actual life for he has physical and social power. Here, change can only occur through force from the ruler or from within the system itself. This despotism, this tautology of dominator and dominating, and the democracy from which it derives, maintains itself by denying the possibility of an alternative, by discounting the possibility for discussion and commentary outside the conventional forms of expression. What Flory fails to recognise is that although he appears to be trapped within a language that offers no alternatives, he could still engage in the self-examination of his individual world that the narrator's commentary implies is needed.

These enclosed worlds are very much a part of the authority and autonomy of the novel. While the writer is directly criticising the social and political, he is also commenting on writing that imposes upon its reader. On a thematic level *Burmese Days* offers no solutions, but its structure explicitly indicates commentary and active discussion as alternatives. And within the relationship of reader and writer there lies the implicit commentary of the writing which suggests not just that authorial novels have no right to impose, but that readers have choice of activity. Flory's suicide is often condemned because it is seen as an indication of the negativity of thematic aspects in the book, yet it has a far more valuable side to it.[9] Instead it may be read as the culmination of a passive, victimised and dominated reading of his political situation. If you condemn Flory's suicide in this way, you also condemn all passive readings of the book. Here there is the beginning of a shift of emphasis away from the extraordinary power of the duality of *defining* or *being defined* by, of dominating and dominated, to a recognition of possible alternatives. Hence the difference between the controlling ironies of the initial narrator and the open, more extensively constructed and varied narration of commentary. But it is not yet explicit, and it is a drawback in the writing not to have moved far enough out of the authorial stance that it criticises.

These tentative criticisms of the autonomy of the naturalistic novel are more fully explored in *A Clergyman's Daughter* where the writing is disastrous in terms of the generic expectations of the reader. Nor is the writer particularly generous to the reader: the experimentation is far too controlled. However, at the same time, what is being attempted is a variety of narrator and character relationships that provide analogies not only for the interaction between individual and public but also for that between writer and reader.

At the start of the book the reader finds Dorothy, the clergyman's daughter of the title, imprisoned in a series of social, sexual and religious stereotypes. The process of the book through its five distinct parts is to present her education in the recognition of the delusive assumptions she lives by. She speaks in a mixture of colloquialism and cliché, stirring herself into action with hearty girls'-school exhortations.[10] The narrator's voice is, by contrast, more observing, less hectic and makes use of far wider vocabulary. As the narratorial voice emerges it becomes apparent that it has many authorial features. If the narrator is not making judgments he is usually reinforcing prejudices with the presentation of accepted stereotypes or the use of unquestioning irony. Nearly every character but Dorothy herself is caricatured through a generalised commentary that leaves nothing to counteract the narrator's opinion, so that he simply voices the conclusions that his presentation has already made obvious. The relationship between narrator and character in Part One is strictly authorial and reflects the closed world of authority presented in the fiction.

Under extreme pressure from her work and situation, Dorothy breaks down. She suddenly loses her memory and 'comes to' on a street corner somewhere in a large city. What the writer has provided is a situation in which the character has no previous assumptions; she must reconstruct herself, her language and her history. At the same time, the narrator is not allowed to interfere with the process. He tries to speak as Dorothy sees, as far as possible without bias. He moves into the past historical tense, a reported past which clearly represents his function. There is far more use of dialogue and less of the dominating, generalised voice that controlled and spelt out the reader's reactions. This stance dwells on precision of detail, qualification of description and explanation, rather than judgment, and is similar to the narrative voice in the second half of *Down and Out in Paris and London*: the 'plain prose style' of 'factual' documentary is again being attempted.

However, Dorothy's resumption of history, language and self in this part of the book belies the possibility of any such 'neutral' presentation. Her first realisation is that language exists outside her; more strictly, that an ideology of language surrounds and defines her. Once she recognises this she becomes 'aware of *herself* ... discovered her separate and unique existence'. The use of words represents a set of assumed rules, an ideology that is basic to man's concept of everything else he views. Awakening to that use re-establishes a past in all the assumptions it carries, and choosing to use words in this way places one irretrievably within the bounds of the history that that use signifies. Just so, the narrator's voice, for all its limited self-questioning, carries the weight of an ideology with it. But it is very easy to take these assumptions for granted, and that is exactly what, under the weight of physical exhaustion, Dorothy does. She 'accepted everything' and was 'far too tired to think', and so becomes again one of the unconsciously dominated. When her memory returns fully, she tries to return to her old life, but because she is not actively taken back, she becomes locked into the passive structure of her new life, reduced to the escape of reading magazines that become 'strangely, absorbingly interesting'.

The third part of the book consists of a scene of down-and-outs keeping company in Trafalgar Square for the night. These people, and Dorothy with them, are at the bottom of the pile. Completely passive and of no use to society because they are not even aware of their domination by it, they have stepped outside the tautological world of individual and public fantasy, into an entirely private, anarchic world of their own. Almost by corollary, the narrator is detached and external, at first presenting only the dialogue of the beggars; but as Dorothy becomes part of their world, finds out its conventions and sinks passively into them, the narration resumes some of its observing familiarity and its air of report.

Dorothy has moved from the unwitting compromise of her early life, to the compromises induced first by physical and then by mental exhaustion. While compromise of some kind is shown to be necessary and although it is made clear that exhaustion 'stuns' one, confuses the real with the unreal and makes it almost impossible to act in any way at all, in each case Dorothy is in part responsible for her situation because she has entered that compromise. In Part Four a *deus ex machina* in the form of a rich uncle is provided to get her out of the situation; she returns to civilisation, to the public world of recognised authority and goes to work in a school. For the first time in her life she has both the awareness and the energy not merely to compromise but to participate actively in the life around her, and she does so. The girls' magazine vocabulary slips away, she observes and learns, creating an active identity.

At the same time the narrator becomes far more involved with the character. Many of the techniques of the narrator in Part One are taken up once more but with far greater openness about the inbuilt limitations they carry. For example, caricature again abounds, but this time it is a very obvious use of stereotype. The names are almost epithets: the alcoholic Miss Strong, earnest Miss Beaver and incompetent Miss Allcock. Mrs Creevy, the hypocritical and grasping headmistress, is presented as an out-and-out caricature of all that is wrong with the private school system. But the important thing is that the central character is shown to be aware of the caricatured nature of these people. It alerts her to deficiencies within the school system and she is able to assess the situation and develop an active role in how she thinks it should work.

However her new approach to teaching, which is based on '*making* something instead of merely learning', is stopped by the head mistress who tells her that she must educate by memorisation and rote-learning, thus preserving the social status quo. And Dorothy capitulates: she prostitutes herself to fulfil someone else's fantasy of education. Creevy even tells her how to worship, and it is in the comparison between religious authority and Creevy's educational despotism that Dorothy begins to understand the nature of her dilemma. The dangers of complete personal freedom have been underlined, not only by the negative anarchy of the beggars in Trafalgar Square, but also by the vulnerability of that freedom, by its potential for control in the freedom of Creevy to dominate her in the name of an anonymous public. Dorothy comes to think that it is 'better to follow in the ancient ways, than to drift in rootless freedom'.

In the fifth and final part of the book she returns to her father and resumes her duties, but this time with an awareness of the domination involved. The conflation throughout much of this part between the narrator's and character's voice reinforces this awareness as the reader watches the commentary taking place in Dorothy's mind rather than being expressed for her, and the final pages of the book present her assessing mind reaching its compromise. Yet while we have learned the need for compromise we have also learned the need for continual reassessment. At the end, the narrator tells us that Dorothy's final compromise is not yet 'consciously' formulated, and the result is a highly unsatisfactory ending. If it had not been for the careful and extensive education that the reader is put through in this novel, one could simply take Dorothy's compromise as it stands. But the entire movement of learning by both character and reader contradicts her express conclusions. The problem may lie in the fact that, though the writer has withdrawn the comforts and escapes of permanent compromise from the reader, the alternatives are ambiguous and diffuse because the narrator is cut out of consideration. Despite the blatantly different voices that the narrator takes on, and which do involve the reader in evaluating the issues, the final conflation of narrator with character leaves one with no way to assess the basis for his commentary. As Orwell was later to say, the one thing wrong with a first person novel was that it made commentary impossible; the reader could never adequately evaluate the stance of the writing.

In *Keep the Aspidistra Flying* the narrator and character are carefully separated from the start. The narrator reveals his prejudices by relating the novel closely to the topics of literature, literary clichés, and the way one goes about writing. And here the narrative ethos is directly related to the literary ethos of the writer and more explicitly to the facades through which the individual relates to the public. *Keep the Aspidistra Flying* makes explicit the process of a mind that escapes by giving the prose over to the main character, Gordon Comstock, at the beginning. The character starts with a voice that types, generalises, uses conventions and pretences, and which rationalises from incorrect grounds. By contrast, the narrator is more observing, he generalises only after going into detail, concentrating on concrete particulars; he also undercuts, qualifies and places his own statements in an ironic perspective that yields even-handed judgements. Yet the interaction between the two very different voices, the one being escapist and enclosed and the other more open and active, is often very close.

Throughout the first chapter Gordon's mind ranges over a series of issues as he muses on a few lines of his own pessimistic verse: books, advertisements, the state of civilisation and money. He condemns 'the extinct monsters of the Victorian age,'[11] and although he is at first aware that his condemnation arises because 'the mere sight of them brought home to him his own sterility,' he passes this off with yet more sweeping generalisations that reduce all such questions to money. Later classifications of literature as 'dead stars' and 'damp squibs', with only the occasional writer like Lawrence or Joyce rising above the abysmal level, are revealed as devices to provide further justification for his own book 'Mice' having been remaindered after the sale of one hundred and fifty-three copies.

Initially in contrast with the pessimism of his attitude to literature is the 'goofy optimism' of the advertisements across the street from the bookshop where Gordon works. The slogans are established by a series of repetitions on Gordon's part as he looks at them 'mechanically'; yet even these 'pink vacuous faces' become distorted through Gordon's mind. The movement is associational, beginning with the 'rat-faced' man in the Bovex advertisement who is turned into 'Modern man as his masters want him to be. A docile little porker, sitting in the money-sty ...', and culminating at the end of the chapter in the 'humming of aeroplanes and the crash of the bombs' that Gordon hopes will destroy the civilisation that he sees.

To Gordon money makes possible both literature and advertisements. Given life ruled by a money ethic, they both reflect back a meaninglessness that leaves his modern world empty and ripe for destruction. Yet the process by which he arrives at these conclusions is superficial. They are generated by a mind flitting unthinkingly from associated image to associated image. Gordon's mind works the way the advertisements do; both create types, present clichés and invent desirable fictions. They and he manipulate logic to invent a world in which people can evade responsibility. Gordon, like Flory, is trapped in a personal world of escape that can only wait passively for the destruction of what lies outside it, rather than envisage anything positive.

In direct contrast the narrator's mind is more detached and prosaic, slightly ironic, and while generalising does so without caricature. The balance is made possible by the history the narrator provides for each character or event, and the history he provides for Gordon's life that establishes the distanced backdrop for Gordon's private attempts to escape. The narrator is not given to clichés, and he tries fully to explain situations, pointing wherever possible to the faults in the reasoning that lies behind them. The narrator knows his account cannot be absolute; it must be 'as the biographers say', fictionalised history. Throughout the chapter on Gordon's history the narrator indicates his stance in relation to Gordon, as someone who understands why the character has created his personal escapist world, and because of that can provide a perspective on it. While Gordon ignores the fact that his attempt to evade compromise is in itself a compromise, the narrator's voice is that of someone aware of the compromise.

And it is to the question of compromise that the external issues of money, civilisation, literature and advertising are relevant. Money is the ultimate compromise of Gordon's life. He wants to escape it, yet he can only escape it fully through having it. The history he is provided with hints at Gordon's background in Victorian materialism and the possible reasons for his obsession; but whatever the cause he wants to escape the money-world, reject the belief that 'Money is what God used to be. Good and evil have no meaning any longer except failure and success.'

The economic compromise is directly parallel to that between poetry and advertising. Gordon, while working highly successfully on advertisements, was able to produce a book of poetry. The poetry was made possible by that compromise. But having written it he leaves the firm. The key point is that he does not especially want to write, but thinks that it will get him 'out of the money-world'. Literary 'taste' may also simply be personal habit, and Gordon watches this in action in the bookshop where he goes to work. He suggests that the woman who prefers Galsworthy to Ethel M. Dell is neither better nor worse than her friend who prefers the opposite. Taste is often socially condoned selection, satisfied by similarly self-enclosed worlds. He and Rosemary, his girlfriend, discuss the weakness of 'Burne-Jones maidens', 'Dickens heroines', 'Rackham illustrations' and James Barrie's fantasies. These artists are as able to stupefy the mind, prettify and make acceptable the world they present, as the romances and adventures that satisfy the library-goers.

Later, just like Dorothy, Gordon tries to find solace in the magazines, comics and twopenny newspapers of the sordid little library he is reduced to managing after he leaves the bookshop. They are ' "escape literature" … Nothing has ever been devised that puts less strain on the intelligence.' The narrator notes that in this state Gordon thinks he is in the 'safe soft womb of the earth', 'failure and success have no meaning', and he lies beyond responsibility. Tied up in the ambiguities is the importance not of compromise but of one's attitude toward it. In the same way advertisements, which are initially held up against literature, are later directly compared with the effect of Burne-Jones maidens. Each has its skilful and involving aspect, something that Gordon only understands at the end of his attempted escape into low-life, and which makes possible his return to advertising.

The compromise in literary terms is not between good and bad taste, but between an involving or a mindlessly accepting attitude to writing. The writer may see some need for compromise at some time, in some areas, but if he goes ahead and produces an active participatory writing this is of little practical importance. Similarly, there is a responsibility on the reader not to read as if all assumptions were being reinforced, but actively to assess and reassess them. Gordon comes to read the trashy novelettes with the ironic emphasis of '*ro*mances', rather than as mindless escape. Irony indicates discrepancies, and the narrator's early irony points to the character's evasiveness and denial of discrepancy. When Gordon takes up the ironic voice at the end of the book, the irony lies in the reading of irony itself for here its conscious use by the character indicates not Gordon's evasiveness but his awareness of compromise. Immediately one has an indication of his change of attitude. He has to discard his enclosed, womb-like world before he can break the vicious circle that unconscious compromise imposes on people. Unconscious compromise is utterly selfish. It is entirely private and makes impossible public communication, genuine interaction with an external world. But having reached this conclusion, there are no guarantees for the reader. Gordon may give way to the escape into domesticity, and the irony become negative. Again, it is not the compromise that matters but one's attitude toward it. The mutually exclusive voices of narrator and character have to continue to engage the reader. Orwell is not providing specific answers, but a stance toward activity.

A major topic of these early works is indeed the complexity of the interdependence of dominated and dominator. But Orwell is fully aware of the complexity. He portrays the self-perpetuating, often vicious circle at work in social, religious and sexual spheres, and makes explicit analogies with the linguistic and the literary. But the complexities of these topics are not overtly resolved. To do so would be to perpetuate the problem by moving into an authorial stance that imposed upon the reader. Instead, through the direct analogies with writing, Orwell tries to suggest in the changing structure of his narrator-character relationships the value of establishing a clear stance for the narrator. This goes hand in hand with the more fundamental need to provide a practical text in which reader and writer meet and engage, for by clarifying the stance of the narrator the reader has a basis from which evaluation and assessment may proceed.

Notes

1 S. Orwell and I. Angus (eds.), *The Collected Essays, Journalism and Letters of George Orwell*, Vol. 1, Harmondsworth, 1970, p. 23. Referred to hereafter as '*CEJL*'.
2 See for example Tom Hopkinson, *George Orwell*, London, 1954, p. 7; L. Brander, *George Orwell*, London, 1954, pp. 210-2; or A. Zwerdling, *Orwell and the Left*, New Haven and London, 1974, p. 147.
3 For example F. Gloversmith, 'Changing Things: Orwell and Auden', in *Class, Culture and Social Change*, Brighton, 1980, in which he says that

Orwell was unable to cope with presenting the working classes. Hence he 'types' characters in *The Road to Wigan Pier* as in his early novels. But this observation is used to denigrate the later work, and misses the point that types are used specifically so that readers should recognise the injustice of their limitations.

4 See the introductory chapter of L. Hunter, *George Orwell: The Search for a Voice*, Milton Keynes, 1984, for a detailed account of this background.

5 George Orwell, *Down and Out in Paris and London*, Harmondsworth, 1984, p. 6.

6 See for example R. Lee, *Orwell's Fiction*, Notre Dame, 1969, which proposes that *Burmese Days* is primarily about the study of communication.

7 George Orwell, *Burmese Days*, Harmondsworth, 1982, p. 14.

8 *CEJL*, Vol. 1, p. 58.

9 See for example T. Eagleton, 'Orwell and the Lower Middle-Class Novel' in R. Williams (ed.), *George Orwell: A Collection of Critical Essays*, Englewood Cliffs, 1974, where he comments on Flory's 'passive compromise'. He recognises Orwell's complexity but leaves little place for the reader's interaction with the text.

10 George Orwell, *A Clergyman's Daughter*, Harmondsworth, 1975, p. 5.

11 George Orwell, *Keep the Aspidistra Flying*, Harmondsworth, 1980, p. 12.

Andy Croft

Worlds Without End Foisted Upon The Future – Some Antecedents Of Nineteen Eighty-Four

1. 'The Ultimate Family Gift Book of the Year'
Not another essay on *Nineteen Eighty-Four*? Readers may be forgiven if their enthusiasm for the novel has faded of late. 1984 began with a six-part TV biography of Orwell, a televised dramatisation of life on Jura, and countless TV discussion programmes, profiles and chat-shows, all acutely conscious that this was *the* year. At the time of writing there is a film of *Nineteen Eighty-Four* currently in production, starring John Hurt; the National Theatre has just presented its controversial version of *Animal Farm*; and the RSC have bought the rights to *Down and Out in Paris and London*. Earlier in the year the Barbican ran a 'Thought Crimes' exhibition, and Orwell now sits at his typewriter in Madame Tussauds – while something from *Star Wars* looks over his shoulder. There is a rock album by Rick Wakeman in the shops, a top-ten single ('Somebody's Watching Me'), an as-yet unperformed musical and two operas. You can buy T-shirts announcing, according to taste, either 'Big Brother is Watching You' or 'Doublethink About It'. Wigan Pier and the down-and-outs in Paris and London have all recently been revisited in print. There can be few national weekly and monthly magazines, daily and local papers, that didn't carry articles about the novel and its author this year. From *Marxism Today* to *Encounter* and the *Barclaycard Magazine*, from the *Morning Star* to the *Daily Telegraph* and the

spoof *Not the 1984 Times*, there was little doubt about *the* subject of the moment. Even the British Tourist Authority journal *In Britain*, beginning the year with an article on current livestock husbandry in Suffolk, felt justified in announcing on its front page, 'The Orwell Animal Farms in 1984' ...

When *Nineteen Eighty-Four* was first published Secker and Warburg gave it a print-run of 25,000 copies; it sold twice that within the year in the UK alone. Since Penguin first published the novel in 1954 they have sold 250,000 copies each year; in 1984 they expect to sell 500,000 copies of what they are calling 'the ultimate family gift book of the year'. Richard Orwell expects to earn £250,000 in the royalties from UK sales this year, and £100,000 from overseas sales. If you have a spare £25 you can buy a facsimile of the original manuscript, or for a mere £400 Secker and Warburg will sell you a de-luxe edition of the Collected Works ...

The commercial success of the novel has been exceeded only by its critical success. When first reading the manuscript Frederick Warburg described it as 'amongst the most terrifying books I have ever read ... a great book'; 'a brilliant and fascinating novel' wrote Diana Trilling. The novel's place in Orwell's *oeuvre* is rarely doubted. For Dame Veronica Wedgewood it was 'the most valuable, the most absorbing, the most powerful book that he has yet written'; for Herbert Read it was 'undoubtedly his greatest'; for Philip Rahv 'far and away the best of Orwell's books.' Its place in the genre of political fiction appears unchallenged in the same way. For the critic Ruth Ann Leif it is simply 'the political novel *par excellence*'; for Philip Rahv 'this novel is the *best* antidote to the totalitarian disease that *any* writer has so far produced.' Anthony Burgess believes that it is 'the *most* nightmarish of *all* the fictional prophecies *ever* written', that if we 'regard his *Nineteen Eighty-Four* as competing in the Worst of all Imaginary World Stakes (it) has won by many lengths.' Bernard Crick argues that *Nineteen Eighty-Four* is to the twentieth century what Thomas Hobbes' *Leviathan* was to the seventeenth', and J.A. Morris that it is 'the most political of the major anti-Utopias'. Critical claims for the novel don't end here. The blurb on the cover of one recent edition describes the novel as nothing less than 'the classic novel of our time'. For one writer *Nineteen Eighty-Four* has earned its place – alongside *Animal Farm* – 'in the scenery of every civilised mind'; the novel demonstrates how the materialist and rationalist idea of progress, the 'hedonist utopia' had been 'shattered'; for another 'from the perspective of literary and intellectual history, *Animal Farm* and *Nineteen Eighty-Four* mark the close of an era that has lasted since the end of the eighteenth century ... *Nineteen Eighty-Four* changed the world by representing the past and present so as to modify people's expectations of the future.'[1]

What are we to make of all this? Is it explicable, or justifiable, in merely literary terms? Or is it just a book-seller's dream run riot? In particular, what response should the left make to this commercial, cultural and political phenomenon, quite without precedent in British literary history? The questions raised by the novel, and by its popular and critical success, cannot be disregarded by the left, since the novel was written by a declared 'democratic socialist' and supporter of the Labour Party, and since it deals with the 'perversions to which a centralised economy is liable', dramatised through something called 'Ingsoc' and addressed primarily as a 'warning' to the 'English-speaking' left.

Much of the left's response to *Nineteen Eighty-Four*, and to its political marketing has been simply hostile, going to great lengths to attack both the novel and its author.[2] Understandable though this may be, particularly during the worst years of the Cold War when many reviewers were recommending *Nineteen Eighty-Four* precisely as an anti-socialist novel and an attack on the Attlee Government, this has meant in practice abandoning the novel to the literary right. And there is no doubting *their* enthusiasm for the novel, or the political uses to which it has been put.[3] There is a *genuine* tone to the outrage which has greeted various belated attempts to 'reclaim' aspects of Orwell's thinking, even *Nineteen Eighty-Four*, for the left. Thirty-five years after the publication of the novel, the work of Raymond Williams and Bernard Crick in particular must appear to many as unlikely and impossible attempts at political body-snatching.

Just possibly *Nineteen Eighty-Four* is no longer worth fighting over, at least not in the *political* terms that have defined the arguments so far. Those arguments were fought and lost a long time ago.[4] If only we can take our eyes for a moment away from the transfixing political influence and importance of this one novel, it may be possible to offer some comparative *literary* assessment of it; it may even occur to us that we don't actually need to keep on re-reading *Nineteen Eighty-Four*. It is this essay's contention that *Nineteen Eighty-Four* was a much less original novel than it may seem today; that rather than being 'the *most* nightmarish of *all* fictional prophecies *ever* written' (my italics), it was only the tail-end of a more original and important literary and political development in this country in the late 1930s and 1940s, and that the novel's extraordinary reception and reputation have more to do with commercial and political considerations than with literary ones. Arguing endlessly about the political 'message' of this one novel only serves to confirm its exceptional status. This at any rate is one essay about *Nineteen Eighty-Four* which doesn't intend to say anything more about it.

2. Fantastic Realities and Fantastic Novels

There was nothing new, of course, in dramatising imagined systems of government some years in the future, not even in dramatising the political worst. Orwell himself was, in Anthony Burgess's words, 'an afficionado of cacatopian fiction'.[5] H.G. Wells was a favourite boyhood author of Orwell's, and *A Modern Utopia* his favourite Wells novel. Samuel Butler, Jack London and Swift he read at school. Other 'scientific romances' that Orwell certainly knew, and which may have influenced his writing *Nineteen Eighty-Four* at least in some details, were Chesterton's *The Man Who Was Thursday* (1917), John Mair's *Never Come Back* (1941) and Robin Maugham's *The 1946 MS* (1943). Above all, as he made clear in a comparative discussion about Huxley's *Brave New World* (1932), Orwell's greatest conscious literary debt in *Nineteen Eighty-Four* was to Zamyatin's *We* (1920).[6]

The 1930s was an especially rich period in the development of utopian and dystopian writing in Britain. All sorts of writers turned their hands in this period to writing at least one utopian or dystopian novel – Malcolm Muggeridge, Eric Linklater, C.S. Forester, R.C. Sherrif, Harold Nicholson, Herbert Read, C.P. Snow, Hilaire Belloc, John Buchan, J.B. Morton, Stephen

King-Hall, and of course, Wells and Huxley.[7]

The sheer ideological variety of these novels is significant enough. They range from Christian utopias like E.C. Taunton's *If Twelve Today* (1937), feminist utopias like Gresswell's *When Yvonne was Dictator* (1935) and G. Cornwallis West's *The Woman Who Stopped War* (1935), to pro-fascist utopias like *The Shadow of Mussolini* by Wilfred Ward (1931) and Dennis Wheatley's *Black August* (1934). The bulk of this fiction was however *negative* in tone, imagining their author's *worst* fears, from R.A. James' anti-Catholic *While England Slept* (1932), Julian Sterne's anti-masonic *The Secret of the Zodiac* (1933), Huxley's anti-Taylorist *Brave New World* to a great many anti-socialist, anti-communist novels, like William le Petre's *The Bolsheviks* (1931) and Morris Sutherland's *Second Storm* (1930).

Clearly something happened to the British literary imagination in the 1930s, to turn so many novelists' heads towards the future. The fear of another war, especially a technologically-advanced one that would not exempt civilian populations, the enduring economic crisis and long-term unemployment, the increasing polarisation of European politics, the seizure of power by fascism in so many continental countries, the developing size and influence of the Communist parties – all these factors seem to have stimulated, in various part, this sudden and diverse imaginative effort to set contemporary events in a long-term perspective.

Peter Widdowson has argued that

> the real interest of fiction in England in the 1930s (and this explains the literary judgement which disregards it) lies in the uncertainty of direction, the tense irresolution, the novels so commonly reveal. At the formal level this uncertainty expresses itself in the diverse modes of fiction employed and their operation in practice; the structural and textual discoveries of modernism, formal realism, documentary reportage, fable, allegory, satire and dystopia ... Faced with what Christopher Isherwood once called the 'fantastic realities' of the 'everyday world', the novelist's problem, acutely in the 1930s, was how to address them.

Moreover Widdowson asserts that this fictional dilemma of

how to come to terms with the 'fantastic realities' of the period is a manifestation of the ideological crisis of liberal humanism.[8] While this may go a long way to explain this literary development, it disregards the most sizeable, subtle and important part of this development – those novels produced on the left.

3. Socialist Fantasy

It was in the 1930s of course that British socialists wrote and secured publication for imaginative literature – poetry, plays, short-stories, novels – on a scale never seen before or since. In particular it was a time when the left began to produce *fiction* to increasing commercial and critical success. Almost two hundred and fifty novels appeared in print between 1930 and 1940 with clear (though of course different and often conflicting) socialist concerns. There were socialist-realist novels, historical novels, comedies, thrillers, detective-stories, fantasies, fables, allegories, experimental novels, romances, satires, *bildungsromans*, family sagas – and utopias and dystopias.[9] Over thirty of these titles chose non-realist locations, fabulous, mythical, futuristic or time-travelling; over twenty were specifically set in the political future.

The first thing to note about these thirty or so non-realist and fantastic novels is the variety of their authors, their wide-ranging social and literary allegiances. Some were already published writers with existing reputations, like Storm Jameson, Patrick Hamilton and Kennth Allot. Some had never published fiction before, like Rex Warner, Barbara Wootton and Ruthven Todd. Some were well known for other activities, like the poet Cecil Day Lewis, the nutritionist Frederick le Gros Clarke, the art-historian Anthony Bertram. For some like Joseph Macleod, Fenner Brockway and 'Murray Constantine' it was their only contribution to the canon of socialist fiction. Harold Heslop and Leslie Mitchell were working-class writers; Terence Greenidge was a close friend of John Betjeman; Philip Toynbee and Amabel Williams-Ellis both belonged to great families of the English 'intellectual aristocracy'. Some, like Storm Jameson, Barbara Wooton and Rex Warner, were active in the Labour Party; Fenner Brockway was a leading member of the ILP; many were Communists, like Maurice Richardson,

Frederick le Gros Clarke and Edward Upward, or close sympathisers, like Joseph Macleod, Amabel Williams-Ellis and Bruce Hamilton. Some were published by the publishing houses of the left, Gollancz and Lawrence and Wishart. But the overwhelming majority were published by mainstream London firms, large and small – Constable, Collins, George Allen and Unwin, the Fortune Press, the Bodley Head, the Hogarth Press, Cape, Boriswood, Faber, Heinemans, the Cressett Press, and Penguin.

Despite the frequently recurring ideas, arguments, settings, even details, in this body of writing; despite its size, its authors seem to have had little sense of being part of any sort of common literary phenomenon. Ruthven Todd, for example, whose fabulous satire *Over the Mountain* (1939) contains a great many specific correspondences with Rex Warner's *The Wild Goose Chase* (1937) (not least the hilarious and brutal 'laughing policemen') claimed that his novel was

> conceived and written before I had read Rex Warner's ... and I was, I think, a little chagrined to realise that they were scions of the same ancestry, and that they both bore the same evidence of the political atmosphere of the period of their adolescence ...[10]

The second thing to note is the small number of these novels that specifically dramatised a critique of capitalism. The only real example of this sort of writing was Amabel William-Ellis's *To Tell the Truth* (1933), written after a visit to the Soviet Union. Set in the 1940s it turned the conventional anti-Soviet travelogue on its head, by imagining the comic consequences of a Soviet defector who visits a Britain of continuing long-term unemployment and large-scale poverty, and who gradually sheds his illusions about bourgeois democracy. In *London's Burning* (1936) set in 1940, Barbara Wootton forsaw a time when unemployment might reach such terrible proportions that rioting erupts in British cities, when the government of the day loses control, and revolution is in the air. It is significant however that in her autobiography Barbara Wootton remembered the novel as an *anti-fascist* one, depicting 'a fascist uprising in London and its effects upon a nice, liberal-minded, peaceable, moderately intellectual and socially-minded business man and his family.'[11] This trick of memory is symptomatic of the way in which the political emphasis shifts in socialist fiction during the 1930s. For it was *anti-fascism* above all that informed the majority of non-realist fiction in the middle and late 1930s, and largely contributed to the development of socialist fiction as a whole.[12]

The third point to note is the small number of attempts at socialist utopias in these years. It cannot be incidental that over half of those that *were* written appeared before 1935. By then the full implications of events in Germany were clear to most people on the left – the suppression not only of the Communists, but also of the Social Democrats and the trade unions. *The utopian spirit was, for the time being, on the defensive.* Even Robert Young's *The War in the Marshes* (1939) and Richard Heron Ward's *The Sun Shall Rise* (1933), both vaguely socialist novels about attempted revolutions in this country, end with their *failures*, their military suppression.

It could also be argued that the millenarian vision of many socialists in the 1920s and 1930s found a concrete political and geographical location in the Soviet Union. For British Communists there would have been little reason to project their political aspirations into fantastic literary locations. Indeed the one pro-Soviet science fiction novel of this period, Frederick le Gros Clarke's *Between Two Men* (1935) concluded by turning *against* political fantasy, with a sharp reminder of contemporary political realities, and of the utopian quality of the international working-class movement. Here utopia is to be found in the *actions* of those people struggling to achieve it. A 'biological fantasy', it described the birth of a new super-species which threatens to replace humanity as the next evolutionary step. At the end of the book the embriologist Sandraval, who is responsible for killing the new creature, travels on the continent, doubtful of the rightness of his decision. There he realises he acted properly, and that there is after all a new kind of humanity,

> the men who toil at their machines and on the earth. German workers with their throbbing ache of revolt against the shadow of the swastika – Russians with their Bolshevik energy that forged creation beneath the naked sky – they were the very pulse of

creation itself; and in whatever sphere life burst forth, they would have received it gladly.[13]

A.L. Morton observed in the *Daily Worker* that the novel was exciting 'because it breaks through in a new place, leaving a broad gap through which later assailants may march.'[14] Though there were a number of other 'biological fantasies' written on the left in the 1930s, few exhibiting this sort of *optimism*. If the example of the Soviet Union continued to exert a utopian pull on the *political* imaginations of many of the left in the 1930s, this had little or no analagous literary representation. After all, if fascism posed a threat liberal imagination, it constituted above all a threat to the continued existence of the Soviet Union.

One utopian novelist worth mentioning is the Scottish writer Leslie Mitchell (better known as Lewis Grassic Gibbon, the author of *A Scots Quair*), who produced two utopian novels in the early 1930s, *Three Go Back* (1932) and *Gay Hunter* (1934). In these Mitchell used the device of time-travelling to catapult a political cross-section of contemporary society 20,000 years into the past and future respectively. In both the time-travellers discover a golden age of primitive communism, unspoilt by class, property, religion and marriage. The eponymous heroine Gay Hunter finds her experience of the future confirms her worst fears for her own times. She remembers

> books of speculation she had read on the future – books of the early Wells, of Flammarian, of their hosts of imitators: books that pictured the sciences mounting and growing, piling great, crystalline pyramids of knowledge and technique unto alien skies, with men their servitors, changing and altering with them, physically and psychically ... or the younger Huxley, with a machine-made world of machines and humans undergoing a fantastic existence, conditioned by the bleak lunacy of their author's anthropological beliefs ... worlds without end that had been foisted upon the future.

(So much for the left's 'hedonist utopia'.) The old democracies, Gay learns, collapsed with atomic war, to be replaced by a Fascist Federation and centuries of permanently warring fascist

'Hierarchies' ruling vast numbers of 'sub-men'. In the end an international revolt by the 'sub-men' and global civil war has all but destroyed humanity. Although the novel is largely a celebration of the primitive communist society of the hunters ('neither prophecy nor propaganda ... though the Hierarchs may never happen, I have a wistful hope for the Hunters'), it is significant that the other two time-travellers are fascists (one in *Three Go Back* is an arms-dealer) who try and introduce warfare to the hunters, to re-establish 'civilisation'. Even Mitchell, whose (partly Trotskyite) Marxism was mixed with Diffusionist anthropology, and whose fiction always contained a shining vision of an *inevitable* communist future – even Mitchell could not disregard the factor of fascism, its implications for ideas about inevitable human progress. Gay realises the danger posed to the hunter society by Major Ledyard's appeal to 'Service, Loyalty, Hardness and Hierarchy'.

> Some seed of desire for safety, security, to poison the minds of men and set them to climbing the bitter tracks to civilisations' bloody plateau, lit by the whorling storm-shells ... war religion, blood sacrifice, all the dreary and terrible mummery of temple and palace and college. Kingdoms would rise again on the earth, poets sing battle again, the war-horses stamp on the face of a child, the women know rape and the men mutilation ...[15]

The growing threat of fascism, the challenge it posed not only to socialism, but to the liberal idea of 'progress', may explain the small number of straightforward socialist utopias in the 1930s. The appearance of fascism constituted a decisive interruption in the imaginative literature of the British left.

Another exception to this is worth noting, Fenner Brockway's *Purple Plaque* (1935). In this highly romantic novel Brockway depicted a revolution on a luxury liner, quarantined indefinitely because of a 'purple plague'. The third-class passengers abolish the class distinctions, the work, food and cabins are shared according to need, a newspaper, a university and currency are established (and nudism permitted).

The mutiny of the dancing-girls which precipitates the revolution was based on a real incident on a trans-Atlantic liner in the early 1930s, when, on Brockway's instigation, a troupe had refused to dance only for the first-class passengers. Brockway's trips to the USA in these years were in part to meet with the Trotskyite Jay Lovestone, recently expelled from the leadership of the CPUSA. The ILP at this time, after a brief attempt to work with the Comintern, was moving rapidly into an ultra-left position, and Brockway in particular was developing a critique of the workings of the Comintern along the lines of Lovestone's.[16]

In the novel therefore, the leadership of the ship's revolution is split between 'Nathan, the Revolutionary Socialist and Wells, the Moscow-minded Communist' ('a difference not so much of principle as of spirit and method'.) It is Nathan who concludes that the ship is

> only a microcosm of society. America and Britain had their first-class and tourist-class, their third-class and crew – the possessing class, the middle-class and the working-class. America and Britain had their luxury for the possessing class and their overcrowded poverty for the working-class. A *revolution* in America and Britain ...[17]

In the same year that *Purple Plague* was published, the Comintern at its Seventh Congress finally shed the last remnants of its 'Class Against Class' policy, and urged the creation of 'People's Fronts' against the threat of fascism. In Britain the Communist Party temporarily dropped the slogan 'For a Soviet Britain'. At the Soviet Writers' Congress the previous year the cultural implications of the new policy had been largely anticipated, in the final suppression of the sectarian proletcult tendencies within Soviet literature, by Radek's conflation of the categories of 'revolutionary', 'progressive', 'working-class', 'proletarian' and 'anti-fascist' writers, and by his call for 'revolutionary writers' to study

> fully and specifically, the fate of literature under the rule of fascism ... the fate of literature under the fascist sceptre (*sic*) constitutes the very gravest warning, the 'writing on the wall' for *all writers*.[18]

In Britain the British Union of Revolutionary Writers, founded in London in December 1933, and part of the proletcult-dominated International Union of Revolutionary Writers, became by its second meeting in February of the next year the British Section of the Writers' International (WI), a much more broadly-based non-Party organisation. The writers whom the Section hoped to attract were primarily those who saw fascism as

> a menace to all the best achievements of human culture ... who are opposed to all attempts to hinder unity in the struggle, or any retreat before fascism or compromise with fascist tendencies.

This statement was published in the first issue of *Left Review*, founded later that year as the organ of the British Section of the WI, and a replacement for the proletcult *Storm*. In its first six months the editors of *Left Review* decisively defeated an ultra-leftist attempt to influence the magazine. As one of the editors, Tom Wintringham, put it,

> our main work as revolutionaries is to get a 'united front' for common action *among all those who are not revolutionaries*, but feel the need to defend culture and literature against the effects of modern capitalism, against fascism, war from the air, throttling of free discussion.[20]

This was a strategy that could have no place in the increasingly ultra-leftist argument of the ILP, and one that was repeatedly criticised by ILP writers – including Orwell – as 'reformist.' So simple a 'revolutionary' novel as *Purple Plague* could only have been written from someone in Brockway's increasingly isolated position.[21]

4. *'A Really Satisfactory Way of Writing About the Age'*
The first of the great many anti-fascist novels written in this country in the 1930s was Montagu Slater's *Haunting Europe* (1934). This was a careful realist account of German working-class life from 1929 to 1933, of the inescapable involvement of one Berlin family in the political turmoil of those years. When the novel appeared Tom Wintringham was generally enthusiastic about it in the *Daily Worker*. He was, however, unhappy about the novel's rather triumphalist

ending, when an underground Party cell is established in the street. 'The final chapter seems odd and strained' he wrote, 'because it implies the conversion to Communism and acceptance into a Party cell of such unlikely people as an old comfortable reformist secretary and a little Nazi nark.'[22] There is another ending to the novel, even more triumphalist, which Wintringham did not mention, set 'some time hence' when a Soviet German Republic has been established, China has gone Communist, the Vatican has been turned into a museum, and the middle classes survive – only in Britain. Both endings, and the terms of Wintringham's criticisms mark the novel out from subsequent anti-fascist and anti-Nazi novels, and date it from a time when the Comintern still expected the KPD to survive underground, and the Hitler government to over-reach itself.[23]

Yet at the same time the second ending of *Haunting Europe* shows how far Slater caught, possibly helped to create, the dominating imaginative feature of anti-fascist fiction – its long-term fantastic and dream-like quality. While he was working on the novel Slater also wrote two anti-fascist plays 'Domesday' (1933) and 'Cock Robin' (1934). The first was a three-act picture of the future establishment of fascism in Britain ('indebted to London's *Iron Heel*'), in the second the hero relives the struggle against (British) fascism while under anaesthetic.[24] The combination of anti-fascism, a sense of impending political defeat, a commitment to the (very) long-term defeat of fascism, the location of a native fascist threat, and the non-naturalistic form are all important and recurring features of anti-fascist British writing. What is most remarkable about these plays however, is that they were never published, never performed. Somehow in these two plays (possibly the first British dramatic attempts to deal with fascism) unknown and by several years, Slater anticipated the non-realist qualities of most subsequent anti-fascist, anti-Nazi, anti-Mosley literature.

In the following year Naomi Mitchison's *We Have Been Warned* was published. This long panoramic novel, with its 82 named and indexed characters was severely criticised by Reg Bishop in the *Daily Worker*, in terms significantly different to those with which Wintringham had criticised *Haunting Europe*. Despite its clear pro-Communist sympathies, Bishop could find few positive things to say about the novel. For its first 547 pages the novel dealt with the contemporary political situation in a fictional parliamentary constituency, its various political activists and their domestic lives. The last six pages however suddenly took on another quality altogether, when one of the female and very pregnant characters has a vision of the future of 'Sallington' – a fascist one.

> First three armed Specials came out, and then the prisoners bunched together, their eyes blindfolded already, and their hands tied behind them. They were strung out along the wall. Nearest to her was Taylor, the man who disbelieved in violence. Then Sam Hall, with a scalp wound plastered with dark blood. Then Dorothy's Bill. Then Reuben Goldberg. Then Mason. But they hadn't tied his hands because his arm was broken; his coat was buttoned over it and he shook a little. Then Tom. With his trouser cut off at the knee and his leg bandaged. Beyond Tom were two women. 'Tom!' she yelled suddenly. 'Tom, we'll remember, we'll – ' And then there was a hand over her mouth, she staggered and was shoved back, gagged ...[25]

Reg Bishop was quite clear about the novel's ending – 'The best thing in the book, a picture of England under fascist terror'.[26] And when was this last chapter written? According to the novel's foreword, 'before the events of summer 1933 in Germany, and before the counter-revolutions of 1934 in Austria and Spain.'

Why did anti-fascist novelists invariably turn to non-realist ways of writing? Firstly, non-realistic writing was the easiest way for British writers to deal with a subject of which they had little personal experience. Realist anti-fascist fiction was generally written by those who had direct contact with fascism, either German – Edward Fitzgerald's *Crooked Eclipse* (1938), Patrick Kirwan's *Black Exchange* (1934), Phyllis Bottome's *The Mortal Storm* (1937), Christopher Isherwood's *Mr Norris Changes Trains* (1934), *Goodbye to Berlin* (1939) – or British – Simon Blumenfeld's *Jew Boy* (1936), *They Won't Let You Live* (1939).

For those whose acquaintance with fascism was largely derived from books and newspapers, the realist novel was clearly a difficult medium in which to write about fascism. Day Lewis described this phenomenon thus:

the slump and the rise of European fascism compelled writers to look over their garden walls ... to divert some of their attention from the bed, the subconscious and the drawing room to the impact of unemployment, political and economic insecurity, upon the lives of ordinary people. And since most middle-class writers lacked any idea about life outside their own class, this dearth of experience outside a class they have rejected has turned ... Communist writers to allegory.[27]

Even Isherwood, the most understating of naturalist novelists, wrote in 1939:

Like many other Europeans, I have come to feel that Franz Kafka, alone among modern novelists, discovered a really satisfactory way of writing about the age in which we live. As, amidst the thickening shadows, we wander farther and farther down the path, from the Reichstag to Madrid, from Madrid to Munich, we recognise in him the Virgil who will be our guide through the unfolding horrors of the contemporary inferno. Prophetically, he has described it all – the vague, overpowering sense of terror; the dream-events vividly and simply remembered but only later seen as inverted and insane; the crisis indefinitely delayed. His is the nightmare world of the dictators.[28]

Michael Roberts in a study of T.E. Hulme had argued that the 'tragic view' was the only possible one to take in the late 1930s, and that Kafka's *The Trial* (published in English the previous year) was one of the best examples of this 'tragic view'.[29] Samuel Hynes has argued that this essay in particular and the interest in Kafka in general reveals a shift away from political commitment to despair in the late 1930s.

The revolutionary view had come to seem, for most writers, untenable, and the tragic view one that history and observation confirmed ... In such a time politics – men's efforts to govern rationally – becomes a tragic activity; and so political parables are tragic parables, ending in defeat and death.[3]

This is of course another variation on the Orwellian judgement that 'on the whole the literary history of the 1930s seems to

justify the opinion that a writer does well to keep out of
politics'. It is also to limit our understanding of who 'most
writers' were (Hynes refers of course to the plays of Spender,
Isherwood and Auden), and it is to misunderstand the
presence of Kafka and socialist fiction of the time. No matter
how 'tragic' and superficially pessimistic were the anti-fascist
dystopias of the late 1930s, almost all were written as political
interventions, as *warnings* about what *might* happen. This is for
example clearly the sense of Naomi Mitchison's title.

In the 1940 Left Book Club edition of *Swastika Night* (1937)
by 'Murray Constantine' – a dystopia imagining Europe after
seven hundred years of the Third Reich – a publisher's note
indicated that the

> picture painted must be considered symbolic of what would
> happen to the world if Hitler were to impose his will (as he must
> not) upon it … While the author has not in the least changed his
> opinion that the Nazi idea is evil, and that we must fight the Nazis
> on land, at sea, in the air, and in ourselves, he has changed his
> mind about the Nazi *power* to make the *world* evil.[31]

For others a certain authorial disingenuity served to point
their readers in the right direction. Terence Greenidge noted at
the beginning of his dream-story *Philip and the Dictator* (1938)
'It should hardly be necessary to state with a story of this kind
that the characters and Institutions contained in it are
fictitious', though just in case any of his readers might miss the
similarities he added, 'General Carstairs has nothing to do
with General Franco'.[32] 'Shamus Frazer' prefaced his satirical *A
Shroud as Well as a Shirt* (1935) with the admission that having
finished the novel

> it was brought to my attention that there already existed in Great
> Britain a fascist party. I should like to take this opportunity of
> saying that there can be no possible resemblance between the
> Cricketshirt Party and those ardent, patriotic souls who are at
> present striving to make this country – 'that we love so well' –
> worthy of the Blackshirt policy.[33]

As well as being a self-consciously imaginative response to

fascism, this sort of writing was secondly a highly *intellectual* response. There seems to have been a strong perception among British intellectuals of the implications of fascism for intellectual and academic life.[34] This was demonstrated most clearly in Rex Warner's *The Professor* (1938), the story of one liberal intellectual's fate at the hands of fascism, loosely based on the events in Austria of that year. The eponymous hero, a classical scholar of international standing and a well-known liberal, is asked to serve as Chancellor of his small landlocked state, politically divided and lying in the shadow of a powerful fascist neighbour. The story of his betrayal by the fascists within the country, his flight, capture, torture and execution is full of long speeches, political and philosophical arguments, classical soliloquies, yet it also contains a lot of physical action.

The Professor refuses his son's advice to arm the working-class districts of the city, he trusts his Chief of Police Colonel Grimm, and he believes that the conflicting interests of the social-democratic forces in the country will be resolved in the face of the external enemy. In the end Colonel Grimm takes power and asks for the assistance of the troops from across the border; the National Legion is given its lead to burn the University library and round up the opposition; the social-democratic leaders are forced into hiding; the Professor is betrayed by his wife, and he is finally shot as he is released from prison.

It is a study in liberalism as much as fascism, a critique of the Professor's failure to understand the implications of fascism for democracy. The ideological climax of the book is a long argument between the Professor and his old academic rival Julius Vander, now a leader of the 'National Legion'. Vander attacks the Professor's 'ethical idealism'. This, he argues is a class-based set of values that never had real universal support.

'Perhaps you'll tell me exactly what you're doing yourself about this "wider Morality"?' 'Love is the highest value we know.' 'Really. How many people do you love?' 'All men are brothers.' 'Indeed. How is it then that you are living so much more comfortably than the other members of the great family? Those books of yours, for instance, they'd fetch a good price. Enough to keep a nigger for several years, I daresay. Oh, come off it

Professor. Why not admit that you're living off other people just as I am, and that you like it? ... You have succeeded in imposing on the man in the street, your "wider" or "higher" morality, and the man in the street, who is not a half-baked philosopher, loathes it ... however, the ordinary man has a natural and healthy distaste for all this business of love and brotherhood ... In fact only one thing has, in the past, saved people like you from being hustled off the stage of history for good and all, and that thing has been your characteristic timidity and hypocrisy. You have never made any serious effort to carry your principles logically into practice, and very lucky for you, too.'[35]

The novel, and Vander's character in particular, is the most sustained fictional examination of fascist ideology in this period. The argument between the Professor and Vander serves the same horrifying purpose in the novel as the interview between Winston and O'Brien in *Nineteen Eighty-Four* and much of O'Brien's argument is couched in Vander's terms. The difference between the two novels and the two scenes is that Warner gives Vander a specific *political* location, gives the 'National Legion' a social, cultural and philosophical content, and that Warner offers an alternative to fascism's too-easy success. At the end of the novel the Professor is recovering from a bout of 'interrogation'.

> Then he remembered that abject and broken moaning of the prisoner in the next cell, and he thought of the countless innocent and obscure men and women who at this moment were being tortured and lacked any means of hope or relief. His mind went out to Jinkerman and his son, and he wished them success, even in enterprises that would involve violence or civil war, so long as there was any hope of abolishing what to him seemed now the worst thing of all, a lawless and irrational oppression ...[36]

5. *A New Sort of Thriller*

A third reason why anti-fascist novelists chose to write about the political future rather than the present, in fabulous rather than immediately pressing settings, is that this permitted many of them to write in popular forms, to introduce comic or thriller elements to their work. It would have been difficult, possibly even in bad taste, to describe the real anti-fascist struggles in East London, Berlin, Vienna or Madrid, in these terms, since this might trivialise the risks and dangers run by the men and women involved in those struggles.

A number of writers clearly sought to popularise socialist politics in the early 1930s by setting them in the form of popularly-readable novels, for example, Ellen Wilkinson's *The Division Bell Mystery* (1932), Harold Heslop's *The Crime of Peter Ropner* (1934), Montagu Slater's *Second City* (1931), Graham Greene's *It's a Battlefield* (1934), and some of the Coles' novels. This is worth remembering, since the thriller, country-house mystery and detective-story genres in the 1920s and 1930s were overwhelmingly used by deeply conservative, often 'anti-Bolshevik' writers. And there was, at the same time, a suspicion on the left towards these sorts of writing.[37]

A popular novelist who used political ideas and events to give his writing greater immediacy and urgency was the prolific Rupert Grayson. *Gun Cotton – Murder at the Bank* (1939), was his fifteenth novel. In many respects it is of a piece with the other twelve 'Gun Cotton' novels, pitting the predictable hero against predictably impossible odds. What is remarkable about the novel however, is that the villain is of a new kind:

Gun had been watching Relff carefully, and he realised that the man was something more than a mere criminal. His self-restraint was admirable; his geniality a splendid cloak – but beneath all that Gun could see in the glint of his eyes and the note behind his voice that the fellow was a fanatic. Fanatical in his hatred of England, fanatical in his devotion to, as Gun felt pretty certain, the cause of International Fascism ... And all the more dangerous for *that*, Gun thought to himself.

'We have behind us almost unlimited resources. For, though it may not be generally recognised, practically every capitalist in the world is with us! Capitalism has been tottering for some years as a system, and the only thing that can save it is world fascism. And so, though mostly in secret, almost every capitalist is a fascist at heart. And some of them – many of the wealthiest of them – are quite prepared to back the cause secretly with their money. No more to say about that. With enough money and man power almost anything in the world can be conquered – even the Bank of England ...'[38]

That even a professional thriller writer like Grayson should choose to characterise his villain as a fascist, that it is a British fascism he depicts, that Relff should connive to articulate a basically Marxist analysis of fascism – this is all testimony to the extraordinary developments within the thriller genre in the late 1930s, and the penetration of anti-fascism into our literary life.

Cecil Day Lewis' (as 'Nicholas Blake') in *The Smiler with the Knife* (1939) pitted his well-connected heroine Georgina Strangeways against the dastardly Chilton Canteclo, leader of the fascist 'English Banner' stockpiling arms beneath Nottingham Castle. In Eric Ambler's *The Dark Frontier* (1936) the quiet and non-political physicist Henry Barstow, himself reading a spy-story about 'Conway Carruthers' suddenly *becomes* 'Conway Carruthers' and dashes off to the Ruritanian country of Ixania, and he engages in the anti-fascist struggle there. Amabel Williams-Ellis set her *Learn to Love First* (1939) in a similar geography, in 'Carolia' in the mid 1940s. There her aristocratic heroine Renata zu Lichtenhof is driven by love to murder the fascist leader Stecker and make contact with the Communist-led resistance. In Andrew Marvell's science-fiction *Minimum Man* (1938) a fascist coup by the 'Party of New Freedom' in Britain in 1950, is only resisted by the socialist underground joining forces with the telepathic and flying foot-high mutants, the 'minimum' people. The narrator of Storm Jameson's *In the Second Year* (1936) is on the run from fascist 'National State Party' police in Britain 1941. Bruce Hamilton's *The Brighton Murder Trial: Rex v Rhodes* (1937) purports to be a case history of a trial of an anti-fascist in 194–. The story is written in 1950, in 'these days of expectation and activity' when 'the eyes of Soviet Europe are turned towards the future', and when the fascist tyranny of the 'National Youth' government has been overthrown at last.

Finally in Bruce Hamilton's *Traitor's Way* (1938) and Graham Greene's *The Confidential Agent* (1939) the left produced two of the best chase-thrillers of the decade. Greene's novel was set in Britain during the (unspecified) Spanish Civil War, where agents for the Republican and fascist forces are competing for a crucial coal-contract. As the Republican 'D' is racing against time, and his opposite number 'L', he is on the run from the

British police on a framed murder-charge. Through an exciting plot that doesn't stop turning till the last page, 'D' is never sure whom he can trust.

> You could trust nobody but yourself, and sometimes you were uncertain whether after all you could trust yourself. *They* didn't trust you, any more than they had trusted the friend with the holy medal, they were right then, and who was to say whether they were not right now? You – you were a prejudiced party; the ideology was a complex affair; heresies crept in ... He wasn't certain that he wasn't watched at this moment; he wasn't certain that it wasn't right for him to be watched. After all, there were aspects of economic materialism which, if he searched his heart, he did not accept ... And the watcher – was he watched? He was haunted for a moment by the vision of an endless distrust ...[39]

In *Traitor's Way*, set in the early 1940s, the hero Noel Mason escapes from Parkhurst, only to find himself in unwitting possession of evidence about a fascist plot to embroil Britain in a war with the Soviet Union.

> I sat down on the edge of the bed and sweated. It was to come at last, the second great world war which had hung like a cloud over Europe for a decade and more. That Great Britain should be found lined up in the ranks of the tyrants surprised me less than it would have before I went to prison, for things had changed since then ... we were on the very brink of the pit. In two short months the world would be at war ... hazard made me, an escaped convict with every man's hand against me, a participant in this deadly secret. It was I alone who had, if fortune favoured me, a chance of preventing the hideous consummation. The idea was a terrifying one, and for a few moments I felt dizzy and shaken ... I ran to the basin and immersed my head two or three times in icy cold water. The terror passed, and I could think once more.[40]

Wanted by the police, hiding from the large fascist underground network, not knowing whom to trust, realising too late that the contact to whom he has given the papers has let slip more than he should have known, Mason finally reaches the safe address he has been given – only to realise that he has come to the fascist headquarters ...

There was of course, a good deal of comedy in all this, as the authors could not always resist drawing attention to their sense of the genre, and characterising the fascists as stage devils. There were at the same time a number of anti-fascist novels whose *main* emphases were comic. Shamus Frazer's picaresque *A Shroud as Well as a Shirt'* (1935) was a sustained satire on the absurdities, vanities and brutalities of British fascism. The 'True Born Britons' model their uniforms on cricket shirts, their idea of political ethics are based (at first) on public-school games, and they come to power on a wave of nationalism created by a Test Match at the Oval.

Easy targets for the satirists were the uniform fetishes of fascist organisation. In *The Virgin King* (1936) by Francis Watson, a whole Ruritanian fascist movement is inadvertently started by a dress-designer with a passion for yellow shirts and jodhpurs; in Terence Greenidge's *Philip and the Dictator* (1938), the dandy Francoist party on the island of St Michael are known by their dress as the 'Silver Coats'; in *The Rhubarb Tree* (1937) by Kenneth Allot and Stephen Tait, the absurd British Nazi 'Sons of Empire' wear red, white and blue shirts; Joseph Macleod ended his *Overture to Cambridge* (1936) with a vision of the world permanently divided into antagonistic but identical fascist camps, the 'Blues', 'Yellows', 'Oranges', and 'Purples'.

The inanities and contradictions of fascist rhetoric were a recurring joke too. In *The King Sees Red* (1936) Anthony Bertram inverted the race theories of Nazism in his Ruritanian dictator Rosenbaum. A new salute has been introduced in Steinbergen, 'shoulders raised ... the arms being kept close to the sides ... the hands were bent outwards with the palms raised.'

'Oy, oy, oy,' Rosenbaum had begun. Thunderously the Steinbergians had answered 'Oy'. 'Men of the Lost Tribe of Steinbergen, what have you done with your birthright? Where is the freedom your fathers won with their shining swords and that we shall win again with our indomitable will to victory. Where is it? It has been given away. It has been given to effete parliaments of uncircumcised dogs. Who gave it? Who are the traitors? You cannot answer. But I can. I will tell you. I, your leader, who am

always right. I am right in what I think; I am right in what I say; I
am right in what I do. (Oy, oy). I speak with the voice of the
people. You are my people. I am your leader. I am you. In
mystical union from my cradle in Whitechapel my soul has burnt
in a pure white flame with the souls of the people of Steinbergen.
One people: one race; one blood: the standard-bearers of culture
and the sharp sword of the hero and the irrevocable will to victory.
I tell you that it is the men of the impure race who have betrayed
us.'

In Steinbergen it is not Jewishness but virginity that is a
crime.

The day after next will be a National Fertilisation Day. After that
all virgins, or anyone having more than one grandmother who
was a virgin, or any man committing racial disgrace with a virgin,
would forthwith be deprived of their civic rights [41]

None of these novels however lost sight for a moment of the
seriousness of their subject matter. As Bertram put it, 'apart
from the shooting, beating, mutilating, imprisoning or exiling
of individuals, Rosenbaum had so far avoided using force.' In
each case the jokes turn sour before the end. In Maurice
Richardson's *The Bad Companions* (1936) two con-men leave
prison with a plan to establish a bogus fascist organisation,
fronted by a distinguished-looking lunatic they have found.
Their idea is to make money out of all the retired
crypto-fascists in the Home Counties. Unfortunately the plan
is more successful than they had ever imagined, and the real
fascists move in ... The comedy of Lady Sybil Tatham's
political equivocations in *The Rhubarb Tree* as she changes her
'Life' of Lenin overnight to a 'Life' of Hitler, according to the
fortunes of the British Nazis, gives way at the end of the novel
to a picture of her working in a tin mine, a political prisoner of
the new régime she supported too late. The opportunist
Rupert in *A Shroud as Well as a Shirt*, whose cynicism provides
most of the jokes about the Cricketshirts he has joined, realises
too late what he is involved in. He tries to make a pacifying
speech to defuse international tension, but is assassinated; this
is blamed on the Soviet Union, and world war breaks out. 'A

marble Rupert Might stood in front of the Horse Guards at Whitehall – its arm raised in eternal salute. It was one of the few things in London that remained standing after the Great Air Raid ...'[42]

6. *The Sources of Fascism*

Part of this writing about fascism and a possible fourth reason why anti-fascist writers should chose non-realistic, 'prophetic' forms, is that it permitted them to make connections between existing political practices (of the BUF or the National Government) and events on the continent. In other words, to satirise what they saw as the *latent* fascism of elements in British society.

This, for example, was clearly the intention of Ruthven Todd's *Over the Mountain* (1939). In this short novel, the hero climbs an impassable mountain to arrive in a strange and terrifying, but familiar country. Its inhabitants 'seemed to be emphasised versions of the sort of people that I could vaguely remember in my country. Everything they said seemed to be slightly in excess, they seemed to be caricatures of their types and professions.'[43] The police in this place are dangerous mental defectives, the press and the Church entirely in the pocket of the nakedly fascist government, and public schools run on paramilitary lines. He eventually escapes, climbs the peak and returns to his own land, only to realise of course that he has never in fact left it ...

By putting fascism in power in Britain in 1940, Storm Jameson in *In the Second Year* (1936) was able to make a series of such connections. As the title indicates, Jameson examines the consolidation of fascism in its second year of real power, the concentration camps, the purging of the Universities, the public anti-semitism. In particular she describes the government's clash with its more radical supporters, clearly based on the events in Germany in 1934, when the idealists within the 'National State Party' are brutally exterminated. The novel proposes a pattern of events likely to lead to a fascist government in Britain – the failure of industrial militancy without political leadership, the collapse of the trade-union movement, large-scale unemployment, the acceptance by the Labour Party of a patriotic and fiscal consensus, the

continuing ineptitude of the National Government, the
disunity of the left, and a growing disillusionment with
parliamentary politics. Moreover Jameson suggests some of
those elements most likely to succour fascism – financiers like
Sir Thomas Chamberlayne, young idealists like Ernest Sacker,
by-standing intellectuals like Tower, careerist social democrats
like Sir Alexander Denham, anti-Communist trade-union
leaders like George Body, men of action like Richard Sacker,
and not least those like Hebden,

> the violent and vicious sub-life depicted in ... a certain kind of
> American novel and film steps off the page or the screen and plays
> its horrid part in what is called the regeneration of his country. A
> disgusting cinematograph psychology becomes actual, as in a
> nightmare.[44]

In *The Brighton Murder Trial*, Bruce Hamilton used the device
of apparently writing from the future to pass comment on his
own time. The legal historian who is ostensibly the author of
The Brighton Murder Trial explains that British fascism failed in
the late 1930s because it had its thunder stolen.

> The final retirement of Mr Baldwin, the purging of the National
> Government of 'the taint of socialism', the introduction into the
> Cabinet of the Churchills, Amerys, Lords Lloyd, Rothermere and
> Beaverbrook, had seemed to provide an administration of
> sufficient 'strength'

to make overt fascism unnecessary. The case Rex v Rhodes
takes place whiile this government is in power, and although it
is a murder trial, it is apparent from the Attorney General's
speech for the prosecution that it is the anti-fascism of the
accused that is really on trial.

> Communism is not on trial here. If it were, I have little doubt as to
> what your verdict as responsible citizens would be. However, it is
> James Bradlaugh Rhodes who is on trial, and the only question of
> politics is how far teachings imbibed from that great oriental
> regime of terror, Anti-Christ in modern dress, the Soviet Union,
> makes it likely that James Bradlaugh Rhodes should have

committed this crime ... the Party to which he belongs, a party
which our perhaps too easy-going political system has so far
permitted a legal existence ...[45]

The inconsistencies of the police evidence, the perjury of
some of the fascist witnesses, the judge's misdirection of the
jury, the political allegiances of the Attorney General, amount
to an extraordinary indictment of the contemporary British
legal system, impossible to make if the novel had not been set
in the future.

A fifth reason why anti-fascist writers chose future and
fantastic locations for their novels is that these enabled them to
make a long-term analysis of fascism. By casting fascism in the
future, as a successful and permanent force of *government*,
novelists were able to examine its political content and its
popular appeal.

A novel like *Swastika Night* (1937) by 'Murray Constantine'
imagining Europe after seven hundred years of Nazi rule, was
able to offer a feminist critique of Nazism impossible in any
other fictional circumstances. The world of the novel is divided
between the Nazi and Japanese Empires, permanently warring
over their sources of labour and materials in the colonies.
Women are kept together in cages, their heads shaved, their
male children taken away at eighteen months; sexual contact
with men is only possible under the cover of darkness, and
permanent relationships not permitted; rape is not recognised
as a crime.

> To love a woman, to the German mind, would be equal to loving
> a worm ... Women like these, hairless, with naked shaven scalps,
> the wretched ill-balance of their feminine forms outlined by their
> tight bifurcated clothes – that horrible meek bowed way they had
> of walking and standing, head low, stomach out, buttocks bulging
> behind – no grace, beauty, no uprightness, all these were male
> qualities. If a woman dared to stand like a man she would be
> beaten.

In the novel a young English 'dissident' is entrusted by one
of the Knights with the only existing copy of a 'true' history of
the world. Alfred learns from this that Hitler was not a God,

that there once existed other Empires, other social systems, that Germany had suffered military defeats in the past, that there had once been something called 'Memory' and something called 'Socialism', and that women were once considered beautiful and equal to men. Above all he learns that the Nazi Empire faces a demographic crisis.

> For the Knight knew, what the women themselves did not know, all over Germany, all over the Holy German Empire in this year of our Lord Hitler 720, more and more boys were being born. It had been a gradual loss of balance, of course, but now it was causing acute uneasiness ... if women were to stop reproducing themselves, how could Hitlerdom continue to exist? It seemed as if, after hundreds of years of the really whole-hearted subjection natural under a religion which was entirely male, the worship of a man who had no mother, *the Only Man*, the women had finally lost heart ... every German of the literate knightly class had nightmare dreams of the extinction of the sacred race, but it was a truth that must not be spoken freely, above all not spoken to the women themselves ... If they once knew that the *Knights*, and even der Fuehrer, wanted girl-children to be born in large quantities; that every fresh statistical paper with its terribly disproportionate male births caused groanings and anxieties and endless secret conferences – if the women once realised all this, what could stop them developing a small thin thread of self-respect? If a woman could rejoice publicly in the birth of a girl, Hitlerdom would start to crumble ...[46]

7. Orwell and Anti-Fascism

Swastika Night is a powerful and unique criticism of fascism, an argument that it was originally mysoginist and ultimately self-destructive, and that its racial theories had roots in sexual hysteria. *Swastika Night* remains undoubtedly the most sophisticated and original of all the many anti-fascist dystopias of the late 1930s and 1940s. Needless to say, it is wholly forgotten today. In a number of specific details – the photograph that is seen by the 'dissident'; the party leader who explains the true history and workings of the Party; the book which proves that change is possible, and memory inviolable; the official rewriting of history; the permanent vilification of the enemy ('the four arch-fiends' Lenin, Stalin, Roehm and Karl Barth); the abasement of sex and the outlawing of love; the state of perpetual and unwinnable warfare ('we're dying, both the huge Empires side by side, of our own strength') – *Swastika Night* clearly anticipates Orwell's *Nineteen Eighty-Four* by several years.

There is no evidence that Orwell ever read *Swastika Night*, or indeed that he read any of the anti-fascist novels mentioned above. Whether or not he was influenced, either in general or specific ways by this body of writing is not important. What is important is that, with the exception of Isherwood, Greene and Day Lewis, these anti-fascist novelists have been disregarded by literary history, and their novels are long out of print. Anti-fascist fiction in this country was a much more varied, original, widely-based and influential body of writing than is generally allowed. Pessimistic in the short term, committed to a victory over fascism in the long term, addressed primarily as a warning, a call to vigilance, looking to the future as a way to talk about the present, drawing upon all sorts of styles and forms – there is just space for *Nineteen Eighty-Four* on the end of this shelf-full of novels. But that novel begins to look a lot less original, a lot less clear and important a contribution to the dystopian tradition, to our imaginative understanding of tyranny, when it is put alongside all these other titles.

And it must be remembered of course that Orwell had no access to any of this earlier dystopian writing, since it was the product of a literary culture he rejected. This literary phenomenon arose out of the arguments for a Popular Front current in the late 1930s in parts of the Labour Party and in the Communist Party, and influential far beyond them both. Not all the writers discussed above were socialists, few belonged to any political party, but all were participants in a remarkable anti-fascist literary alliance that Orwell went to repeated lengths to abuse.

As late as July 1939 he was characterising the anti-fascist movement as a

sort of monstrous harlequinade in which everyone is constantly bounding across the stage in a false nose – Quakers shouting for a bigger army, Communists waving Union Jacks, Winston Churchill posing as a democrat ... How can we 'fight fascism' except by bolstering up a far greater injustice? ... What meaning would there be, even if it were successful, in bringing down Hitler's system to stabilize something that is far bigger and in its different way just as bad?[47]

For Orwell at this time the struggle against British imperialism abroad and the revolutionary struggle against capitalism at home took priority over the threat of fascism.

A couple of years earlier he had argued

I do not see how one can oppose fascism except by working for the overthrow of capitalism, starting, of course, in one's own country. If one collaborates with a capitalist-imperialist government in a struggle 'against fascism', i.e. against a rival imperialism, one is simply letting fascism in by the back door.[48]

This was the line taken by the ILP which Orwell had recently joined, now only a dwindling fraction of its earlier size and influence, increasingly hostile to what they saw as the 'reformism' of the Popular Front idea. Even after the outbreak of war Orwell was to describe the late 1930s thus:

Comintern slogans suddenly faded from red to pink. 'World revolution' and 'Social fascism' gave way to 'Defence of democracy' and 'Stop Hitler!' The years 1935-9 were the period of anti-fascism and the Popular Front, the heyday of the Left Book Club, when red duchesses and 'broad-minded' deans toured the battlefields of the Spanish war and Winston Churchill was the blue-eyed boy of the *Daily Worker* ... By 1937 the whole of the intelligentsia was mentally at war, left-wing thought had narrowed down to 'anti-fascism'.[49]

'Narrowed down'? 'Narrowed down'? This is a hard phrase for any political development able to generate such an extraordinary and diverse literary culture in so short a time. But then for Orwell writing in *Inside the Whale* in 1940 the whole anti-fascist canon could be reduced to the collected works of Auden, Spender, MacNeice and Isherwood, in particular to Auden's poem *Spain* (and to two lines of that poem.) Edward Thompson has argued that

> in this essay, more than any other, the aspirations of a generation were buried; not only was a political movement, which embodied much that was honourable, buried, but so also was the notion of disinterested dedication to a political cause.[50]

Orwell, he wrote, 'falsifies the record.'

More than this, surely. What else can we conclude of someone who complained in 1944 that 'English literature' had failed to contribute to 'the special class of literature that has arisen out of the European political struggle since the rise of fascism' and that

> England is lacking, therefore, in what one might call concentration camp literature. The special world created by secret-police forces, censorship of opinion, torture and frame-up trials is, of course, known about and to some extent disapproved of, but it has made very little emotional impact

– what else can we conclude but that – as so often – Orwell didn't know what he was talking about?[51]

Our sense of the sheer size, liveliness and richness of British anti-fascist literature has been denied us for over forty years, largely because of the critical judgements of George Orwell. There is some irony in the fact that the consequent gap in our understanding of the sources of tyranny, of the way in which the human imagination has responded to tyranny, has been filled for so long by one novel only, and that this novel should have been written by, of all people, George Orwell.

Notes

1 F. Warburg, Publisher's Report on *Nineteen Eighty-Four*, 13 December 1948. See *All Publishers are Equal*, London, 1973; D. Trilling, *Nation*, 25 June 1949; V. Wedgewood, *Time and Tide*, 11 June 1949; H. Read, *World Review*, June 1950; P. Rahv, *Partisan Review*, July 1950; R.A. Leif, *Homage to Oceania*, Ohio, 1969, p.26; A. Burgess, *1985*, London, 1978, p.52; B.

Crick, *George Orwell: A Life*, Harmondsworth, 1982, p.570; L. Spencer, '*Animal Farm* and *Nineteen Eighty-Four*' in *George Orwell*, Leeds University Adult Education Department, Bradford Centre Occasional Papers No 3, 1981, p.81; W. Steinhoff, *The Origins of Nineteen Eighty-Four*, Ann Arbor, 1975, pp.216, 222.

2   See for example J. Walsh, *Marxist Quarterly*, January 1956: S. Sillen, *Masses and Mainstream*, August 1949; A. Calder Marshall, *Reynolds News*, 12 June 1949; I. Deutscher, *Heretics and Renegades*, London, 1955; Jack Lindsay, *After the Thirties*, London, 1956, p.66. For an extensive survey of critical responses to the novel see J. Meyers (ed.), *George Orwell: The Critical Heritage*, London, 1975.

3   See for example P. Rahv, loc.cit.; R.A. Leif, op.cit., p.134; R. Conquest, 'And Guess Who's Watching Big Brother?' *Daily Telegraph*, 28 January 1984; P. Johnson, *Spectator*, 7 January 1984; C. Cruise O'Brien, *Observer*, 18 December 1983, 25 March 1984; L. Labedz, 'Will George Orwell Survive 1984?' *Encounter*, June 1984.

4   See E.P. Thompson, 'Outside the Whale', in E.P. Thompson (ed.), *Out of Apathy*, London, 1960.

5   A. Burgess, op.cit., p.52.

6   See Orwell's review of *We* in S. Orwell and I. Angus (eds.), *The Collected Essays, Journalism and Letters of George Orwell*, Vol.4, Harmondsworth, 1970, p.95, referred to hereafter as '*CEJL*'.

7   See I.F. Clarke, *Tale of the Future*, London, 1972; *The Pattern of Expectation*, London, 1979; *Voices Prophesying War*, Oxford, 1966.

8   P. Widdowson, 'Between the Acts: English Fiction in the Thirties' in J. Clarke, M. Heinemann *et al* (eds.), *Culture and Crisis in Britain in the Thirties*, London, 1979, p.134.

9   For discussion of this wider literary development see G. Klaus 'Socialist Fiction in the 1930s; in J. Lucas (ed.), *The Thirties: A Challenge to Orthodoxy*, Brighton, 1978, and Andy Croft, 'Socialist Novels from the 1930s', *Bulletin of Marx Memorial Library*, September 1982. Though for reasons of space the present essay restricts itself to a discussion of novels published in the 1930s, it should be recognised that this literary development was sustained throughout the 1940s.

10   R. Todd, Preface to *The Lost Traveller*, New York, 1968.

11   B. Wootton, *In A World I Never Made*, London, 1967, p.83.

12.   Three notable exceptions to this were Rex Warner, *The Wild Goose Chase* (1937), Edward Upward, *Journey to the Border* (1938) and Patrick Hamilton, *Impromptu in Moribundia* (1939). Each was concerned, however, not so much to attack capitalist society as its sustaining ideology, and each sought to expose the fascist potential of idealism. The lengthy gestation of both Upward's and Warner's novels, and the exceptional position of Hamilton's within his own 'exaggerated-naturalist' writing, partly explains the exceptional nature of these titles. By the time *Journey to the Border* was published, it is clear that Upward thought of it as an *anti*-fantasy novel.

13   F. le Gros Clarke, *Between Two Men*, London, 1935, p.272.

14   A.L. Morton, *Daily Worker*, 12 June 1935.

15 L. Mitchell, *Gay Hunter*, London, 1934, pp.47, 178. For a discussion of the influence of Marxism and Diffusionism on Mitchell's work see I.S. Munro, *Leslie Mitchell*, London, 1966 and D.F. Young, *Beyond the Sunset*, Aberdeen, 1973.

16 See F. Brockway, *Inside the Left*, London, 1942.

17 F. Brockway, *Purple Plague*, London, 1935, p.263 (my italics).

18 See K. Radek, 'World Literature' in H.G. Scott (ed.), *Problems of Soviet Literature*, London, 1935, p.108 (my italics); republished as *Soviet Writers' Congress, 1934*, London, 1977.

19 *Left Review*, October 1934.

20 *Left Review*, 'Controversy', March 1935 (my italics). See also *New Writing*, Spring 1936, where John Lehmann declared that it should be 'first and foremost interested in literature, and though it does not intend to open its pages to writers of reactionary or fascist sentiments, it is independent of any political party' – in other words it was to be simultaneously non-political, literary-based *and* anti-fascist.

21 Significantly, when in 1937 Philip Toynbee's first novel *The Savage Days* was published, describing a successful Communist led revolution in this country, the establishment of Soviets and the extermination of the 'Whites', it was severely criticised in the *Daily Worker*. 'Gabriel' noted with some impatience that the novel was written by 'an Oxford undergraduate who ... has not yet come of age' and that while 'this young man should be encouraged to keep on writing' he should 'for a time at least, be discouraged from writing.' *Daily Worker*, 17 March 1937. Raymond Williams recalls (in *Politics and Letters*, London, 1979) that he wrote such a novel at the age of sixteen called 'Mountain Sunset', which was rejected by Gollancz. The miner and novelist Harold Heslop also wrote such a novel, 'Red Earth', about a successful British revolution set in 1941; he could never get it published in this country.

22 *Daily Worker*, 11 April 1934.

23 See, for example, *The Communist Party of Germany Lives and Fights*, enthusiastically reviewed in the *Daily Worker*, 27 December 1933.

24 See A. Rattenbury, 'Some Poems and a Play by Montagu Slater' in J. Lucas (ed.), op.cit.

25 N. Mitchison, *We Have Been Warned*, London, 1935, p.552.

26 *Daily Worker*, 8 May 1935.

27 C. Day Lewis, *New Masses*, 7 June 1938; John Lehmann made a similar point the following year when he said that this sort of political fantasy 'could only have been produced in a country which was at the same time isolated from the "gradual ruin spreading like a stain" and deeply involved in the long run in its consequences.' *New Writing in Europe*, Harmondsworth, 1940, p.61.

28 C. Isherwood, *New Republic*, 8 March 1939; see also J. Symons, *The Thirties*, London, 1960, pp.16, 28; and J. Lindsay, op.cit., p.33.

29 M. Roberts, 'The Tragic Way', *T.E. Hulme*, London, 1938.

30 S. Hynes, *The Auden Generation*, London, 1976, p.315; J.A. Morris makes a similar point when he argues that the effect of Kafka was to encourage the 'examination of the role (or plight) of the individual, rather than the

group ... Thus the new 'political' literature tended to be, paradoxically, anti-political.' *Writers and Politics in Modern Britain*, London, 1977, p.68.

31 'Murray Constantine', *Swastika Night*, London, 1937; publisher's note to 1940 edition.

32 T. Greenidge, *Philip and the Dictator*, London, 1938, author's note.

33 'Shamus Frazer', *A Shroud as Well as a Shirt*, London, 1935, preface.

34 See for example, J. Macleod, *Overture to Cambridge*, London, 1936 and J. Lindsay, *Adam of a New World*, London, 1937; one of the most extraordinary anthologies of the period, *In Letters of Red*, carried a number of highly experimental and fantastic pieces, including extracts from work by Warner, Upward, Frank Tilsley and Herbert Hodge. The collection had no introduction, only a short quotation from Sir Peter Chalmers Mitchell on fascism as a 'pathological condition'; *In Letters of Red*, London, 1938.

35 R. Warner, *The Professor*, London, 1938; Harmondsworth, 1944, pp.64-7.

36 Ibid., p.166.

37 See for example Alick West's series on the detective novel in *Left Review*, 1938. For an excellent discussion of the politics of the genre see K. Worpole, *Dockers and Detectives*, London, 1983. It is worth noting that some of the most virulent anti-semitic and pro-fascist novels of this period adopted the thriller genre, for example Josephine Ward, *The Shadow of Mussolini*, London, 1931 and 'JJJ', *Blueshirts*, London, 1926; for a contemporary discussion of fascist thrillers see L. Filatova, 'Fascism and Recent English Literature', *International Literature*, No.6, March 1934.

38 R. Grayson, *Gun Cotton – Murder at the Bank*, London, 1939; p.258; mention should be made here of S. Fowler Wright's series of novels depicting the 'coming war' between Britain and Germany, e.g. *Prelude in Prague*, *A Story of the War of 1938*, London, 1935, describing the German occupation of Czechoslovakia.

39 G. Greene, *The Confidential Agent*, Harmondsworth, 1982, p.10.

40 B. Hamilton, *Traitor's Way*, London, 1938, p.97.

41 C.A.G. Bertram, *The King Sees Red*, London, 1936, pp.206, 209; another fictional inversion of fascist race 'theories' was *Zulu in Germany*, London, 1939 by 'Usikota'. Since the author Carl Brinitzer was a German anti-fascist exile, and was therefore part of a seperate though close anti-fascist literary culture, it is beyond the scope of this essay.

42 'Shamus Frazer', op.cit., p.343.

43 R. Todd, *Over the Mountain*, London, 1939, p.63.

44 S. Jameson, *In the Second Year*, London, 1936, p.46; under the pseudonym 'James Hill' Jameson wrote one of the few British novels dealing with the Spanish War, *No Victory for the Soldier*, London, 1937.

45 B. Hamilton, *The Brighton Murder Trial*, London, 1937, pp. 305, 329.

46 'Murray Constantine', op.cit., pp.1213; the name 'Murray Constantine' was the pseudonym of a successful woman novelist, permission to reveal whose identity I have been unable to obtain from her agents; for a detailed examination of the correspondences between *Swastika Night* and *Nineteen Eighty-Four* see D. Patai, 'Orwell's Despair, Burdekin's Hope; Gender and Power in Dystopia' in *Women's Studies International Forum*,

Vol.7, no.2, pp.85-95. Frank Tilsley made the same connection between patriarchy and fascism, domestic and European politics in *Little Tin God*, London, 1939.

47 G. Orwell, 'Not Counting Niggers', *Adelphi*, July 1939, *CEJL*, Vol.I, p.434.
48 Letter to Geoffrey Gorer, ibid., p.318.
49 'Inside the Whale', ibid., p.563. For an excellent discussion of Orwell as an ultra-leftist and as a propagandist see C. Fleay and M. Sanders, 'Becoming a Dragon: George Orwell and Propaganda', Middlesex Polytechnic *History Journal*, Vol.1 No.4, supplement spring 1984.
50 E.P. Thompson, op.cit.
51 G. Orwell, 'Arthur Koestler', *Focus*, 2, 1946 (*CEJL*, Vol.3, pp.271-2).

Stuart Hall

Conjuring Leviathan: Orwell on the State

Orwell was a representative, as well as a controversial, figure –
just as *Nineteen Eighty-Four* became a 'representative' as well as
a prophetic book. Both came to 'stand for' something
significant in the political and intellectual life of the age. This is
not surprising. Though Orwell was only forty-six when he
died, he lived through tumultuous times, was personally
involved in events which became turning points in
twentieth-century history, and engaged directly with themes
and questions which have dominated much of our political
thinking since. He saw, at first hand, the 'twilight of Empire'
(in the Burma police), the 'Hungry Thirties' and the
Depression. He witnessed the rise of fascism and made the
archetypal anti-fascist response – he went to fight in Spain. He
also saw at first hand the grim impact of Stalinism on the
socialist movement in Europe. His political outlook was deeply
shaped by the Second World War, and then by the 'Cold War'.

In addition to 'being there', Orwell also wrote about these
events in that direct, plain-spoken, self-expressing 'documentary' style which became characteristic of him and of his
period. Through this witnessing of events, he helped to *define*
what those events meant as political experiences – giving each
the stamp of his peculiarly 'English' point of view. In trying to
come to terms, now, with what those events 'really meant', we
are obliged to reckon, one way or another, with Orwell. That is
why we keep asking, 'Was Orwell right?' A hopeless approach,
since he was so often right *and* wrong, sometimes in succession,

217

more often in the same moment. Despite the claims on moral clarity and political honesty which his style makes for him, his political writing was shot through with ambiguities and, in the final analysis, deeply contradictory. For example, the best case of these 'boiled rabbits of the left' who are hesitant about sinking their differences with the right simply because they are both against fascism (and whom Orwell excoriates in that inexcusably casual brutalist phrase, 'My Country Right or Left') is, of course, none other than Orwell himself, writing in exactly that sceptical vein about the dangers of sinking differences only a few months earlier in 'Not Counting Niggers'. He was almost always partial: but the parts he saw, he saw *into* with an astonishing penetration. Even when wrong, he makes us think again about our certainties. That is why there are so many 'Orwells'. There were so many to choose from. In addition, there are those we have felt obliged to make up for ourselves. It now seems wholly wrong to read Orwell for his 'correctness'. We read him for his contradictoriness, for his vulnerability, his gift of exposure. Of the mountain of critical observations, favourable and dismissive, which exists about Orwell, the one observation which in my view comes closest to the truth is that of Raymond Williams:

> Instead of flattening out the contradictions by choosing this or that tendency as the 'real' Orwell, or fragmenting them by separating this or that period or this or that genre, we ought to say that it is the paradoxes which are finally significant.[1]

That, at any rate, is the approach adopted in this sketch of the evolution of Orwell's ideas about the state, which eventually found such powerful expression in the nightmare vision of *Nineteen Eighty-Four*.

Despite his socialism, Orwell was instinctively an *individualist*. He held independent, sometimes idiosyncratic views; he was always 'his own man'. George Woodcock, his anarchist friend, called him 'an iconoclast'. He fought with others for causes he believed in – but always in his own way. He hated to be told what to do, bossed around, regimented or made to toe the party line. He belonged to the *libertarian* socialist, rather than the collectivist socialist, tradition. This had consequences for his instinctive attitudes towards authority, discipline and power – and hence for his view of the state. What he hated about the fellow-travelling, left-wing intellectuals was their willingness to subordinate themselves to the party line and to give up thinking for themselves. What he loved about Catalonia was the spirit of radical egalitarianism: 'no military ranks ... no titles or badges, no heel-clicking and no saluting.'[2] One of the greatest strengths of the English, he argued, was the weakness of its militarist tradition: the sergeant-major was a universally hated figure. 'Fascism' and 'totalitarianism' came to signify the jackboot, the torture chamber and the rubber truncheon: the iconography of naked, violent, unqualified state power, with the individual at its disposal – the basic structure of imagery in *Nineteen Eighty-Four*. The proles are unable to become the basis of the opposition to tyranny, and Winston and Julia go down alone, holding aloft the flickering candle of individual liberty, private emotion and personal dissent. Orwell's individualism gave him a basic orientation to politics which was fundamentally alien to the statist notion of 'bringing socialism to the masses' through the imposition of state dictatorship and, indeed, to the whole tradition which identified socialism with collectivism and state control. *Nineteen Eighty-Four* owed a great deal to Orwell's instinctive libertarianism.

Orwell also had a very independent political formation *as a socialist*, which distinguished him from the majority of intellectuals who turned to the left in the 1930s. For whereas they fell under the orbit of the Communist Party and the Popular Front, Orwell's formation was mainly in the orbit of the ILP, an independent party of the left, opposed to the statism of both the Labour Party and Stalinism: 'the only British party ... which aims at anying I should regard as Socialism';[3] which Crick describes as 'left-wing, egalitarian, a strange mixture of secularized evangelism and non-Communist Marxism'.[4] His route to Spain was via his ILP contacts – which is how he came to join POUM rather than a Communist battalion. He came to accept the ILP line that Stalin had betrayed the revolution and was holding back the pace of the social revolution in Spain. When he returned from Spain, he briefly joined the ILP in 1938, though he was an inveterate non-joiner. Though he admitted that, in England, there was only one socialist party that 'really mattered' in a mass sense – the Labour Party – he never wrote or spoke of it seriously as a political vehicle which could bring about a fundamental shift of power.[5] It was to the short-lived Commonwealth Party that he looked for leadership of the popular movement he thought was developing during the radicalizing years of the war.

On his return from Spain, the anarchists tried to recruit him, but he never formally joined them. However, undoubtedly, his experiences in Spain strengthened the natural 'anarchism' of his politics and this, too, carried with it implications for his attitude towards the state. Catalonia remained with him as a radical, egalitarian utopia. POUM's brand of oppositional communism and anarcho-syndicalism, and the egalitarian working-class character which Barcelona assumed under its inspiration, strongly appealed to him. It was the destruction of POUM and the imprisonment of anarchists and others, including many of his ILP friends, which conclusively demonstrated to him the consequences of the Stalinist betrayal of the revolution. These events deepened his anti-Communism. But they also set in motion one of the most powerful themes in Orwell's thinking (and in *Nineteen Eighty-Four*): the idea of the growing convergence between the fascist and the Stalinist dictatorships, and of totalitarianism as the basis for a new type of state formation.

When he tried to tell the truth about Spain as he saw it, once he had returned to England, he encountered a wall of silence and hostility: the left did not want to hear. It preferred to believe what he saw as a falsification of history. This is why, in *Nineteen Eighty-Four*, the question of ideological control (the control of thought and language), the erosion of historical memory, the falsification of records and the re-writing of history are so basic to his view of the essential mechanisms of the totalitarian state. It is why Winston – when he drinks a toast – puts 'the past' above all else. Subordination to the party could make intelligent people accept ludicrous ideas. But under 'totalitarianism' *doublethink* became a necessary way of life: '$2 + 2 = 5$'.

Were Orwell's views on the state 'Trotskyist'? The Spanish communists and the Comintern labelled POUM 'Trotskyist'.

When T.S. Eliot politely advised Fabers not to publish *Animal Farm*, he labelled Orwell's viewpoint 'Trotskyite'. Warburg, who did publish it, was incorrectly described as 'the Trotskyite publisher,'[6] Yet Orwell was never a member of the Trotskyite movement, had little connection with its sects and, though impressed by some of Trotsky's writings, expressed doubts as to whether things would have been radically different had Trotsky's opposition to Stalin succeeded. Goldstein's 'testament' in *Nineteen Eighty-Four* is clearly modelled on Trotsky's writings, as indeed was its dialectical style of argument and the description of Goldstein himself – 'long, thin nose, near the end of which a pair of spectacles was perched'. But Goldstein and his testament are composite creations, with elements of the American anarchist Emma Goldman, and the testament of the POUM leader Andrés Nin, as well as Trotsky himself. Goldstein's position in *Nineteen Eighty-Four* and Orwell's attitude to him remain ambiguous.

Though Orwell did not become a Trotskyist, he did take up, at different times, positions not dissimilar from some of those held by Trotskyists. One example of this is his wavering adherence to the thesis that the defeat of Franco and the deepening of the revolutionary process in Spain had to go hand in hand – a position which he later transposed into an argument about the war against Hitler, and the development of an English socialism.

Orwell's thesis about the growing convergence between East and West and the emergence of a new kind of state based on the rule of a powerful élite and a collectivized group – what he called at first 'oligarchical collectivism' – has many similarities with the theories of 'bureaucratic collectivism' which some Trotskyists later used to explain what had happened in the Soviet Union and to define the character of the Soviet state. For example, in the 1960s, a leading American ex-Trotskyist and Trotsky's translator and literary executor, Max Schachtman, published *The Bureaucratic Revolution* in which he tried to analyse the deformation of the Stalinist state using the theory of 'bureaucratic collectivism'. Even more directly influential for Orwell were the views of James Burnham who, in the 1940s, left the American Trotskyist movement and produced *The Managerial Revolution*, a book which depicted the drift towards a system of managed collectivism which, he argued, pointed up the growing similarities between Hitler's Germany, Stalin's Russia and Roosevelt's New Deal.

Much of this reflected the evolution of Trotsky's thinking about the character of the Soviet dictatorship. After his exclusion from power, Trotsky had described the Soviet state as 'degenerated' through the growth of a privileged bureaucracy which found its political representative in Stalin. Economic backwardness, shortages and the isolation of the Russian revolution had produced, not a new type of capitalist ruling *class* but a bureaucratic *caste*. The state was drawn by the need to extract forced surpluses for modernization to exploit and coerce its own class. But from 1939 onwards (Schachtman gives as a critical reference Trotsky's 'The USSR in the War', published in the *New International* in November) Trotsky advanced the proposition that the Stalinist dictatorship was not, as he had supposed, a workers' state which had suffered temporary bureaucratic 'degeneration', but rather 'the first stage of a new exploiting society' which, on the basis of the nationalization of property, the party and state bureaucracy had become a new exploiting and dictatorial 'ruling class'. Splits between the different.Trotskyist sects depended in part on which of Trotsky's theories were thought to be correct.

Orwell's thinking did not follow the intricate twists of these internal sectarian debates. But he began to envisage a 'new type of social system', with its roots in, but by-passing, its revolutionary and democratic origins, which would continue to exploit the masses on the basis of collectivized property and the oligarchical rule in a repressive state of a dictatorial élite. The lineaments of this system we clearly discernible in his description of Oceania in *Nineteen Eighty-Four*

There is another way in which Orwell related to the question of 'Trotskyism'. In order to secure his rule, Stalin obliged the left opposition groups to confess that they had acted in ways which were 'objectively' inimical to the Soviet Union or were actually agents of Western capitalism. In Stalinist language, the term 'Trotskyite' became synonymous with 'enemy of the state': and the assault against these enemies within was exported into the Communist parties and movements throughout Europe – including Spain where Orwell encountered it at first hand. Professor Crick in his biography records that Alba, a historian of Catalan Marxism, reported that three days before the POUM leader Andrés Nin was expelled from the Republican government (the beginning of the drive against POUM), the Soviet newspaper *Pravda* announced that, 'In Catalonia the elimination of Trotskyites and anarcho-syndicalists has begun. It will be carried out with the same energy as it was carried out in the Soviet Union.'[7]

In a remarkable passage on the manipulation of political language, which carries echoes down to our own day, Orwell reflects on how this particular syllogism – Trotskyist = revolutionary socialist = traitor – has been reworked by the left (as later the term 'Trotskyist' was to be mercilessly worked over by the right):

> And what is a Trotskyist? This terrible word – in Spain at this moment you can be thrown into jail and kept there indefinitely, without trial, on the mere rumour that you are Trotskyist – is only beginning to be bandied to and fro in England. We shall be hearing more of it later. The word 'Trotskyist' (or 'Trotsky-fascist') is generally used to mean a disguised fascist who poses as an ultra-revolutionary in order to split the left-wing forces. But it derives its peculiar power from the fact that it means three separate things. It can mean one who, like Trotsky, wished for world revolution; or a member of the actual organization of which Trotsky is head (the only legitimate use of the word); or the disguised fascist already mentioned. The three meanings can be telescoped one into the other at will. Meaning No. 1 may or may not carry with it meaning No.2, and meaning No. 2 almost invariably carries with it meaning No. 3. Thus 'XY has been heard to speak favourably of world revolution; therefore he is a Trotskyist; therefore he is a fascist.' In Spain, to some extent even in England, *anyone* professing revolutionary socialism (i.e. professing the things the Communist Party professed until a few years ago) is under suspicion of being a Trotskyist in the pay of Franco or Hitler.[8]

Orwell thought that the Depression and the war had demonstrated the rottenness of capitalism and the need to plan. The war not only made the case for planning: it had advanced it practically. Many did see, in rationing and production for the war effort, the emergence of a sort of 'war socialism'. Planning, however, was not a straightforward question for Orwell, because of its overtones of regimentation and state control.

This may explain why so many of the stark images of the Oceania landscape in *Nineteen Eighty-Four* reflect, not some grim Soviet future, but 'the drabness and monotony of the English industrial suburb, the "filthy and grimy and smelly" ugliness ... the food rationing and the government controls which he knew in war-time Britain.'[9] The picture of society given in *Nineteen Eighty-Four*, Julian Symons noted in his review in the *Times Literary Supplement*,

> has an awful plausibility. In some ways life does not differ very much from the life we live today. The pannikin of pinkish-gray stew, the hunk of bread and cube of cheese, the mug of milkless Victory coffee with its accompanying saccharine tablet – that is the kind of meal we very much remember ...[10]

This has the effect, as Symons noted, of involving us more directly, since so much of it is only an extension of familiar things: a 'near future'.

But was it only the stylistic requirements of naturalism which made Orwell express the totalitarian nightmare through the imagery of Britain's war-time rationing, planning and controls? It may not be far-fetched to see this in the context of a deeper ambiguity in the novel – the position he ascribes in *Nineteen Eighty-Four* to INGSOC, whose sacred principles are 'Newspeak, doublethink, the mutability of the past': even though INGSOC is clearly an acronym of '*Eng*lish *Soc*ialism' – the term used very positively in 1940 for the kind of socialism which Orwell himself evoked so positively in *The Lion and the Unicorn*.

There is also the question of how much *Nineteen Eighty-Four* was a caricature of Soviet totalitarianism, and how far it is pointed at totalitarian tendencies latent in all the superstates, including Western capitalism. Orwell himself, in the statement he dictated to Warburg to clarify his intentions about *Nineteen Eighty-Four*, not only gives the latter reading his positive warrant, but links it with the final elements in the chain of ideas which went into the making of *Nineteen Eighty-Four* and his 'last thoughts' about the state. This final phase was dominated by the descent into the Cold War, the division of the world into the armed superstate blocs, each with their spheres of influence, the state of 'permanent war' generated between them as a requirement of their survival, the dependence of each on the arms race, and the frozen postures imposed by the advent of atomic weapons. Here Orwell is on the edge of a theory of 'exterminism' – to use E.P. Thompson's phrase – where the military complex has acquired a sort of autonomous, self-sustaining impetus of its own within the superstates.

> George Orwell assumes that if such societies as he describes in *Nineteen Eighty-Four* come into being there will be several super states. This is fully dealt with in the relevant chapters of *Nineteen Eighty-Four*. It is also discussed from a different angle by James Burnham in *The Managerial Revolution*. These super states will naturally be in opposition to each other or (a novel point) will pretend to be much more in opposition than in fact they are. Two of the principal super states will obviously be the Anglo-American world and Eurasia. If these two great blocs line up as mortal enemies it is obvious that the Anglo-Americans will not take the name of their opponents and will not dramatize themselves on the scene of history as Communists. Thus they will have to find a new name for themselves. The name suggested in *Nineteen Eighty-Four* is of course Ingsoc, but in practice a wide range of choices is open. In the USA the phrase 'Americanism' or 'hundred per cent Americanism' is suitable and the qualifying adjective is as totalitarian as anyone could wish.[11]

Clarification of this kind was necessary because even Warburg, when he first read the draft of *Nineteen Eighty-Four* – and unknown to Orwell – had gained precisely the impression which Orwell was so anxious to avoid:

> The political system which prevails is Ingsoc = English Socialism. This I take to be a deliberate and sadistic attack on socialism and socialist parties generally. It seems to indicate a final breach

between Orwell and socialism, not the socialism of equality and human brotherhood which clearly Orwell no longer expects from socialist parties, but the socialism of Marxism and the managerial revolution. *Nineteen Eighty-Four* is among other things an attack on Burnham's managerialism; and it is worth a cool million votes to the Conservative Party; it is imaginable that it might have a preface by Winston Churchill after whom its hero is named. *Nineteen Eighty-Four should be published as soon as possible, in June 1949.*[12]

Warburg was by no means alone in interpreting *Nineteen Eighty-Four* in this way. Sillen, in the American Communist journal *Masses and Mainstream*, might have been expected to gloss *Nineteen Eighty-Four* an 'anti-socialist polemic'. But more sympathetic critics, like Diana Trilling in *The Nation*, did see *Nineteen Eighty-Four* as 'an assimilation of the English Labour government to Soviet communism', documenting the thesis that 'by the fourth decade of the twentieth century all the main currents of political thought were authoritarian. Every new political theory ... led back to hierarchy and regimentation.' Golo Mann, the German historian, tried to separate Orwell from the charge of crude anti-communism – since *Life, Reader's Digest* and other American magazines had 'pounced upon *Nineteen Eighty-Four* and given the book the widest possible publicity as an anti-Communist pamphlet.' Shortly before his death, Orwell was obliged to clarify his intentions again to the United Automobile Workers, who wanted to recommend *Nineteen Eighty-Four* to their members. In the press release quoted above Orwell had emphasised that the book was a *warning* rather than prophecy: 'The moral is ... *Don't let it happen*![13]

Orwell hated everything to do with fascism from the beginning. Everything in his life to that date predisposed him to do so. After the emergence of Stalinism in the Soviet Union, the purges and the Moscow Trials, he came to hate everything that Stalinism stood for, too. He became convinced that the 'reign of terror, forcible suppression of political parties, a stifling censorship of the press, ceaseless espionage and mass imprisonment without trial' which he had seen perpetrated by both the fascists and by some Communists in Spain meant that, paradoxically, Communism too had become 'a counter-revolutionary force'.[14] His concept of 'totalitarianism' was born out of this equation: the growing similarities in the tendencies and character of types of state which appear superficially to belong to different species.

Orwell knew that fascist Germany and Stalinist Russia had different economic, political and ideological systems and subscribed to totally opposed political philosophies: the record of anti-fascist struggle by Communists throughout Europe in the 1930s was well documented. Orwell argued that the two societies had begun to reveal striking similarities at the level of their *underlying tendencies*. Later, he came to include Western-style monopoly capitalism as belonging to the same 'family' of states, exhibiting the same underlying dynamic. It therefore became possible to speak of 'totalitarianism' as a general historical movement towards a distinctive, new, terrifying *type* of state.

For Orwell, 'totalitarianism' was a loose, general concept: more a political image than an analytic construct. Yet it is interesting that when he reviewed a book about the Soviet Union called *Assignment in Utopia* by Eugene Lyons (a United States Agency correspondent), Orwell began with what he now regarded as the difficult but key question: 'Is it socialism or is it a peculiarly vicious form of state capitalism? ... The system that Mr Lyons describes does not seem to be so very different from fascism.'[15] This statement, however, did not lead Orwell on to an analysis of the similarities and differences in economic, social and political structures between the three types of state. The discussion pivots instead around a set of images dominated by a single element: the repressive character and the reign of terror on which totalitarian states are founded. 'If you want a picture of the future of humanity imagine a boot stamping on a human face – for ever.'

Another indication of the drift of his thinking is found in his reviews of the work of Franz Borkenau. In July 1937 he reviewed Borkenau's justly famous book, *The Spanish Cockpit*, very favourably because it matched his own experiences in Catalonia. At that time he thought Borkenau was simply a distinguished observer of the international scene. In fact he was an Austrian Communist who had been a Comintern agent.

Borkenau's history, *The Communist International*, which Orwell reviewed in 1938, documents the impact and working out of Comintern policy on other European parties, including the Spanish. Orwell's review of Borkenau's *The Totalitarian Enemy* (1940) explored a new set of themes: the 'striking resemblance between the German and Russian régimes', the friendships between opposites 'cemented in blood' (the Hitler-Stalin pact), and the fact that 'The two régimes, having started from opposite ends, are rapidly evolving towards the same system – a form of oligarchical collectivism.'[16] One of the main forces driving these two régimes towards one another, he added, is the 'socialistic' effect of preparing for *war*.

'Oligarchical collectivism' is a term which belongs to a 'family' of concepts which were used, especially in Marxist debate, to define the character of the Soviet Union and, sometimes, other types of social system. 'Oligarchical' refers to the fact that power is held in and wielded by a small, compact but powerful *élite*. 'Collectivism' signifies the 'corporate', planned, centralized and integrated nature of the economy, and the massive and direct involvement of the state in a much expanded role in the economy and society. 'Collectivism' was, historically, an ambiguous concept, linked with but by no means identical to 'socialism'. It was assumed that 'socialist' states would be planned, centralized and integrated, with expanded state regulation, and therefore they would be 'collectivist' in character. But historical 'collectivism' had also been at the turn of the century a programme for national regeneration sponsored by the social-imperialist right as a way of integrating the classes into an organic conception of the nation, and as an alternative to both classical *laissez-faire* and redistributive, egalitarian socialism.

At the turn of the century, imperialists and tariff-reformers, as well as the Fabians, were collectivists without being egalitarian or democratic. Many believed that the need to make society more efficient, followed by the need to organize for war and to achieve national mobilization, were the factors which most powerfully shifted the old *laissez-faire* capitalism in a 'collectivist' direction.

The term 'oligarchical collectivism' thus raises a number of questions about Orwell's ideas about the state at this time. For in addition to characterizing the Soviet state, it refers to the proposition that 'advanced' or 'monopoly' capitalism could move, at the planning/collectivist level, in the direction of socialism and yet preserve its most 'capitalistic' features, e.g. the exploitation of waged labour; and that so-called 'communist' or 'socialist' societies could similarly become state-collectives and planned in character without delivering socialism, in the sense of ending the exploitation of the masses.

In his BBC broadcast 'Literature and Totalitarianism', Orwell remarked that 'When one mentions totalitarianism one thinks immediately of Germany, Russia, Italy, but I think one must face the risk that this phenomenon is going to be world-wide'.[17] This is the second part of the equation on which the 'totalitarianism' thesis was based: the proposition that fascism, Stalinism *and* capitalism in its monopoly phase *all* belonged to a new and distinctive species of totalitarian state. One of the places where this line of argument is most fully developed is in Orwell's essay on James Burnham's *The Managerial Revolution*, a book premissed precisely on such a thesis. Orwell thought that Burnham had greatly exaggerated some things but that, in his identification of basic trends and tendencies across the globe, Burnham was broadly correct. (Orwell did not, of course, share Burnham's affirmative attitude towards the growth of 'managerialism'.) Orwell summarized Burnham's thesis as follows:

> Capitalism is disappearing, but socialism is not replacing it. What is now arising is a new kind of planned, centralized society which will be neither capitalist nor, in any accepted sense of the word, democratic. The rulers of this society will be the people who effectively control the means of production: that is, business executives, technicians, bureaucrats and soldiers, lumped together by Burnham under the name of 'managers'. These people will eliminate the old capitalist class, crush the working class, and so organize society that all power and economic privilege remain in their own hands. Private property rights will be abolished, but common ownership will not be established. The new 'managerial' societies will not consist of a patchwork of small, independent states, but of great super-states grouped round the main industrial centres ...[18]

Burnham himself gave an account of the evolution of the managerialism thesis in his Preface to *The Managerial Revolution*. He had been a member of a Trotskyist organization in the 1930s – the 'Fourth International' – and originally subscribed to the analysis of the character of the Soviet state which at that time carried Trotsky's imprimatur. This was that, though Stalinism represented a bureaucratic dictatorship, the Soviet Union was still a 'degenerated workers' state or proletarian dictatorship, and therefore the Soviet régime still had to be defended by those who wished to preserve the victories achieved by the Bolshevik revolution. Burnham says that the thesis began to disintegrate for him as soon as he attempted to fit the formulas to reality. For the workers, as far as he could see, were as far away from wielding power as they had been under the Tsar, the country was ruled by a dictatorial party apparatus backed by the police, and the country did not appear to be moving in a socialist direction. How, then, were Marxists to understand and analyse the nature of the Soviet state?

In classical Marxist terms, there could only be two possible types of state in the modern industrialized world: a capitalist/bourgeois state or socialist/workers' state (leading eventually to communism and the withering away of the state). Burnham came to the conclusion that, since the Soviet Union was neither of these, there must be in embryo a 'new form of society', perhaps combining features of both but representing a novel line of development. This he christened 'managerialist'. Once established, there was no reason to restrict its application to the Soviet Union. It became possible

> to interpret long-term structural developments in other major nations as moving, though by different paths, towards the same or a similar form. The analogies were especially convincing in the case of Nazi Germany and New Deal America. I thus arrived at a general hypothesis that world society is in the midst of a major social transformation that may be called 'the managerial revolution'.[19]

The most novel aspect of this formulation is that Burnham considered Roosevelt's New Deal to be also a very primitive movement in the 'managerial' direction. By the end, 'The future of the US' (as his final chapter was called) had become the centrepiece of Burnham's preoccupations.

This therefore connects the debate, and Orwell's thinking, not only with attempts to understand the evolution of the exceptional fascist and communist states, but also with the analysis of the developed capitalist industrial system. Within Marxist circles this debate began with Lenin's attempt, in his theory of the 'imperialist' stage of capitalist development, to establish Marxist terms for analysing the post *laissez-faire* phase of monopoly capitalism, drawing on such works as Hilferding's studies of finance capital, Bukharin's thesis concerning the fusion of state and private capital, and Hobson's study of capitalism and the imperialist system.

The phrase 'state capitalism' was not, of course, restricted to this analysis of twentieth-century capitalism. Lenin had favourably characterized his New Economic Policy – a partial retreat from full collectivization in the Soviet Union after 1921 – as 'state capitalist', on the model of the German state's superintendence of private capital in the interest of the nation during the First World War. But the Menshevik critics who believed that the phase of capitalist development could not be short-circuited in the Soviet Union used the term to describe the Bolshevik system as such; and later Trotskyists also appropriated the concept. (Tony Ciff's view that after 1928 capitalism had been restored in the Soviet Union through the state's role in forcing through industrialization is one of the most elaborated of these appropriations.) The concept therefore progressively acquired a critical edge.

The debate, however, was not restricted to Marxist circles. With the growth of an economy dominated by large-scale corporate enterprises, and the development – in the period of the 'New Deal' under Roosevelt – of much greater state intervention and federal regulation of the economy as a remedy for recurrent economic crises, there also developed amongst 'bourgeois' economists and theorists a debate about the character of modern capitalism. The principal ways in which corporate capitalist economies were said to differ from the 'classic' *laissez-faire* model were in a) the extent of state intervention; b) the decreasing role of the private capitalist entrepreneur and of the 'private ownership' of industrial property; c) the growth of 'corporate' property, sometimes including the state ownership of basic industries; and d) the separation of 'ownership' from 'control'. The *effective* control, it was argued, now rested not with the capitalist class as such but with the *managers*, who may or may not own large chunks of corporate property, but who have a massive stake in the long-term accumulation of capital, the strategic management of corporate policies and enterprises, who derive immense wealth, privilege and power from their control of the means of production, and who share a 'collectivist' and 'capitalist planning' ideology with their counterparts in the expanding state bureaucracy with which they are increasingly connected.

In support of his rather speculative and 'Machiavellian' propositions. Burnham developed another important aspect to his theory: namely, a critique of the classic argument that ownership of capital and property – capitalist 'property-rights' – is the sufficient guarantee of a capitalist system; and that, therefore, the abolition of those property rights is a sufficient guarantee that the society is becoming socialist. Burnham argues against this syllogism. It is possible, he says, for property rights to be abolished – as they have been in the Soviet Union and in those parts of capitalist economies with large, nationalized or state-owned sectors – and yet for the *control* over the means of production to continue to be concentrated in the hands of a small élite, with no passage of power to the working class.

Another intriguing aspect of Burnham's case is how he deals with the 'New Deal'. For, though the New Deal did mark an important transition point in the development of American capitalism, it clearly differed radically from the line of development of either Nazi Germany or the Soviet Union. He recognized the New Deal as 'the most primitive and least organised' of the managerialisms. But, he argued, there was a historical bond, even if not a formal identity, between Stalinism, fascism and 'New Dealism', in their common movement away from competitive capitalism, their reliance on planning and the state and their corporate, managerialist, 'anti-capitalist' ideologies. Above all, he argued, 'the direction is what is all-important; and New Dealism points in the same direction as the others.'[20] This may seem far-fetched in retrospect. But it may not be so clear to us now, after decades of 'mixed economies', 'welfare capitalism', corporatist bargaining and Keynesianism, just how radical a departure the New Deal was, and how distinctive were the corporate and political ideologies which cohered around it. It was the first real attempt to set Keynesian theories to work in a practical way, in a large-scale advanced capitalist economy, as a remedy against recession, unemployment and slump. Its planning and collectivist ideology was a radical modification of the 'liberal-free-enterprise' ideology which has always been so strong in the US. It did appear to be a sort of half-way house between capitalism and socialism or, like Keynesianism itself, the reforms required by the system to prevent and forestall more wide-ranging structural changes. The difference is that whereas, according to the latter view, the New Deal was a 'historic compromise' between two fundamentally alternative systems – a compromise sealed by the evolution of the new corporate capitalist forms – Burnham saw such a hybrid not as reverting to one or other of the fundamental models, but rather as *going forwards* to the evolution of a new type, a new stage.

When Orwell came back to Burnham, in 1947 (in a review of his *The Struggle for the World*), it was to note and reflect on a major development of the 'managerialist' or 'totalitarian' thesis.[21] For in that book, Burnham projects his speculative theses about the state on to the world stage. It concerns the world of rival armed blocs, of East vs West, the Cold War, above all the shadow of atomic weapons and the arms race. Again, it parallels, to some extent, the direction of Orwell's own thinking, though he continued to have a quite different attitude towards the developments which Burnham described. Burnham's argument here – a familiar doomy prediction amongst the Cold War converts – was that world Communism was well on the way to world domination. This would mean 'not so much conquest by Russia as conquest by a special form of social organization' – a system which is 'technically collectivist, but concentrates all power in a very few hands, is based on forced labour and eliminates all real or imaginary opponents by means of terrorism.'[22]

It does not take a moment to see that the managerial/ totalitarian society, which Burnham was predicting as the future of all major societies, has now been conveniently assigned to Communism *alone*; and that, unpredictably, Burnham has – as Orwell wryly noted – under the pressure of the Cold War, reverted to the position of 'champion of old-style democracy' which he believes has somehow survived all the transitions he described and is still alive and well in the United States. Indeed, 'old-style democracy seems somewhat optimistic a description, because Burnham, with his characteristic intemperateness, now recommends that the only option open to the US is to seize the initiative and establish 'what amounts to a world empire now'; the first move of which should be a pre-emptive nuclear strike against the Soviet Union. It was a strange and unpredictable place for the theory of 'managerialism' to end. It must be added that a number of ex-Trotskyists, whose anti-Communism became their whole political *raison d'être*, coupled with their overwhelming antipathy to and hatred of the Soviet Union, did, under the multiple pressures of the Cold War, tread a very similar path, and end up on the extreme right of the American political and strategic-policy spectrum.

Orwell did not go in Burnham's direction in this respect. He reported that he had heard many conversations in Britain about the division of the world between two camps dominated by the USA and the USSR, which ended with the reluctant admission, 'Oh well, of course, if one had to choose, there's no question about it – America.' He himself moved increasingly into the position of feeling trapped between these alternating and competing world systems, with much that he believed in crushed out of existence by both. This is another way of saying that Orwell remained more faithful to the pessimistic conclusion that there might be very little to choose between 'Eurasia' and 'Oceania'. That is what ultimately defined the structure of thought, the play of concepts and the deep pessimism which underpinned *Nineteen Eighty-Four*. The novel was predicated on the stark proposition: 'what if totalitarianism *is* the future of all societies?'

The centre-piece of this conception of a general totalitarian form of the modern state was the concept, not of class, but of *power*. Power came to have *two* principal dimensions for Orwell: terror and torture – the apparatus of organized violence and 'thought control' or what Orwell called in his review of Bertrand Russell's *Power*, 'the huge system of organized lying upon which dictators depend'.[23] In another review on Soviet government, Orwell concluded a discussion of aspects of Russian modernization and the standard of living of the average Soviet citizen with a very strong emphasis on 'something entirely unprecedented' about modern dictatorships:

> The radio, press-censorship, standardized education and the secret police have altered everything. Mass suggestion is a science of the last twenty years and we do not yet know how successful it will be.[24]

The ideological dimension thus played an increasingly important role in Orwell's use of the totalitarian concept. It was also, subsequently, elaborated in theoretical terms by other writers of whom, at this stage, Orwell seems to have had little or no knowledge. Theorists of the neo-Marxist 'Frankfurt School', such as Herbert Marcuse or Theodor Adorno, for example, who were expelled from Germany by the Nazis and emigrated to the USA, argued later that the manipulation of propaganda and the exploitation of the mass mentality by powerful élites had been substantially enhanced by the new media of propaganda and communication. The Nazis particularly had brought the art of mass propaganda to a high pitch of development. But, they argued, this danger was also present, if in a different form, in the mass culture of Western capitalist societies like Britain and the USA. This argument also drew attention to the concentration of power in the hands of a small élite, the breakdown of older, class-based social systems into new kinds of division between 'élites' and 'masses', the power of élites in manipulating mass consciousness through the use of authoritarian symbols – like the Fuehrer, Stalin, or 'Big Brother'.

Orwell wrote a great deal – and with insight – about popular culture. But when he expanded on the thought control aspect of 'totalitarianism' he did so less in relation to 'mass culture' and more in terms of rather more traditional themes: the place of the writer in a totalitarian world; the threats to the writer's individual voice; the corruption of political language; the falsification of historical records, the obliteration of the memory of the past and the ubiquitous presence of *doublethink*. His essay 'Looking Back on the Spanish Civil War' (1942) contained a lengthy reflection on the fact that 'the very concept of objective truth is fading out of the world' and 'the chances are that those lies, or at any rate, similar lies will pass into history'.[25] It toyed with speculation about a 'nightmare world' in which 'the Leader or some ruling clique controls not only the future but *the past*.'[26] By 1947, when Orwell's plans for *Nineteen Eighty-Four* were developing fast, the 'organized lying' is conceived as 'something integral to totalitarianism', which demands the 'continuous alteration of the past', and a 'schizophrenic system of thought, in which the laws of common sense ... could be disregarded' by some, and people would see nothing wrong in 'falsifying an historical fact.'[27] The idea of writing books by machinery which crops up again in *Nineteen Eighty-Four* is already here – and on this occasion the description of totalitarianism steps over very easily into a caricature of contemporary culture in the West.[28] The distinctions – fascism, Stalinism, capitalism – were beginning to break down.

Interestingly, there was a passing encounter between Orwell and someone who did espouse a view close to that, not from the ex-Trotskyist right, but from a classic liberal position. The theme comes through very powerfully in Orwell's review of Hayek's *Road to Serfdom*, which appeared in 1944. This book, by the distinguished European liberal philosopher, was a vigorous denunciation of the drift into 'despotism' taking place in all directions, and an eloquent restatement and defence of *laissez-faire* capitalism and liberalism, which has become a *locus classicus* of modern neo-liberalism. In the 1970s and 1980s Hayek became one of the most powerful ideologues of the 'New Right' and a philosophical precursor of Thatcherism.

Orwell summarized his argument thus:

By bringing the whole of life under the control of the state, socialism necessarily gives power to an inner ring of bureaucrats, who in almost every case will be men who want power for its own sake and will stick at nothing in order to retain it. Britain, he says, is now going the same road as Germany, with the left-wing intelligentsia in the van and the Tory Party a good second. The only salvation lies in returning to an unplanned economy, free competition, and emphasis on liberty rather than on security.[29]

Underlying Hayek's argument is the premise that the freedoms of the individual (liberty) and free market competitive capitalism (the market) are identical, mutually interdependent and indivisible. Any movement away from them is a small step on the primrose path to totalitarianism. Hayek accepts the Orwell/Burnham thesis that fascism and communism have come to resemble one another more and more. But Orwell thought that it was Hayek's aim to show that the post-war attempt to introduce the welfare state and centralized planning into a liberal-democratic type of system also opens the floodgates to a totalitarian future.

Hayek argues that in order to ensure the wide consensus necessary for planning, the state will need to use the means of education and information to *create* a unity of purpose. As it replaces the hidden hand of the market – the ideal way of reconciling competing interest for Hayek – processes of planning will progressively spill over, from the strictly economic, into all other aspects of society. Planning must, for these reasons, become 'total' – and, pivoting, so to speak, on this double meaning of the word, Hayek says that democratic planning will thus become increasingly totalitarian. So, from the loftiest of motives, the attempt to supercede the market will have driven us slowly down the same path as the other 'totalitarianisms': 'The road to serfdom'. The similarities between this argument and Mrs Thatcher's charge of 'creeping state socialism' are obvious.

Orwell's response is to argue that there is little evidence of the old 'free market' existing, even if that were what we wanted, since the predominant trend in capitalist economies was *not* towards liberty, competition and choice but towards concentration and monopoly.

Considered in the way outlined here, we can see that

Orwell's ideas about the state evolved against a rich theoretical and political background, and engaged questions and issues which, more than ever, lie at the centre of contemporary preoccupations. This sketch of the evolution of his ideas should also help us to approach *Nineteen Eighty-Four* and Orwell's controversial position in the closing years of his life in a way significantly different from that which has become conventional wisdom on the left. *Nineteen Eighty-Four* was, of course, a work of imaginative fiction, a 'book of anticipations', not a text in political theory; and Orwell's characteristic mode was deeply antipathetic to anything overtly abstract, analytic or intellectual. (His overt anti-intellectualism is one of his most consistent, and least attractive qualities.) One cannot therefore expect to disinter fully-formed explanatory theories from Orwell's fictional and journalistic writing. On the other hand, Orwell was a deeply political animal and *Nineteen Eighty-Four*, right or wrong, was no mere exercise in literary utopianism. He was always thinking about the big, troubling questions of his time, trying to record and explain the contradictory pressures of being alive as a certain kind of socialist at one of the cross-roads of history. His work, therefore, gives evidence not of theory but of *thinking*.

It is clear, for example, that although *Nineteen Eighty-Four* had deep roots in Orwell's anti-Communism, his experience of Stalinism and his conviction of the revolution betrayed, its central impetus is not exclusively an attack on Soviet Communism, or even the failure of the promise of socialism, but something else: a general historical tendency in modern states – the collectivizing impetus and its fateful consequences – which he regarded as well-advanced in Communist and post-liberal capitalist societies alike. This led him to depict, not a country or even a continent, but a whole world system in the inexorable grasp of a new type of authoritarian system. Also, if it is true, on the one hand, that Orwell was driven by his experiences to the very edge (and some would argue over the edge) of 'cold warriorism' as the world sharply polarized in the great freeze of the 1940s, he was also one of the first people to stare the grim realities of the modern arms race in the face, and one of the first to see how the Cold War would strengthen and underpin the authoritarian tendencies in *both* major camps as an inevitable consequence of that mutual interdependence in the great dance of the dead we call deterrence.

What, then, of the general accuracy and cogency of his thinking on the question of the state? On a whole host of points Orwell's thinking can be shown to be interesting, insightful, even original, in some ways prophetic – but deeply flawed, one-sided, or just plain wrong. For example, convergence theory had its hey-day but quickly lost its explanatory power. Overemphasizing the common features arising from the process of technologically-advanced industrial development, it flattened out all pertinent the historical differences which are required to explain the linked but quite distinctive historical evolutions within the capitalist and communist 'families' of state.

Even more flawed was Orwell's isolation of the *power* principle from the whole complex of social relations which make up an actual, working social formation. Social relations have a reduced, abstracted, disembodied character in *Nineteen Eighty-Four*. The system works by the exercise of power and violence alone, as ends in themselves. This is a useful imaginative licence or exaggeration to make a polemical point, but of course it is not an adequate account of any society or state. Even the most totalitarian state we know is rooted in a complex of class and other social relations and cannot be adequately explained as a system of power alone. There is something, after all, to Isaac Deutscher's complaint of a lack of analytic or explanatory complexity in Orwell's thinking, in spite of the 'testament' – of a totalitarianism abstracted out of its embedding within a set of social relations or a well defined economic or class system. A criticism which led Deutscher, unfairly, to say that Orwell tells us 'how' totalitarianism works but not 'why' – an absence which leads, Deutscher argued, to a 'disembodied sadism'. This is something more than the usual, accurate complaint that, though Orwell used some of the language and concepts of Marxism, his analysis of the state was not deeply informed by it. The criticism of 'disembodied sadism' points to another, related, weakness: the concentration on *coercion* as the principle modality of the totalitarian state, and the absence of the equally puzzling and in some ways more lethal question of the consent of the masses to power under the 'normal' régime of the liberal democratic capitalist state.

All that and more having been conceded, one is also obliged – taking his thinking about the state in its wider context – to acknowledge how piercingly Orwell penetrates to the heart of some of the key questions for the left, not just in his time but in *ours*. The problem of the state and the linked questions of the disciplinary power of the state apparatuses and the bureaucracy is the great unsolved question both of actual-existing socialism *and* of democratic socialism itself. The great paradox remains: it is only through the intervention of the state that the great processes of capitalist accumulation and the market can be modified or transformed; but then the state itself becomes a weight of authority and power resting on the backs of the people, an instrument of their disciplining and exploitation, with a life of its own. The failure of the Soviet model, the disintegration of the reformist tradition and the monopolistic, corporatist and authoritarian tendencies within modern capitalism all, from their different and opposed points in the political spectrum, come back to rest on the unresolved enigma of the state.

Orwell may not have been correct to follow the line of thought which traced all these divergent paths to the same, mono-causal point of origin – totalitarianism; but at a less literal level he was not wrong in what he glimpsed of certain historical tendencies in the advanced societies of the world, and of the fatal incipient trend toward authoritarianism built deep into the very competitive process itself in post-liberal capitalist societies, which has become more, not less, apparent as the century advances. The *statist* character of socialism, in any of its actual-existing varieties – East and West – remains one of the greatest unsolved problems for the left, one of the greatest inhibitions to the renewal of socialism in our time – and the right's greatest, most persuasive weapon.

Orwell did not 'solve' the problem, either; but he pointed straight at it and hence enables us to learn from him – even, as Brecht put it, from his 'bad side'.

Notes

1 Raymond Williams, *Orwell*, London, 1971, p. 87.
2 Bernard Crick, *George Orwell: A Life*, Harmondsworth, 1982, p. 322, referred to hereafter as '*A Life*'. *Homage to Catalonia*, Harmondsworth, 1970, p. 29.
3 S. Orwell and I. Angus (eds.), *The Collected Essays, Journalism and Letters of George Orwell*, Vol. 1, Harmondsworth, 1970, p. 374, referred to hereafter as '*CEJL*'.
4 *A Life*, pp. 252-3.
5 *CEJL*, Vol. 2, p. 113.
6 *A Life*, p. 339.
7 Quoted in ibid., p. 329.
8 'Spilling the Spanish Beans' in *CEJL*, Vol. 1, pp. 306-7.
9 Isaac Deutscher, *Heretics and Renegades*, London, 1955, p. 43.
10 In J. Meyers (ed.), *George Orwell: The Critical Heritage*, London, 1975, p. 252.
11 Part of the text of a clarificatory press release based on notes prepared by Orwell and issued by Secker & Warburg, quoted in *A Life*, p. 566.
12 Frederic Warburg in J. Meyers (ed.), op.cit., p. 248.
13 *A Life*, p. 566
14 *CEJL*, Vol. 1, p. 302.
15 *CEJL*, Vol. 1, pp. 369-70.
16 *CEJL*, Vol. 2, pp. 40-1.
17 *CEJL*, Vol. 2, p. 162.
18 *CEJL*, Vol. 4, p. 192.
19 James Burnham, *The Managerial Revolution*, London, 1960, p. vi.
20 Ibid., p. 197.
21 *CEJL*, Vol. 4, p. 360.
22 Ibid., p. 361.
23 *CEJL*, Vol. 1, p. 414.
24 *CEJL*, Vol. 1, p. 419.
25 *CEJL*, Vol. 2, p. 295.
26 Ibid., p. 297.
27 *CEJL*, Vol. 4, pp. 85-6.
28 Ibid., pp. 92-3.
29 *CEJL*, Vol. 3, p. 143.

Christopher Norris

Language, Truth and Ideology: Orwell and the Post-War Left

'The limits of my language are the limits of my world' wrote Wittgenstein, drawing the conclusion that we had best not talk about matters too deep for our language properly to comprehend. George Orwell's thinking about language and politics might well provoke a similar reflection. The limits of that thinking are plain enough in the puzzles, perplexities and downright confusions which critics have often pointed out. More specifically, Orwell's homespun empiricist outlook – his assumption that the truth was just there to be told in a straightforward, common-sense way – now seems not merely naive but culpably self-deluding. Raymond Williams sums up this line of attack when he writes of Orwell's 'successful impersonation of the plain man who bumps into experience in an unmediated way and is simply telling the truth about it'.[1]

Williams's point is that this plain-man role was closely bound up with Orwell's failure of political and moral nerve. Claiming as he did to demystify politics, to speak up for the average 'decent' character against all those typecast leftist intellectuals, Orwell was unable to see beyond the blinkered common-sense ideology which shaped both his politics and his language. This role started out as a handy polemical device for debunking what he saw as the chronic bad faith of party-line Communists and self-styled 'left' intellectuals. It ended up as second nature, not only for Orwell but for a whole generation of collusive Cold-War ideologues, anxious to disguise their breakdown of political nerve by retreating into postures of cynical indifference. All this in the name of a painfully honest endeavour to simply *speak the truth* as perceived by a mind disabused of all fashionable creeds and ideologies.

Such, in rough outline, is the case against Orwell mounted by Williams and others who have sought to explain the Orwell phenomenon. It is an argument complicated by all manner of sharp ideological tensions and disagreements. Orwell cannot easily be lumped together with the run of socialist defectors, those (like many of the group around Auden) who simply switched sides like a new suit of clothes. He remained, if confusedly, a spokesman of the left, and one who could moreover look back and declare that every word he had ever written had been in the cause of 'democratic socialism'. This is what makes him such a difficult figure to come to terms with for anyone writing, like Williams, out of that same socialist tradition. It is not just the fact that Orwell was kidnapped by the forces of reaction, his style taken over as the basic currency of what E.P. Thompson has aptly called 'Natopolitan' doublethink. Neither is it simply that the 'good' bits of his writing – the occasional sharp-eyed socialist perceptions – need to be winnowed from the great mass of obscurantist rhetoric and prejudice. More urgent is the fact that Orwell arrived where he did by clinging to an attitude – call it the 'common-sense' outlook – which few British socialists are willing to break with, revise and refine it as they may. This tension remains deeply inscribed within the discourse of those who have attempted – like Williams and Thompson – to think their way beyond it.

Put simply, it is the issue between 'British' and 'Continental' styles of Marxist debate. On the one side stands the empiricist conviction that reality exists independently of the mind which perceives or interprets it. The unmediated *facts* of real-life experience are appealed to as a bedrock guarantee that we can, after all, tell the truth of that experience by sticking to straightforward accurate description and not letting words or ideologies get in the way. It is an argument familiar enough in the history of British commonsense responses to rationalism, scepticism and other such threats to decency and truth. With Orwell it takes a particularly bluff and dogmatic form. If you deny his position – so the rhetoric implies – then you line up effectively with those, like the craven state functionaries in *Nineteen Eighty-Four*, who treat the factual record of history as a mere 'text' to be erased and re-written at whatever latest whim of political command. Hanging on to past truths provides the one small hope that commonsense and decency may prevail over the powers of totalitarian mystification. Letting go of those truths is the mark of an intellectual treason linked to a last-ditch phase of political decline. It is a knock-down argument against those who would object that truth is not such a simple matter, or that Orwell's plain-dealing common-sense line produced a potent mythology all the more mischievous for its widespread appeal. Only a fool or a villain (or maybe a 'clever' left intellectual) would cling to some sophisticated theory of truth in the face of Orwell's arguments.

So much for the empiricist politics of language bound up with Orwell's characteristic style. It is a position – as his critics ruefully admit – which evokes certain powerful ready-made sympathies among readers brought up on the 'British ideology' of native common-sense empiricism. As the left has come to question that rooted tradition, so it has moved toward a more articulate critique of the ideas and assumptions that sustain it. Such is the strain of 'Continental' Marxist theory which Williams and others of a broadly New Left persuasion have increasingly taken into account.[2] To summarise its main lines of argument – as I shall over the next few paragraphs – is to show how they comprise, in effect, a very pointed critique of Orwellian thinking about language, politics and ideology. The desire to get a critical, diagnostic view of the culture which had thrown up such an ambiguous 'radical' spokesman was no doubt a part of William's motivation in turning to these new theoretical sources. But there remain certain unresolved problems and tensions. More specifically, there is a residual pull toward the native, 'commonsense' tradition which leaves Williams himself ambiguously placed with regard to that complex of ideological motives which he terms 'the Orwell character'. Williams cannot entirely divest his writing of the homespun individualist-empirical style which animates Orwell's prose. He can certainly acknowledge the weight of implied ideology which goes along with the resistance to theory in its cruder, neo-Orwellian forms. But the same resistance is at work in his own way of treating theoretical issues as part of an evolving social *experience*, a combination of documentary record and personal work-in-progress. And it is this deep ambivalence that gives such a sharply paradoxical edge to his dealings with Orwell over the past two decades.

The Orwellian malaise can be understood straightforwardly from the standpoint of an Althusserian Marxism secure in its own theoretical rigour. Orwell represents the confused and self-destructive motives of a liberal humanism finally run aground on its own bankrupt ideology. That the individual subject is a fiction sustained by that ideology, held in place by a process of imperative socialization, is a message not to be found in Orwell's writing. Or rather, it is there to be found easily enough, but in the guise of a warning against what *could happen* if 'democracy' gave way to the forces of totalitarian social control. Orwell, one could say, perceives the mechanism at work but projects it onto an alien and feared political 'system' by way of preserving his own deluded belief in the sufficiency of human (individual) dignity and truth. What *Nineteen Eighty-Four* thus documents – reading symptomatically, or 'against the grain' – is the nihilistic horror unleashed upon itself by an ideology wedded to the values of liberal humanism but forced to acknowledge their precisely *ideological* character. Winston Smith's revolt, like those of a long line of Orwell heroes, from Flory in *Burmese Days* to Bowling in *Coming Up For Air*, becomes a kind of grim working-out of the paradoxes attendant on humanist belief. It begins with a gesture of faith (however muted) in the autonomous individual as preserver of truth against the forces of political repression. It ends with the wholesale destruction of these hopes, with Winston's resistances broken down and his 'individual' voice wholly reinscribed within the slogans of a sovereign doublethink.

Althusserian Marxism holds that this is the enabling condition of all ideology.[3] The autonomous, self-acting 'subject' of humanist discourse is in fact a mere figment of the mystified political unconscious, a symbolic realm where relations of power are both inscribed and effectively disguised. The *illusion* of autonomy – of independent selfhood – is precisely what ideology requires if subjects are to keep their place without recognising what holds them there. Ideology is that which 'interpellates' the subject, inserts him or her into a dominant order of social relations. This order is ceaselessly produced and confirmed by the various agencies of power which define all available subject-positions. Thus language operates as the first and most basic socializing structure, consigning the 'individual' to a certain clearly-marked role within the discourse of family and institutional life. As the child learns its place *vis-à-vis* the authority of parental language, so the subject gains access to a larger realm of symbolic interaction and mediated social relations. The power thus acquired – the possession of language and, along with it, social identity – also entails an unconscious adaptation to the role laid down by that pervasive ideology. This ambiguous sense is inscribed within the very word 'subject': on the one hand the locus of (imaginary) selfhood and freedom, on the other the seat of all *subjection* as imposed by whatever socio-political constraints.

Such, in rough outline, is the core of Althusser's theoretical programme. He declares a total break with those varieties of 'humanist' thinking which assume that men and women create their own history by coming to understand the forces at work in that same complex but intelligible process. Such thinking, even when found in the early texts of Marx, betrays (according to Althusser) a strain of pre-critical ideology which it is the task of Marxist 'science' to expose and criticise. Only thus can theory lay claim to a wholly demystified (or 'scientific') knowledge whose concepts are sufficiently rigorous to validate its own production. Otherwise thought remains trapped within a purely imaginary order of discourse where subjects fail to recognise the ideological character of their own (spontaneous or common-sense) modes of understanding. This strain of 'theoretical anti-humanism' is the aspect of Althusser's philosophy which sets it most firmly apart from the mainstream of Western Marxist tradition. It entails what many would regard as a thoroughly disabling break with the ideal of potential human self-knowledge and fulfilment held out by the 'early' Marx. It denies that human agents have the power to comprehend their own present role in the 'overdetermined' structures of historical cause and effect. Again, it is the inveterate delusion of humanist ideology which places 'man', the self-conscious willing individual, at the centre of his or her own political destiny. Rather we must recognise, says Althusser, that 'man' is the product of a certain (mainly nineteenth-century) ideology, a figure whose imaginary essence is wholly bound up with that superannuated discourse.

Marx remained captive to that same delusion so long as he subscribed to a generalized notion of human fulfilment as the end-point and redemptive upshot of historical change. Then occurred what Althusser terms the 'epistemological break' in Marx's thinking, the decisive shift of analytical terrain which signalled the emergence of a genuine 'scientific' Marxism. Subjectivity must henceforth be conceived as an *effect* of certain partial and distorting ideologies, rather than a *cause* or self-sufficient ground of historical self-knowledge. To think otherwise is to collude with ideology by supposing that there might exist zones of private (or relatively private) experience untouched by the structures of political power. It is precisely in such activities – family, schooling, religion, etc. – that Althusser locates the more subtly coercive effects of social conditioning. These are the 'ideological state apparatuses' which keep subjectivity in place by holding out an illusory promise of autonomous self-fulfilment.

It is not hard to imagine how Orwell might have reacted, had he lived to witness this phenomenon of a Marxism which repudiates every last vestige of 'humanist' sentiment. And indeed, in E.P. Thompson's 'The Poverty Of Theory', we have what often reads like a latter-day Orwellian riposte, albeit on a level of argument more intricate and sustained than anything in Orwell.[4] My point is that Thompson takes over something of the plain-speaking, common-sense, empirical 'line', even while deploring what it led to in Orwell's case. His attack on Althusser is conducted in the name of a socialism which properly refuses to write off its own past history as so many episodes of 'ideological' misrecognition. For Thompson, the whole creaking edifice of Althusserian theory is nothing but a species of abstract mystification, a means of keeping *real* history and politics safely at bay. Worst of all, in Thompson's view, is the arrogant intellectualism that reserves 'scientific' knowledge to a tiny minority while consigning the great mass of socialist efforts and activities to the region of mere 'lived' ideology.

Thompson writes, of course, as a chronicler of working-class movements and events whose own best efforts have gone into reconstructing that active pre-history. He likewise argues against Althusser that individuals *can* achieve a consciousness of their historical situation, such that they can act collectively to change the institutions that shape it. To treat those institutions – whether schools, churches or labour movements – as mere emanations of a monolithic state ideology, is to throw away the entire history of working-class experience in a gesture of sovereign 'scientific' contempt. What is more, that 'science' – as Thompson most tellingly argues – amounts to little more than a congeries of empty abstractions resembling the worst excesses of scholastic philosophy. All in all – and in default of any convincing responses from the Althusserian camp – it may be said that Thompson's robust empiricism carries the day.

The Orwell comparison seems apt in two main respects. There is the air of a knock-down common-sense argument, an exasperated appeal to what *anyone* must recognise unless they are in the grip of some half-baked 'theory' or other. It is the tone of some of Orwell's best journalism, and also some of his worst – most prejudiced and obfuscating – tracts for the times. In Thompson, to be fair, the style is more tightly disciplined and never blurs an argument by taking a line of plain-man 'honest' bluster. What Thompson does is to turn against Orwell the same kind of powerful *tu quoque* argument that Orwell employed against his own targets. The following passage (from Thompson's essay 'Outside the Whale') shows the similarity clearly enough:

> Somewhere around 1948 the *real* whale of Natopolis swam along this way through the seas of the Cold War. After watching the splashing about of the disenchanted, with mean speculation in its small eyes, it opened its jaws and gulped – not, indeed, so that the intellectuals could sit in a dignified posture in its belly, but in order to add nourishment to its digestive system ... The Natopolitan intellectual was disabled by self-distrust no less than the Stalinist intellectual was disabled by fear of reverting to

bourgeois modes of thought ... The Western disenchanted
delivered themselves over, by their own hand and in confessional
mood, to McCarthyism, just as an earlier generation of
communist intellectuals had, by their capitulation before the
'infallible' party, delivered themselves over to Stalin and to Beria.[5]

This argument is Orwellian not only in symmetrically reversing
Orwell's charges, but also in the way it appeals to
straightforward honest self-evaluation as the means of seeing
through political fraud and doublethink. The politics and the
rhetoric are inseparable here. The force of Thompson's riposte
comes from his agreeing with Orwell to this extent at least; that
'intellectuals' (whether Stalinist or 'Natopolitan') are in no
good position to act wisely or learn from experience.

What Thompson chiefly objects to in Althusser's thinking is
the pitiless divorce between theory and experience, the latter
reduced to a mere reflex of prevailing ideology. The result of
such high-handed intellectualism is to sidetrack 'theory' into a
dead-end of arid dialectics, and at the same time to evoke
sinister echoes of a Stalinist dogmatism on matters of method
and principle. These charges, explicit in the essay on Althusser,
are also present more ambiguously in Thompson's writing
about Orwell. There, it is the Stalinist 'intellectuals' who are
seen as ideological dupes, victims of a passive conformist
mentality which precisely mirrors Orwell's brand of confused
reactionary sentiment. This amounts to a partial endorsement
of Orwell's anti-intellectualism. It is qualified, of course, by
Thompson's insistence that Orwell got everything upside down
when he came to draw the lessons of his own political
experience. What Thompson *cannot* do, on the other hand, is
take the line so readily available to Marxists of an Althusserian
persuasion: that is, the argument that Orwell's blinkered
ideology – his commonsense empiricist stance – was precisely
what led to his chronic political confusions.

Hence the nagging problem that Orwell presents to thinkers
working in the broad tradition of British socialist politics. He
turned against that tradition while persistently claiming to
speak for it; took over its most rooted assumptions in the
service of antagonistic aims; and produced, in short, a

point-for-point travesty of socialist argument. This confusion is worse confounded by the marked convergence between Orwell's critique of totalitarian thinking and the case which Thompson and others bring against Marxist intellectuals like Althusser. The appendix on Newspeak in *Nineteen Eighty-Four* is precisely an account of how language 'interpellates' the subject by dictating his or her role within a clearly-marked order of juridical limits to the power of independent thought. The destruction of freedom begins and ends – as Orwell repeatedly insists – in the more or less systematic corruption of language. Winston Smith's short-lived revolt is finally snuffed out when he comes to accept the mind-bending paradoxes of Newspeak. That the individual can resist such pressures – hold out for decency and truth – is a hope which the novel in the end shows up as sadly deluded. Thompson might take it as a warning example of what intellect may get up to when divorced from the empirical checks and remembrances of communal history. Certainly this is where Orwell places the one tiny hope of sanity redeemed. Hence Winston's efforts to recover the past through scraps of evidence and folk-memory as yet undestroyed by the wholesale re-writing of official history. But this revolt in the name of empiricist wisdom ends up in abject failure as the forces of ideological coercion reassert their hold. Truth-to-experience can muster small resistance against a state 'apparatus' that controls the very terms by which to make sense of 'experience' and 'truth'. There is no line of exit from *Nineteen Eighty-Four* that doesn't lead back to a message of out-and-out cynicism and despair. This thoroughly undercuts any remaining belief in the strengths and virtues of a 'common-sense' opposed to the abstract machinations of political theory.

Perry Anderson has offered a persuasive account of how this impasse developed within the broad tradition of Western Marxism. It began, he argues, with the chronic divorce between theory and practical politics imposed by the beleaguered situation of left-wing intellectuals in a deeply entrenched liberal-bourgeois culture. This led to an increasing concentration on issues of method and principle, as opposed to the kind of strategic activist thinking which might have issued in a genuine revolutionary politics. 'Where Marx had successively moved from philosophy to economics to politics in his own studies, Western Marxism inverted his route.'[6] Theoretical questions – notably those of epistemology and aesthetics – came to monopolize the high ground of Western Marxist debate. In Anderson's words:

> Major economic analyses of capitalism, within a Marxist framework, largely petered out after the Great Depression; political scanning of the bourgeois state dwindled away after the silencing of Gramsci; strategic discussion of the roads to a realizable socialism disappeared almost entirely. What increasingly took their place was a revival of *philosophical* discourse proper, itself centred on questions of method – that is, more epistemological than substantive in character.[7]

And the upshot of this development, Anderson argues, was a state of theoretical deadlock within the discourse of Western Marxist reason. This had to do with the rival claims of *subject* and *structure*, or – more generally – 'humanist' and 'scientific' modes of explanation. The conflict was signalled in Marx's own writings as a matter of shifting emphases. On the one hand texts like the *Communist Manifesto* laid stress on the ways in which human agents could engage collectively in the class-struggle and thus influence the historical course of events. On the other, such writings as *A Contribution to the Critique of Political Economy* insisted that priority be given to causal explanations in the structural mode, chief among them the conflict between 'forces of production' and 'relations of production'. The one line of thought leads directly to a humanist Marxism founded on the notion of man as the more-or-less *conscious* or willing agent of his own historical destiny. The other renounces such residual elements of 'bourgeois' individualism in the name of a scientific theory opposed to all humanist ('ideological') motives. It is this latter tendency which receives its most extreme formulation in Althusser's structuralist reading of Marx.

Anderson finds this problem epitomised in the finally abortive project of Sartre's *Critique of Dialectical Reason*. In his prefatory essay ('Search For A Method') Sartre focuses on the question: what kinds of knowledge can we bring to bear nowadays on the task of reconstructing an individual life-history? His proposal involves a complex assemblage of ideas from Marxism, psychoanalysis and a refined, socialized form of existentialist philosophy. This amounts to an assertion that classical Marxism is inadequate, as it stands, to comprehend a life in all the vivid contingencies of actual, historical experience. As Sartre famously put it, Paul Valéry may have been a petty-bourgeois French intellectual, but not every petty-bourgeois French intellectual was Paul Valéry. Socio-economic modes of explanation had a real but limited efficacy. They were concerned with large-scale structural determinants which had little bearing on the lived project which made up an individual 'case'. Such theories required the supplementary evidence of a knowledge more finely attuned to existentialist psychology. Only thus could Marxism avoid the charge of abusing its explanatory powers in pursuit of a crudely reductive determinist creed.

Such was the argument of Sartre's polemical preface. But the major part of the *Critique* is devoted to its other, more 'structuralist' project: to describing, that is, the complex *ensembles* of socio-economic relationship which make up the objective conditions of human existence. The 'Search for a Method' had pointed toward biography – albeit a new and sophisticated form of biography – as the touchstone of historical understanding. In the *Critique* proper, as Anderson describes it, Sartre aimed to provide 'a philosophical account of the "elementary formal structures" of any possible history, or a theory of the general mechanisms of the construction and subversion of social groups.'[8] The two projects were intended to generate a unified totalizing method, a synthesis of Marxist explanatory science and existentialist biography. In the event this ambition failed to materialize and Sartre never produced the promised second volume of the *Critique*. What followed was the fashionable swing toward structuralism, a theory which – in Anderson's view – abandoned any genuine attempt to arrive at a workable mediation between subject and structure, experience and knowledge. 'The unresolved difficulties and deadlocks within Marxist theory, which structuralism promised to transcend, were never negotiated in detail within this rival space.'[9] The result was another, more extreme disjunction between reified 'structures' on the one hand, and anarchic subjectivity on the other.

Anderson's diagnosis is open to question in its reading of the current post-structuralist predicament. Nevertheless it offers a useful hold for understanding what exactly it is, in Orwell's thinking about language and politics, that continues to vex his socialist commentators. The painful antinomy of 'subject' and 'structure' is present with a vengeance in Orwell's writing, not least in the confused philosophy of language that runs through his fiction and journalistic essays alike. Anderson undoubtedly puts a finger on this same problem when he argues against the structuralist habit of adopting the Saussurian language-paradigm by way of explaining all manner of cultural phenomena.[10] The relation between *langue* and *parole* is, he writes, 'a peculiarly aberrant compass for plotting the diverse positions of structure and subject in the world outside language'.[11] This because the terms of Saussure's distinction create a polarized contrast between the long-term stability of language-as-system (*langue*) and the short-term, volatile character of speech (*parole*). Neither provides a very apt analogy for the complex, many-levelled interplay of time-scales which operates elsewhere in human society. Linguistic structures, Anderson points out, 'have an exceptionally low coefficient of mobility' compared with other social institutions. And this structural immobility of language has its obverse in the sheer *inventiveness* of speech, the freedom of the subject to improvise at will within the broadest constraints of meaning and context. Yet this very freedom, as Anderson sees it, is 'curiously inconsequential: that is, its effects on the structure in return are virtually nil'.[12] In short, the nemesis of structuralist thinking is a constant vacillation between unworkable extremes of determinist rigour and subjectivist illusion.

Of course I am not claiming Orwell as some kind of homespun proto-structuralist stumbling toward the light. His bluff empirical stance was all too proof against anything resembling a worked-out theoretical 'position'. Yet that very desire to stick with the facts of commonsense experience betrayed Orwell into a version of the same double-bind that Anderson so shrewdly diagnoses. Its effects are most evident in his various pronouncements on the relation between language, politics and ideology. Basically Orwell subscribes to the straightforward empiricist view that language in a normal, healthy condition simply hands over the raw stuff of experience. Abstractions are bad (like clichés and 'dead' metaphors) if they get in the way of this primary purpose. 'What is above all needed is to let the meaning choose the word, and not the other way around.'[13] Or again: 'probably it is better to put off using words as long as possible and get one's meaning as clear as one can through pictures and sensations.'[14] It is an attitude familiar enough from the long tradition of British common-sense philosophy. No ideas but in things, or in words that retain as much as possible of the lively impressions which summon them to mind. Hitting off the right form of words is simply a matter of hunting around until the language fits whatever you want to describe.

As Orwell sees it, the main threat to this healthy state of language is the habit of letting *words choose meanings*, or relaxing the vigilant referential grip which prevents language from conjuring up phantom realities. Such is the fundamental ethics of style which Orwell expounds in 'Politics and the English Language'. The writer's plain duty is to *think without words* as far as possible, and then to make sure that they do an adequate job by simply handing over the sense of what he thinks. Abstraction is a sure sign that language is getting in the way. As Orwell puts it:

> When you think of something abstract you are more inclined to use words from the start, and unless you make a conscious effort to prevent it, the existing dialect will come rushing in and do the job for you, at the expense of blurring or even changing your meaning.[15]

That is, the writer sets out with a clear enough sense of what he or she *means* to say, and then works hard to prevent language from distorting what those thoughts turn out to *mean*. The problems with this are more than just a matter of local ambiguity ('meaning' = either 'sense' or 'intention'). What exactly can Orwell have in mind when he conjures up a pre-linguistic stratum of innocent, original thought as yet untouched by the malign influence of words? How can the writer's 'meaning' begin to take shape before thought becomes intelligible to itself in the process of achieving adequate expression? These are crude formulations, but nowhere near as crude – or hopelessly confused – as Orwell's way of stating the case.

What creates this confusion is the same sharp dichotomy between *langue* and *parole* that Anderson detects in the structuralist paradigm. On the one hand language is a set-up of prevailing significations which threaten to invade and disfigure whatever one wants to say. 'The existing dialect', as Orwell puts it, 'will come rushing in and do the job for you.' On the other, mere honesty requires that the writer 'make a conscious effort to prevent it', opposing his or her vigilantly truthful *parole* to the *langue* of ideological mystification. To this way of thinking there is no middle-ground between language as an alien structure of ready-made, mindless clichés and language as a purely voluntarist expression of the individual will-to-resist. And the upshot of this drastic dualism, as Anderson argues, is a failure to conceive how language could possibly withstand the drift toward systematic reification. For there is no real effect of *parole* upon *langue*, such that the writer's individual efforts might exercise some long-term influence for the good. The 'structural immobility' of language at large is indifferent to the great multiplicity of speech-acts whose conditions it determines, in an abstract way, without their being able to reciprocally act back upon it. As Anderson so rightly observes, 'Even the greatest writers, whose genius has influenced whole cultures, have typically altered the language relatively little.'[16] What structuralism fails to reckon with is this basic asymmetry in the relation between *langue* and *parole*. To extrapolate directly from language to politics is to end up with a stark confrontation of determinist and voluntarist creeds.

Orwell's thinking about language is closely bound up with his reading of political history. 'Prose literature as we know it', he writes, 'is the product of rationalism, of the Protestant centuries, of the autonomous individual.'[17] There is a morality of style, Orwell insists, and its truth-telling virtues have their own very specific historical sources and conditions. The 'autonomous individual' is the last fragile hope that language can be rescued from the traps and snares of collective ideology.

(One recalls, in this connection, that 'The Last Man In Europe' was Orwell's first working title for *Nineteen Eighty-Four*.) The empiricist matching-up of words and experience requires a well-nigh heroic effort of individual will if the untruths of language are not to insinuate their hold. 'Unless spontaneity enters at some point or another, literary creation is impossible, and language itself becomes ossified.'[18] Spontaneity (or sincerity) is the precondition for cutting through the swathes of conventional verbiage and simply telling things as they are. This has been the attitude of a long line of literary critics, from Dr Johnson to F.R. Leavis. Catherine Belsey sums it up as the doctrine of 'expressive realism', and describes it as follows:

> This is the theory that literature reflects the *reality* of experience as it is perceived by one (especially gifted) individual, who *expresses* it in a discourse which enables other individuals to recognize it as true.[19]

Orwell's morality of style conforms closely enough to this general description. What sets it apart from the mainstream of liberal-humanist ideology is Orwell's attempt to think out the consequences in political terms. This attempt may have ended in a state of deadlocked despair, but its lessons are pointedly relevant still.

Orwell never faced up to the deep contradictions in his thinking about language and politics. The Orwellian persona was a means of holding them at bay, warding off doubts and perplexities by an appeal to straightforward common-sense knowledge. A bluff disregard of theoretical problems has always been the hallmark of that 'English' ideology which thinkers from the 'other', Continental tradition have treated with alternating wonder and despair. Unconsciousness, as Basil de Selincourt remarked, is the great virtue of the English, though also – he might have added – the source of much ideological mystification. In Orwell unconsciousness is raised as a guard against the kind of critical self-knowledge that might create problems for his homespun empiricist outlook. Yet the symptoms of that repression are there to be read in the twists and complications of Orwell's writing, fiction and journalism alike. I have suggested how they bear on a diagnostic reading of *Nineteen Eighty-Four* and his essays on language and politics. It remains to analyse more specifically the relation between Orwell's political ideas and the blind-spots of mystified ideology to which they give rise in his texts.

A good case in point is 'Politics Vs Literature', an essay on Swift which Orwell published in 1946. It is a remarkable piece in several ways, not least for its apparently unconscious bearing on Orwell's own predicament as author and ideologue. Politically, says Orwell, 'Swift was one of those people who are driven into a sort of perverse Toryism by the follies of the progressive party of the moment.'[20] If Swift can hardly be labelled 'left', still he is a kind of Tory anarchist, 'despising authority while disbelieving in liberty'. The generalized misanthropy of *Gulliver's Travels* is strangely allied to a passionate defence of individual rights against the manifold abuses of state power. It makes sense to think of Swift as 'rebel and iconoclast', though only if we recognise the perverse element of right-wing 'totalitarian' thinking which went along with his confused populist sympathies.

Up to this point Orwell's version is pretty much in line with standard critical thinking on the matter of Swift's ambivalent politics. There are two things, however, which work to complicate Orwell's reading. First is the fact that he tends to equate Swift with Gulliver, assuming (for instance) that the latter's admiration for the cold, calculating Houyhnhnms may safely be imputed to Swift himself and called upon as evidence of his political views. Second – and connected with this – is Orwell's doubtless unconscious investment in a version of the same contradictory ideology that he discovers in Swift. With Orwell likewise, there is a strain of 'perverse Toryism' produced – as he wants us to believe – by honest disenchantment with 'the follies of the progressive party of the moment'. Orwell sees Swift as a problematic case, a writer forced into tragic isolation by his keen understanding of the follies and corruptions of his day. What he fails to grasp is the extent to which his own reading both mirrors and intensifies the latent contradictions in Swift.

Thus Orwell can write, as if stating the obvious, of 'the

"Reason" which he [Swift as well as Gulliver] so admires in the Houyhnhnms.' There is no allowance here for the way in which Swift – like all inventive satirists – manipulates his fictional narrators so as to keep a firm distance between their views and his. By collapsing that distance Orwell is giving voice to the same ideology of 'expressive realism' that determines the logic of all his thinking on language and politics. He is more clear-sighted at the outset of his essay, where the point is made that Gulliver is a far from unitary 'character', his viewpoint shifting drastically in the course of the narrative from down-to-earth, homely practicality to a well-nigh imbecile misanthropic hatred. 'These inconsistencies', Orwell remarks, 'are forced upon Swift by the fact that Gulliver is there chiefly to provide a contrast.'[21] Quite simply, it is necessary – in the light of Swift's satiric design – that Gulliver should appear sensible in Part I and increasingly erratic or unbalanced thereafter. But this formalist attitude in Orwell turns out to have sharp limits. 'Whenever Gulliver is not acting as a stooge there is a sort of continuity in his character, which comes out especially in his resourcefulness and his observation of physical detail.'[22] This supposed continuity, or 'depth' of character, is the source of Orwell's implicit belief that Gulliver speaks for Swift in admiring the Houyhnhnms and their inhuman socio-political arrangements. And what precisely is the 'Reason' that Swift so admires? Orwell defines it as consisting for the most part in 'either common sense – i.e. acceptance of the obvious and contempt for quibbles and abstractions – or absence of passion and superstition.'[23] Swift assumes in short that 'we know all that we need to know already, and merely use our knowledge incorrectly.'

The trouble with this, as Orwell goes on to argue, is that it leaves no room for rational disagreement, since the truth is always self-evident to those with sense enough to see it. The Houyhnhnms have reached 'the highest stage of totalitarian organization', the stage where dissent is simply unthinkable and reason coincides perfectly with public opinion. Swift, according to Orwell, approves of this kind of thing 'because among his many gifts neither curiosity nor good nature was included'. But this is to ignore what most readers perceive readily enough: that Gulliver's attitude in Book IV is by no means endorsed by Swift, but represents a crazy extreme of cynical paranoia. Orwell concedes that 'Gulliver's horror of the Yahoos, together with his recognition that they are the same kind of creature as himself, contains a logical absurdity.'[24] What he won't acknowledge is that Swift may be manipulating Gulliver's (and the reader's) responses with a view to undermining precisely that absurd misanthropic over-reaction. And it is here, one suspects, that Orwell's reading becomes skewed by his own disenchantment and general dim view of the hopes for political progress. The despairing message has to come from Swift's real-life experience, rather than from Gulliver's merely fictional awareness.

This essay drives home the same grim conclusion, the same paralysis of intellect and will, as afflicts Winston Smith and the other protagonists of Orwell's novels. Swift becomes a spokesman for the rock-bottom cynical commonsense which cleaves to the 'facts' of unmediated experience and admits of nothing beyond them except the contortions of 'totalitarian' intellect. Most readers will see that Book IV of *Gulliver's Travels* is a species of elaborate narrative frame-up which exposes the absurdity of Gulliver's choice between 'Houyhnhnm' reason on the one hand and 'Yahoo' common humanity on the other. Orwell is intermittently aware that the case has been framed in a highly prejudicial manner.

> In comparison with what are the Yahoos disgusting? Not with the Houyhnhnms, because at this time Gulliver has not seen a Houyhnhnm. It can only be in comparison with himself, i.e. with a human being.[25]

There may be something odd, this concedes, in taking so lofty a view of human values and reason as to exclude all humanity from properly claiming to possess them. Yet this is the logical absurdity that Orwell wants to attribute to *Swift*, rather than seeing Book IV of the *Travels* as a brilliant device for exposing such drastic and fallacious choices of attitude. In the end Orwell is unable to conceive of any path between brutish 'popular' instinct and the dictates of pure 'totalitarian' reason. It is the same stark dichotomy in *Nineteen Eighty-Four* that separates the mindless existence of the proles from the cynical acquiescence of Party 'intellectuals' like O'Brien.

What this finally comes down to is Orwell's deep-grained empiricist conviction: that intellect can only corrupt and distort the certitudes of common-sense knowledge. Yet common sense itself proves incapable of rising above the errors and delusions of unreflective experience. Houyhnhnm society has reached that stage, as Orwell describes it, where 'conformity has become so general that there is no need for a police force'. The habits of unreflective thought have been so bedded down into common-sense lore that the Houyhnhnm language has no word signifying 'opinion'. Within such a total ideology there is simply no room for dissenting views. The Houyhnhnms represent all that is rational and virtuous, while the Yahoos serve as convenient foils by embodying the lowest, i.e. the 'human', aspects of animal nature. Orwell was to make his own use of this topsy-turvy logic in *Animal Farm*, published just a few months after the essay on Swift. He was evidently drawn by its capacity to turn the moral tables on anyone claiming superior insight on behalf of whatever ideological creed. But along with the manipulative skill of Orwell's satire there emerges a perverse and self-defeating logic born of political despair. Thus he remarks of *Gulliver*,

> One feels that all these adventures, and all these changes of mood, could have happened to the same person, and the inter-connexion between Swift's political loyalties and his ultimate despair is one of the most interesting features of the book.[26]

This constant equating of Gulliver and Swift – thus muffling some of Swift's most effective satirical points – is symptomatic of Orwell's confusedly personal reading. The essay is a curious mixture of blindness and insight, most revealing as regards Orwell's motives in writing it where it seems most perversely off the point about Swift.

I have argued a connection between Orwell's politics, his ideas about language and the narrative forms in which those two strands of thought were closely intertwined. I have also suggested that Orwell's predicament is that of a peculiarly 'English' ideology forced up against its limits by a last-ditch adherence to empiricist habits of mind. This is why he remains very much on the agenda for Marxist critical debate. What Orwell represents – albeit in a distorted perspective – is that clash between 'common sense' and 'theory' which thinkers like Raymond Williams have striven to surmount, or at least to articulate more clearly. With Orwell it takes the form of a desperate allegiance to factual self-evidence, along with the grim recognition that 'facts' can be manipulated out of existence by those with the power to impose their own versions of truth. From the standpoint of 'Continental' Marxism his case can be diagnosed as displaying all the blindspots and irrational regressions of empiricist ideology. Williams registers the force of this argument when he writes of Orwell's plain-man, common-sense style: his air of perpetually 'bumping up' against the straightforward *facts* of experience. Yet the commitment to empiricism – as a mode of historical experience, if not as a full-blown ideology – continues to exercise a rival claim in Williams's dealings with Continental Marxism. For him, as for Thompson, it acts as a constant qualifying check on the powers of theoretical abstraction.

It is this, perhaps, as much as his renegade politics, that constitutes the standing provocation of Orwell's 'case' in the context of present socialist debate. In *Politics And Letters* Williams says that he now finds Orwell just about unreadable, his writing – as well as his politics – so repugnant as almost to resist further comment.[27] The causes of that reaction, in one of Orwell's most acute commentators, make up a whole complex chapter in the history of post-war British socialism.

Notes

1 Raymond Williams, *Politics And Letters*, London, 1979, p. 385.
2 See for instance Raymond Williams, *Politics And Literature*, Oxford, 1977.
3 See Louis Althusser, *For Marx*, (tr. Ben Brewster), London, 1969.
4 E.P. Thompson, *The Poverty of Theory and Other Essays*, London, 1978.
5 E.P. Thompson, 'Outside The Whale', in ibid., pp. 1-33, p. 19.
6 Perry Anderson, *In The Tracks of Historical Materialism*, London, 1983, p. 17.
7 Ibid., 16.
8 Jean-Paul Sartre, *Critique of Dialectical Reason* (tr. Alan Sheridan-Smith),

London, 1976, p. 36.

9 Anderson, op.cit., p. 55.

10 Ibid., pp. 32-55.

11 Ibid., p. 44.

12 Ibid., p. 44.

13 'Politics And The English Language', in S. Orwell and I. Angus (eds.), *The Collected Journalism and Letters of George Orwell*, Vol. 3, Harmondsworth, 1970, pp. 156-70, p. 168. Referred to hereafter as '*CEJL*'.

14 Ibid., p. 169.

15 Ibid., p. 168-9.

16 Anderson, op.cit., p. 44.

17 'The Prevention of Literature', in *CEJL*, Vol. 4, pp, 81-95, p. 92.

18 Ibid., p. 95.

19 Catherine Belsey, *Critical Practice*, London, 1980, p. 7.

20 'Politics vs Literature: an Examination of *Gulliver's Travels*', in *CEJL*, Vol. 4, pp. 241-61, p. 243.

21 Ibid., p. 242.

22 Ibid., p. 242.

23 Ibid., p. 247.

24 Ibid., p. 254.

25 Ibid., pp. 254-5.

26 Ibid., p. 243.

27 Williams, *Politics And Letters*, op.cit., p. 392.

Antony Easthope

Fact and Fantasy in 'Nineteen Eighty-Four'

> *Nineteen Eighty-Four*, after two decades in which it was read with the utmost seriousness as a political prophecy, is now taking its place … as a science-fiction story.
>
> Patrick Parrinder[1]

When Peter Sutcliffe, the Yorkshire Ripper, was convicted, the BBC showed footage shot through the front window of a car as it ranged at night through the backstreets of Bradford, Barnsley and Leeds. In Orwell's *Nineteen Eighty-Four* Winston Smith sees a similar townscape:

> Were there always these vistas of rotting nineteenth-century houses, their sides shored up with baulks of timber, their windows patched with cardboard and their roofs with corrugated iron, their crazy garden walls sagging in all directions? And the bombed sites where the plaster dust swirled in the air and the willow-herb straggled over heaps of rubble …[2]

Britain in 1984 is like that, ravaged not by war but by five years of Thatcherite recession and deindustrialisation. These are the landscapes not so much of Dorking and Basingstoke but of Bolton, Manchester and Rochdale.

Fact and Truth in 'Nineteen Eighty-Four'

Nineteen Eighty-Four has sold over eleven million copies round the world. Published by Secker and Warburg in 1949, it has

263

gone through forty-one impressions since appearing as a
Penguin in 1954. More than any other novel this century –
certainly more than any English novel – this book has come to
pervade general consciousness. '1984', 'doublethink', 'Big
Brother is watching you' have become shorthand figures,
collective images for the fear of bureaucratic, state-controlled
totalitarianism.

Nineteen Eighty-Four is very widely known and almost
everyone seems to think they know what it is and what it says.
One way to begin to unpack the text is to discriminate between
fact and fantasy, to move forward from reading the text as a
discourse of knowledge to reading it as fantasy in a certain
fictional mode (novelistic realism), as literary discourse for
which truth or falsity is no longer the most applicable
criterion.

Considered as a prediction of the actual political situation in
1984 AD the book has sometimes, but not always, prophesied
correctly. Right that the world would be divided into three
blocks (Soviet, Chinese, North-Atlantic), each living under
continuous threat of war; right also that the purpose of the
Cold War is not really a matter of classic nineteenth-century
competition for markets, but not quite right to regard war as
mainly a means to eat up the surplus of consumer goods
(rather than as politically motivated in the military-industrial
complexes, East and West). Right that the Cold War functions
ideologically for the international benefit of the super-states
'to preserve the special mental atmosphere that a hierarchical
society needs' (p. 161). Dead wrong that the ruling groups used
atomic weapons for a while after 1945 but stopped when they
saw that such use 'would mean the end of organized society,
and hence of their own power' (p. 158).

Of course Britain in 1984 is not a totalitarian dictatorship.
But in the past five years it has moved closer towards that
formation and away from democracy. By letting unemployment rise from around one to four and a half million (the real
figure), Thatcher's government has strengthened the hierarchic
and undemocratic power of capital (both state and private). In
the past five years the army and police have been powerfully
reinforced and now sometimes act in coalition: on 30 October
1983, in an unprecedented step, some women at Greenham

Common were *arrested* by soldiers.[3] Special riot police in shiny new visors now enforce shiny new laws against trade union activity. Central government has effectively taken over the powers of the regionally elected local authorities and is now moving to abolish the county authorities. Poverty has increased. While in 1979 11.5 million people were living below the official poverty line the figure had risen to 15 million by 1981.[4] Under Thatcherism Britain in 1984 is getting more seedy, more run-down, more unhappy, a zone symbolised by silent people waiting in lengthening queues for the bus, the post office, the hospital, the dole. Five years have witnessed the explicable death of social-democratic England.[5]

As Orwell foresaw, secrecy and surveillance have increased. In Britain freedom of information is restricted by the use of D Notices, the Official Secrets Act, laws regarding libel and *sub judice*. Although the television screen does not spy on us, Orwell was right to anticipate the central importance of television in manipulating public opinion. A secret committee of the BBC, the Director News and Current Affairs Committee, meets every Tuesday morning in Room 7082 at Lime Grove to fix the political line to be followed in news broadcasts.[6] During the past few years the state has greatly extended its capacity to monitor individual behaviour electronically, for example, by listening to transatlantic phone calls. And yes, we do now generally use a biro, 'an ink-pencil' (p. 9) rather than a pen with a nib.

Totalitarianism

To read *Nineteen Eighty-Four* for its accuracy and inaccuracy as a political prediction – look here on this picture (Orwell's account) and on this (the world in 1984) – is to read the text referentially, as a matter of facts proved true and false. But traditionally there is another, more general level at which a text may be read as truth. For Aristotle the historian differs from the poet in that the historian tells us about facts and 'what has happened' while the poet tells us 'the kinds of things that might happen' at a level of typicality.[7] Read as a text affirming some general truth about reality, *Nineteen Eighty-Four* can be seen as anticipating and in some way leading to the development during and after the 1950s of a particular area in litical theory (I would reserve the term political science), one which identifies both communism and fascism as *totalitarian*. In 1965, in a chapter called 'The General Characteristics of Totalitarian Dictatorship' C.J. Friedrich and Z. Brzezinski list six features of this form of society: 'an ideology, a single party typically led by one man, a terroristic police, a communications monopoly, a weapons monopoly, and a centrally directed economy.'[8] S.E. Finer later defines 'the totalitarian type' of state according to two features: 'that the entire society is politicised' and that 'the viewpoints which so politicise it are reduced to one alone, from which no dissidence is tolerated.'[9] On this basis the Soviet system under Stalin during the 1930s and Hitler's Nazi Germany can be equated.

Nineteen Eighty-Four aligns itself with this conception, explicitly so in the section which contains Emmanuel Goldstein's 'The Theory and Practice of Oligarchical Collectivism' (pp. 151-174). Noting that the conditions of life in the three super-states of Oceania, Eurasia and Eastasia are very much the same, Goldstein affirms that 'Everywhere there is the same pyramidal structure, the same worship of a semi-divine leader, the same economy existing by and for continuous warfare' (p. 160). The rest of the novel seeks to illustrate this view in detail, for instance by making Goldstein himself a composite scapegoat, both the Stalinist's Trotsky and the Nazi's jew.

As a concept 'totalitarianism' depends more upon ideology than upon science. As Leonard Shapiro says, 'Perhaps as a concept totalitarianism is elusive, hard to define, liable to abuse by the demagogue, and, if wrongly used, a source of confusion when we are trying to find our way through the maze of the many forms which a polity can assume.'[10] His qualifying 'perhaps' is over-cautious. Firstly, because any definition of totalitarianism must efface major social differences between specific examples, even when they may seem as close as National Socialism in Germany and Soviet Communism during the 1930s (for example, while capital was state-owned in the USSR it remained largely privately-owned in Germany). Secondly, because by abstracting and universalising a political system the concept of totalitarianism makes it impossible to understand political effects in terms of specific historical causes, causes as diverse as the development of Stalinist Russia out of Tsarist absolutism and of Nazi Germany from the liberal democracy of the Weimar Republic. Accordingly, Goldstein's 'Theory of Oligarchical Collectivism', despite its satirical force, is pretty short on explanations. It is left for O'Brien to say that it all comes about because 'The Party seeks power entirely for its own sake ... The object of power is power' (pp. 211, 212). And he is not so much anticipating Foucault as reviving Hobbes: the general inclination of mankind is a 'restlesse desire of Power after power.'[11]

Liberalism

The political theory of totalitarianism is deeply penetrated by an ideological commitment to liberal-humanism, as evidenced in the way it works to hypostasise and privilege the liberal-democratic system as *summum bonum* and ideal type of government. Liberal democracy is complicit with the totalitarianism it would condemn in that it supports the undemocratic structures of corporate capitalism and state paternalism. As usual, freedom for the individual really means freedom from social control for the private corporation. Perhaps an extreme instance this, yet no discourse can wholly escape ideology.

A number of somewhat unrelated areas of recent theoretical work, including the Anglo-American philosophic critique of empiricism, the philosophy of science since Kuhn, contributions by Althusser in historical materialism and, within a contrasted problematic, by Derrida, can be summarised, however drastically, in a single statement: since the distinction between 'science' and 'ideology' is not absolute but relative, there can be no corresponding, pure distinction between the cognitive and affective effects of a text, between the text as fact and the text as fantasy. While this may work to the disadvantage of political theory (disablingly so, I would have thought, in the case of the theory of totalitarianism), it works to the advantage of Orwell's novel. It can and has been read in terms of a discourse of knowledge, as a political tract or pamphlet aiming to give access to a reality beyond itself. But it is hard to know what one is doing in trying to *refute* or bring evidence against *Nineteen Eighty-Four*. And if it were compelled to survive as a text only within the discourse of political theory it wouldn't last very long.

Nineteen Eighty-Four is subtitled 'A Novel'. Among other things this means that whatever is read as the text's assertions at the level of knowledge (and no text can wholly escape these even if it is only the assertion that Sophia is the capital of Bulgaria), they will be 'enacted' or 'dramatised' or 'realised' or 'supplemented' by a fictional narration such that these assertions become re-installed within the category of ideology rather than science. In *Nineteen Eighty-Four* the novel's abstractable and discursive 'statement' about totalitarianism becomes inseparable from the pseudo-biography of Winston Smith, his love affair with Julia, his betrayal by O'Brien. Inevitably this fictional narrative becomes dream-like, a vehicle for fantasy.

An argument that opens up at this point is whether the device and artifice of the literary text defamiliarises ideology or naturalises it. While Althusser claims that such artifice enables us to 'perceive' ideology, Macherey tends to argue that it naturalises and neutralises ideological contradictions. I suspect that the literary text does both at once, according to its own specific economy, in a simultaneous movement that is ultimately self-cancelling; I am sure that it is up to a progressive reading to make visible the foundations on which the ideological assertions of a text depend.

Certainly the explicit tendency of *Nineteen Eighty-Four* is to affirm a liberal notion of the freedom of the individual against all totalitarianism. It aims to do so both thematically, in discussion of the nature of reality, subjectivity, and language, and formally, by offering itself to be read as a realist text. And yet (one reason why it is such a good novel?) this liberalism is worked through so thoroughly in the novelistic forms of dialogue, narrative and the dramatisation of character, and brings into play such a range of heterogeneous discourses that the effect of the text – at least in this present reading – is to undermine precisely the liberal assertion it proposes for itself.

Nineteen Eighty-Four is committed to advocating and defining, sometimes even hysterically, a view of human nature. Or rather one view of human nature against another. Against O'Brien's Hobbesian apology for tyranny the book passionately and explicitly proclaims a notion of self-conscious individuality as definition of man and source of all value. Through the rendering of Winston Smith and his fictional world this liberalism is explored and extended in relation to epistemological, ethical and ontological discourses. Like a good Cartesian (or, more surprisingly, like a Beckett hero) the first thing Winston Smith becomes certain of is his own inner speech, 'the interminable restless monologue that had been running inside his head, literally for years' (p. 10). Rather than attributing this to the internalisation of various outward discourses, the novel (with Smith) claims it as the private property of the individual – 'Nothing was your own except the few cubic centimetres inside your skull' (p. 25). Individual self-consciousness is validated by contrast when the word 'unconscious' is applied to the body and the social. 'Orthodoxy', says Syme, Smith's colleague, 'is unconsciousness' (p. 46, but see also the use of the word on pp. 32, 33, 35, 46, 55). Throughout the novel the individual is accorded value as transcendental subject of knowledge. Winston Smith feels vindicated when he discovers by accident a fact, 'concrete evidence' that the Party has lied (p. 66). He returns obsessively to an empiricist conception of truth as pregiven once and for all in the real such that the individual may be present to himself as bearer of that truth. This underlies Smith's horror of what the Party does, and it is constantly reaffirmed by the text's references to doublethink and Newspeak: 'The empiricist method of thought, on which all the scientific achievements of the past were founded, is opposed to the most fundamental principles of Ingsoc' (p. 157). Significantly (it is an issue to which we shall return), Smith cannot interest Julia in becoming a transcendental subject for knowledge as 'She did not feel the abyss opening beneath her feet at the thought of lies becoming truth' (p. 17). He does.

Corresponding to this imputed priority of individual consciousness are the moral values Smith describes as 'privacy, love, and friendship', a sense of personal loyalty located in the family (p. 28), values which are those traditionally subscribed to by the English gentry (and quite admirable they are as far as they go) but which Smith later discovers among the proles:

They were governed by private loyalties which they did not question. What mattered were individual relationships ... They

were not loyal to a party or a country or an idea, they were loyal to
one another. (p. 135)

This is no mere passing phase in Smith's developing
experience. Right at the end, after he has tried to refute
O'Brien's view that 'Nothing exists except through human
consciousness' by pointing to the pregiven truths of geology
('But the rocks are full of the bones of extinct animals ...'
p. 213), Smith's liberalism is forced to admit its claim to
metaphysical guarantees. O'Brien rightly diagnoses that Smith
imagines 'there is something called human nature which will
be outraged by what we do and will turn against us'; and he
speaks Smith's epitaph: 'You are the last man ... You are the
guardian of the human spirit' (pp. 216-217). 'Man', for
Winston Smith and Orwell's text, is an abstract essence
'inherent in each single individual' rather than a heterogenous
being constituted in 'the ensemble of social relations.'[12] It's fair
to add that O'Brien's Hobbesian anthropology ('The object of
power is power') is no less humanist than Smith's liberalism in
resting on a view of man as an abstract essence.

This informing liberalism can be easily recognised as
holding up one side in a series of well-known ideological
contradictions, each handing on a supposedly absolute
opposition: subject/object, mind/body, individual/social.
Once the text has set up a prior conception of the individual as
self-constituted (outside history, language, the psychoanalytic
process) it follows inevitably that *anything* which threatens to
limit this will appear as unfreedom, all 'Orthodoxy' will be
'unconscious'. Posed as abstracts, the couple freedom/totali-
tarianism generate and confirm each other, and in this respect
the novel only presents an extreme version of the social as itself
oppressive, a notion found everywhere from Jane Austen to
D.H. Lawrence. And what is thematically asserted in the
narrative of *Nineteen Eighty-Four* is also worked through in the
novel's narrative form as a realist text.

A Science-Fiction Story

As Patrick Parrinder well argues, *Nineteen Eighty-Four* must now
take its place in the genre of science-fiction, 'not because of the
future setting but because of the "estranged" and yet cognitive

status of the Thought Police, the two-way telescreen, Newspeak, and Oligarchical Collectivism.'[13] These distorted transpositions from our own world become recognisable cognitively but also provide the pleasures of metamorphosis, play and wit. One minor example occurs when Winston Smith expects wine to taste of blackberry jam and have 'an immediate intoxicating effect' (p. 140), and, his palate eroded by years of Victory Gin, is disappointed. Classic science fiction, however, presupposes the realist mode even if in some ways its purpose, like that of coherent meaning in the tendentious joke as analysed by Freud, is to defer and disguise the point so as to make it more suddenly effective.

But *Nineteen Eighty-Four* is not classic science fiction. Relatively low on fantasy situations and high on psychological complexity, it is much closer to the traditional realism of the nineteenth-century novel. On the basis of a rendering of individuals situated in an internally consistent world of everyday reality, a narrative is sustained according to the conventional links by which cause and effect are assumed to hook together. This is Barthes's proairetic code, for which an example might be the way the arrest of Smith and Julia at the end of Part Two is followed by his interrogation in Part Three. And the narrative also operates consistently through the hermeneutic code according to which, for example, the seemingly unmotivated appearance of a rat in the lovers' hideaway to be greeted by Winston Smith's words 'Of all horrors in the world – a rat' (p. 119) is explained when 'the worst thing in the world' in Room 101 turns out to be a cage of rats (p. 228). The consistent application of these codes within the narrated, together with the psychological coherence of the presentation of character, tends to efface the means of representation in the novel in favour of the represented, to offer the narrated as an object not constructed by writing, and so transparently accessible to the subject, the reader thus placed in a position of mastery. And this position is confirmed by the generally anonymous and unmarked novelistic style of the text. Yet within the water of its would-be styleless style there float two other distinct kinds of writing, the long extracts from Goldstein's theoretical work and the Appendix on 'The Principles of Newspeak' (pp. 241-252), as well as various slogans (on p. 86, for example), the voice of the singing prole (pp. 133, 175), slabs of newspeak from Smith's office (p. 34), and a series of extracts (some unpunctuated and all in lower case, as on p. 19) from Smith's diary. In order to substantiate itself as a unity aiming to secure a unitary and transcendent position for the reader, the text establishes these different kinds of discourse and modes of writing within itself only because it is confident it can bind them together into a seamless whole.

'Nineteen Eighty-Four' as Writing

In this the text's project necessarily fails. There are various places where it begins to unravel but possibly two are the most manifest. One is the respect in which *Nineteen Eighty-Four* by directing its attention so forcibly at the topic of writing, comes in conequence to place in the foreground and make a problem of its own discursive origin. Another occurs in the development and dramatisation of Winston Smith's character. Invited, or rather compelled, by the realist narrative to take Smith as the main point of identification, readers find themselves entangled and led elsewhere by a body of fantasy far exceeding the function the text means to assign to it.

A feeling of falling into a Derridean *abîme* afflicts Winston Smith whenever he thinks of 'lies becoming truth' (p. 127). An occupational hazard for him in his work on Newspeak at the Ministry of Truth, it becomes a main constituent in his neurotic obsession with the real:

> As soon as all the corrections which happened to be necessary in any particular number of *The Times* had been assembled and collated, that number would be reprinted, the original copy destroyed, and the corrupted copy placed on the files in its stead. This process of continuous alteration was applied not only to newspapers, but to books, periodicals, pamphlets, posters, leaflets, films, soundtracks, cartoons, photographs – to every kind of literature or documentation which might conceivably hold any political or ideological significance. Day by day and almost minute by minute the past was brought up to date … All history was a palimpsest, scraped clean and reinscribed exactly as often as necessary … (pp. 35-36)

For Winston Smith and for the novel that endorse
process of continuous alteration and reinscription
thing in the world (the rats, as will be argued, a
surrogate for it). Two issues should be separated here. One is
the undemocratic manipulation and suppression of information, something which has got worse in Britain in the years up
to 1984. The other is the impossibility – in every sense – of a
reality which stands (to adapt some phrases from Derrida) as a
fundamental immobility, a natural site, absolutely present
outside discourse and beyond the reach of the play of the
signifier.[14] And yet it is this impossible object which Winston
Smith desires.

In the concluding exchanges O'Brien says that 'reality is not
external' but 'exists in the human mind, and nowhere else'
(p. 200), and again, that 'nothing exists except through human
consciousness' (p. 213). O'Brien's idealism (truth exists only in
discursive construction) shares the same absolutist problematic
as Smith's positivist empiricism (truth exists independent of
discursive construction). Winston Smith's mind – his being –
begins to crack apart first at the encounter with the disjunction
between meaning and referent, then at the slide of signifier
over signified. The meaning of history *is* subject to 'continuous
alteration' since it is a meaning constructed in an ever-moving
present (though it would not follow from this that
historiography does not refer to its own verifiable object of
knowledge). And the meaning of a text *is* transformed if its
linguistic components are re-written, if, for example, the
Lockeian rhetoric of the Declaration of Independence is
translated into Newspeak (see p. 251). But the inherent
arbitrariness of the relation between signifier and signified
does not prevent a stable sign coming about within what
Saussure calls 'the social fact' of discourse.[15]

By continually enforcing an either/or – either the absolute
immobility of the real represented transparently in language,
or the abyss of words which are only words – the novel tends to
negate what it intended. Instead of confirming the truth of the
text it subverts it. Surely the conscientious use of a realist
narrative means us to overlook the means of representation in
favour of what is represented, to accede to the prose style as
something weightless and without origin? And what happens?

Continuous insistence on writing pushes into the foreground the text's own discourse, making us ask what it is and where it comes from. If it originates in the present, how can it have access to this narrative from 1984? And if it derives from 1984, how come it is not written in Newspeak, and what would it be like if it were? Worse follows. For Winston Smith's obsession with finding a truth immune to discursive construction cannot but call attention to the fictionality of this text we are in the process of reading. *Nineteen Eighty-Four*, as a novel, consists of meanings which do not refer to reality; as such, it can't be distinguished from the material in the Ministry of Plenty which 'had no connexion with anything in the real world' (p. 36). The life, love and subsequent suffering of Winston Smith are themselves nothing but a set of 'lies becoming truths'.

Julia is less susceptible to the horror induced in Smith by the way writing makes truth and lies ultimately though not immediately indistinguishable. As far as he and the novel's avowed purpose are concerned, this counts against her. As main representative of woman in the text Julia is essentialised. She belongs to nature rather than culture (Smith finds her breasts to be 'ripe yet firm', p. 112). She is imagined as all woman, her 'short hair and boyish overalls' only making her 'far more feminine' (p. 117). She is seen as exclusively heterosexual, exclaiming at one point 'How I hate women!' (p. 107), a feature strengthened in Winston Smith's eyes by the number of men she has made love with:

> His heart leapt. Scores of times she had done it: he wished it had been hundreds – thousands. (p. 103)

Julia, then, is a figure of masculine fantasy, not unlike Honeychile in Fleming's *Dr No*, the tomboy stereotype of woman, less rational, less conscientious, less aware, less committed to culture, less concerned with absolute truth. 'You're only a rebel from the waist downwards' is Smith's enthusiastic assessment (p. 128).

Part Two follows the course of their love affair, Chapter 2 concluding with their escape from London and the Anti-Sex League into a clearing in the Berkshire woods. Smith reflects that 'simple undifferentiated desire ... was the force that would tear the Party to pieces' and his view is ratified when, after they make love, the section ends 'It was a political act' (p. 104). So they may believe but we may recall Foucault's more sombre conclusion in *The History of Sexuality* that the 'desirability of sex' makes us think we are affirming it

> against all power, when in fact we are fastened to the deployment of sexuality that has lifted up from within us a sort of mirage in which we think we see ourself reflected ...[16]

Once again, *1984* reproduces the ideological opposition between the social and the individual, here articulated as that between politics and sexuality.

Fantasy

The intended perspective of *Nineteen Eighty-Four* overlaps largely with the attitudes and experience of Winston Smith, who is offered to the reader as a main point of identification. Smith constitutes a paradigmatic example of the subject of knowledge privileged by realist fiction, like the detective in that genre. He is also the Romantic hero, expressively writing his novelistic inwardness into existence via the 'hurried untidy scrawl' of his diary, just as the hero's represented identity at the beginning of *David Copperfield* seems hardly distinct from his identity in the act of enunciation: 'Whether I shall turn out to be the hero of my own life, or whether that station will be held by anyone else, these pages must show.' And he is even a version of the existentialist hero. Since orthodoxy is unconsciousness, individuated self-awareness itself is a thoughtcrime meriting death. By entering consciousness Smith acknowledges his contingency, making it over into a motive for action: 'Now he had recognised himself as a dead man it became important to stay alive as long as possible' (p. 26).

Through the rest of the text the reader is invited to follow sympathetically Smith's developing experience, his burgeoning sense of selfhood, his anagnorisis, his love for Julia and their attempt to join the Brotherhood, his arrest, interrogation, torture, and final dissolution into orthodoxy: 'He loved Big Brother' (p. 240). But this psychic passage necessarily betrays the novel into a discourse of the other, a scene for fantasy that ineluctably unsticks the text's avowed unity and its aim to make readers as present to themselves in the face of the text as Winston wants to be within it. *Nineteen Eighty-Four* does this the more radically because it seeks to disavow so curtly the dynamic of the unconscious by ascribing it to a social other (orthodoxy is unconsciousness) or a bodily otherness.

One way to envisage what can figure in the place of an object of desire for Winston Smith is to consider how often and how intensely he recurs to the fantasy of killing a woman – 'He would flog her to death with a rubber truncheon' (p. 16, but examples also on pp. 84, 92, 99, 111, etc.). From this main trajectory his love for Julia brings only a temporary inflection. Traversing the 'official' narrative of the text, running through and across its proferred concatenation of events, there is another narrative. What counts in this other theatre is less the narrative order of events than the order of their narration for Winston Smith. Though a practice of reading will exceed any programmatic analysis, attention can be drawn to some of the more cathected moments of the text.

'The question, as always in classical realism, is one of identity.'[17] *Nineteen Eighty-Four* opens with Winston Smith watched by the castrating gaze of Big Brother and moved by O'Brien's 'curiously disarming' trick of 'resettling his spectacles on his nose' (p. 12). Admitted thus into conscious self-identity and starting a diary, Smith would negotiate the castration complex by locating its site as the maternal body. He hates women, wishes to kill them, dreams that his mother and sister sacrificed their lives for him (p. 27). In the passage from polymorphous perversity to distinct heterosexual preference for a mature object the human subject never loses its bisexual potential. For men the Oedipus complex is both positive (identification with the Father leading to heterosexual object-choice) and negative, a form in which a boy 'displays an affectionate feminine attitude to his father and a correspond-ing jealousy and hostility to his mother.'[18] Insofar as he is placed in the feminine position towards the Father, Smith feels an ambivalent love towards O'Brien, one on which the text constantly (and otherwise inexplicably) insists. O'Brien knows his thoughts (p. 17), O'Brien promises to meet him 'in the place where there is no darkness' (p. 24), O'Brien has 'a remarkable grace in his movements' (p. 143). To the end Smith experiences a 'peculiar reverence for O'Brien'. Paranoia ('Always the eyes watching you and the voice enveloping you', p. 25) is induced by Smith's attempt to foreclose his homosexuality.

Against this negative form at a deeper level Smith's heterosexuality acts in a precarious counter-movement. He discovers hatred towards Big Brother (p. 15); works through in dreaming of her something of his feeling towards his mother; while thinking of his failed relationship with his wife, Katherine, he has intercourse with a female prole prostitute (pp. 54 – 59), just – but only just – overcoming his horror of her mouth ('nothing except a cavernous blackness'); writes that '*If there is hope it lies in the proles*' (p. 59) – understanding of this is deferred; and visits an antique shop owned by Mr Charrington, 'perhaps sixty ... with a long, benevolent nose' (p. 79), from whom he acquires the phallus.

It is symbolised fetishistically:

> It was a heavy lump of glass, curved on one side, flat on the other, making almost a hemisphere. There was a peculiar softness, as of rainwater, in both the colour and the texture of the glass. At the heart of it, magnified by the curved surface, there was a strange, pink, convoluted object that recalled a rose or a sea anemone. (p. 79)

This glass paperweight is 'heavy in his pocket, but fortunately it did not make much of a bulge' (p. 80), even though it 'banged against his thigh at every step' (p. 84).

Armed with the phallus (whereas O'Brien's grace is 'disarming') and following her message to him, 'I love you' (p. 89), Smith in Part Two enters into his love-affair with Julia. They take a room over Charrington's shop, where Smith keeps the paperweight on a table, gleaming 'softly in the half-darkness' (p. 112). 'Inexhaustibly interesting' (more interesting in the text's own estimation than Julia), it gathers into itself the traditional symbolic resonances of Romantic love, an enclave of reciprocated narcissism, the heart of a heartless world, light, eternity, 'a tiny world', 'eternity at the heart of the crystal' (pp. 121, 124, 127, 131). For Smith love is represented fetishistically not only by the paperweight but also, now, by the figure of the singing prole, the phallic mother. As 'solid as a Norman pillar, with brawny red forearms', she had a mouth 'corked with clothes pegs'. Her love-song echoes through Part Two, and at one point she is watched by both Smith and Julia (pp. 175-176). Having found this hope in the proles, Smith is now able to recall his own mother, imaged not as death but in terms of a similar phallicism. Working over his earlier dream he sees in his mother a protective 'gesture of the arm' (p. 131) and admits to Julia, 'until this moment I believed I had murdered my mother' (p. 132). In identification (albeit uneasy) with Goldstein and with the (deceptive) appearance of O'Brien as member of the Brotherhood, Winston Smith starts to take political action against an unjust society. But at the end of Part Two Charrington turns out to be a member of the Thought Police, Smith and Julia are arrested, the glass paperweight is 'smashed to pieces' (p. 179).

Delusional jealousy in men is regarded by psychoanalysis as a defence against homosexuality, a projection that can be described in the formula: '*I* do not love him, *she* loves him'.[19] In the more extreme form of persecutory paranoia 'it is precisely the most loved person of his own sex that becomes his persecutor',[20] and the corresponding paradigm is: 'I do not *love* him – I *hate* him, because HE PERSECUTES ME'.[21] In *Nineteen Eighty-Four* O'Brien is the focus for Smith's paranoiac sense that everyone is watching him and threatening him. At points in the text Smith's homosexual love for O'Brien and his heterosexual love for Julia coalesce in a compromise formation, for example when he fantasises that he might use the paperweight to 'smash her skull in' (p. 84), or again when he tells her, 'The more men you've had, the more I love you' (p. 103). But for Smith the negative Oedipal trajectory wins out in the end.

O'Brien in his role as member of the Brotherhood contacts Smith in the same place and by the same means of a written note as Julia first did (pp. 129-130). In Part Three with the arrest, interrogation, torture and confession Smith finally arrives at his long-promised rendezvous with O'Brien in 'the place where there is no darkness' (p. 196), the constant electric light of the prison-cell. 'I do not love him, he hates me':

O'Brien tortures Smith but still he loves him, says that 'He was the tormentor, he was the protector' (p. 196), and later finds, 'He had never loved him so deeply as at this moment' (p. 202).

Smith's regression from self-identity and heterosexual love for Julia is not completed until the threat of castration is re-instituted in Room 101 (pp. 227-231). Like Ratman in the well-known case-history, he feels that other people, especially O'Brien, know his thoughts. Like Ratman also, who fantasised around the idea of 'a specially horrible punishment used in the East',[22] Winston Smith is menaced with what 'was a common punishment in Imperial China'. But the rats would aim at the head rather than the anus. In Ratman, an obsessional neurotic, the idea took the form of anal eroticism and was related to 'the lady whom he admired':[23] Smith himself has the place of the victim. As usual in the process of the unconscious, the meaning 'castration' is displaced into a marginal signifier, the apparently arbitrary room number. 101, three digits in a binary series, makes up the phallic number with absence at its centre and also connotes the airship which crashed so spectacularly on 5th October 1930.[24] Faced with the worst thing in the world ('they attack the eyes first') Smith entirely repudiates his heterosexuality ('Do it to Julia!'). Afterwards, drunk in the café, he 'froze with horror' at the thought of heterosexual intercourse (p. 234); his paranoia has dissolved with full relapse into the feminine position: 'He loved Big Brother' (p. 240).

Dystopia and Paranoia

Rather than diminishing or reducing the text of *Nineteen Eighty-Four*, the previous account would expand its literary significance. This can be understood in two respects: because fantasy in literature is always imbricated with an ideological formation; because it is a function of literary fantasy to be representative rather than idiosyncratic. There is space here only to point in the directions in which analysis needs to be more fully developed.

Writing not about *Nineteen Eighty-Four* but about the film text, *Dog Day Afternoon*, Fredric Jameson argues that the modern vision of dystopia derives allegorically from 'that immense and decentralised power network which marks the present multinational stage of monpoly capitalism.'[25] While older expressions in the utopian/dystopian mode gave a *personalised* account of power as originating, for good or ill, with individuals, this contemporary film renders a sense, 'rarely accessible in figurable terms', of power as hostile, systematic, and marked rather by the absence of personal agency than its presence; a sense

> inscribed in the spatial trajectory of the film itself as it moves from the ghettoised squalor of the bank interior to that eerie and impersonal science fiction landscape of the airport finale: a corporate space without inhabitants, utterly technologised and functional, a place beyond city and country alike – collective, yet without people, automated and computerised, yet without any of that older utopian or dystopian clamour ...[26]

Whether or not we go along with Jameson's willingness to tie back dystopia onto an economic cause, monopoly capitalism, we may still accept that the modern dystopian mode reproduces an ideological formation around anonymous social repression rather than individual agency.

But the account of literature as ideology does not exhaust its effect as fantasy, and for this we must turn to psychoanalysis. Briefly: everyone has fantasies in the form of day-dreams, invariably of an undisguised and narcissistic nature that is boring for others; the aesthetic text, because it provides 'forepleasure' in the 'purely formal'[27] (that is, the work/play of the signifier), presents fantasies in such a way that makes it 'possible for other people once more to derive consolation and alleviation from their own sources of pleasure in their unconscious which have become inaccessible to them.'[28] While the fantasy in actuality tends towards the merely personal and subjective, the *aesthetic* fantasy moves onto the terrain of the transindividual and intersubjective. And so the fact that *Nineteen Eighty-Four* has been widely read for nearly two generations is itself evidence that the text can perform as a symptomatic literary fantasy for Europe and North America in the twentieth century.

Nineteen Eighty-Four makes available the fantasy of persecutory paranoia (and it would be a misrecognition to say that Winston Smith 'really' is being persecuted by Ingsoc). In the course of arguing that 'no meaning given to history, based on Hegeliano-Marxist premises' is capable of accounting for fascism, for 'the drama of Nazism', Lacan has suggested that paranoia should be referred to the operation of the death drive:

> the offering to obscure gods of an object of sacrifice is something which few subjects can resist ... the sacrifice signifies that, in the object of our desires, we try to find evidence for the presence of the desire of this Other that I call here *the dark God*.[29]

Again, the issue of historical explanation – monopoly capitalism, Nazism – may be left aside in bringing together dystopia and paranoia.

Just as polymorphous perversity is for utopia, so persecutory paranoia – they are attacking me – constitutes the psychoanalytic lining, the unconscious subtext, for dystopia. As such it constantly recurs through images and narratives of unjust imprisonment and interrogation, not only in popular culture, in film and television, but also in high cultural literary modes: in Kafka (there is 'a small, curiously beetle-like man' in *Nineteen Eighty-Four*, p. 52); in Pound's *Pisan Cantos*, in Solzhenitsyn's *First Circle*, and in Pynchon's *V* (especially 'Mondaugen's story'). Linked to a state of global warfare the dystopian/paranoiac fantasy appears in *Catch 22* and *Gravity's Rainbow*; linked to the hospital or psychiatric ward in *Clockwork Orange, One Flew Over the Cuckoo's Nest, Woman at the Edge of Time*. And, in Norman Bryson's description, it forms the basis for one of the best-known paintings of this century:

> *Guernica*, a specific reaction to a single (if emblematic) political event, by raising the spectre of slaughter from the air, becomes a generalised nightmare.[30]

The list could be extended. Despite the specific forms taken by secondary revision in each of these different texts – the state institution as bureaucracy, prison camp, Gulag, military base, psychiatric hospital, secret police (whether KGB or CIA) – all can be read for the fantasy of living in what Pynchon names

'The Zone', subject to institutionalised surveillance and persecution by a wholly malign other.

Applying this view to *Nineteen Eighty-Four*, my argument would be that the text makes the dystopian/paranoiac fantasy more effectively available in Part One of the novel than later, when, via Winston Smith's affair with Julia and relationship with O'Brien, the text becomes increasingly psychologised and denunciatory in the rhetoric of what Jameson speaks of as 'dystopian clamour'. Continuous international warfare (real or invented), the Thought Police, Newspeak, 'the eyes watching you', the seedy townscapes of London under Ingsoc, these state institutional, cultural, linguistic and subjective apparatuses present in figurable terms what is arguably the most typical contemporary fantasy.

The Novel as Paperweight

> There was such a depth of it, and yet it was almost as transparent as air ... as though the surface of the glass had been the arch of the sky, enclosing a tiny world ... He had the feeling that he could get inside it, and that in fact he was inside it, along with the mahogany bed and the gateleg table, and ... the paperweight itself. The paperweight was the room he was in, and the coral was Julia's life and his own, fixed in a sort of eternity at the heart of the crystal. (p. 121)

Since persecutory paranoia is a defence against homosexuality, *Nineteen Eighty-Four* may also achieve typicality in its sexual politics. The homosexuality of Winston Smith's negative Oedipus complex leads to reinforcement of the disavowal of castration in the positive form, his love for Julia. Within his fetishistic imaginary Julia figures as the phallus of his fully present heterosexuality. Unable to live with his own divided sexuality, Smith must fix Julia's femininity in place once and for all according to the traditional phallocentric scenario of Romantic love. Her own sexuality is to be denied so that she can become coral in his paperweight, natural rather than human, mineral rather than organic, like the metallic woman that is Pynchon's V or the Venus Anadyomene in 'Medallion', the last poem in Pound's *Hugh Selwyn Mauberley*:

Spun in King Minos' hall
From metal, or intractable amber ...

Hence the names: Winston Smith, stand-in for the cigar-smoking warlord, Julia his jewel.

Julia in the paperweight, Julia as the paperweight, is meant to be a mirror in whose reflection Winston Smith may appear fully present to himself in the form he wishes to see himself, a transcendent ego. The paperweight represents 'a sort of eternity', a point at which being is infinitely present outside temporal difference as well as spatial difference, a completed circle. But also, in this variegated symbolism, because it is 'almost as transparent as air', this crystal would provide unmediated access to knowledge, with no means of representation acting to bring subject into relation with object. Winston Smith sees himself inside the paperweight 'along with the mahogany bed' and, in total self-reference, 'the paperweight itself'.

If sexual difference is taken up analogously with linguistic difference, Winston Smith's foreclosure of sexual difference (he is to be all man, Julia all woman) corresponds to his denial that meaning is produced in the process of the signifier. Absolutely opposed to Newspeak, the paperweight for him is 'a little chunk of history that they've forgotten to alter' (p. 120), one of 'a few solid objects with no words attached to them' (p. 127). Even after it is broken, Smith during his interrogation struggles like a tragic hero to retain his conception of himself as a man and a sovereign consciousness able to grasp truth outside words. In the name of the Father, O'Brien in room 101 reinstates for Smith the persistence of human consciousness only in words, text, writing. And the novel intends a reader to take Smith's return to the feminine position only as tragic.

Nineteen Eighty-Four tries to supplement its proferred meaning with the guarantee of a metatext, the 'Appendix'. There, the principle of Newspeak is defined as the intention 'to make speech as nearly as possible independent of conscious-ness' (p. 248). Aiming to counterpose itself wholly against the possibility of Newspeak, to present to the reader a consciousness as nearly as possible independent of writing, the novel mobilises the realist mode as a would-be transparent means of access to the truth it would represent. In trying to refound the significance of the text not so much as a picture of reality, to be judged true or false, nor as a general truth about totalitarianism, but rather as a typical form of modern fantasy, this analysis has suggested how the text as writing provokes readings beyond its overt intention. However hard it tries – the more it tries – to tell the truth, *Nineteen Eighty-Four* cannot cover clearly and hold in place the process of the text on which it depends. Literally, a paperweight is something used to hold down pieces of writing. *Nineteen Eighty-Four* cannot be such an object. Nor, for that matter, can this present analysis.

Notes

1 Patrick Parrinder, *Science Fiction, Its Criticism and Teaching*, London, 1980, p. 75.
2 George Orwell, *Nineteen Eighty-Four*, Harmondsworth, 1983, p. 7. All page references are to this edition.
3 *Guardian*, 31 October 1983.
4 *Guardian*, 1 November 1983, report of *Family Expenditure Survey*, published by the Department of Health and Social Security, 1983.
5 For an explanation, see Stuart Hall, 'The Great Moving Right Show', in Stuart Hall and Martin Jacques (eds.), *The Politics of Thatcherism*, London, 1983; for an alternative, see Geoff Hodgson, *The Democratic Economy*, Harmondsworth, 1984.
6 'Screening the News', *The Leveller*, No. 11 (January 1978), pp. 14-17.
7 Aristotle, 'On the Art of Poetry' in *Classical Literary Criticism*, (tr. T.S. Dorsch), Harmondsworth, 1965, p. 43.
8 C.J. Friedrich and Zbigniew Brzezinski, *Totalitarian Dictatorship and Autocracy*, Cambridge, Massachusetts, 1965, p. 21.
9 S.E. Finer, *Comparative Government*, London, 1970, p. 75.
10 Leonard Shapiro, *Totalitarianism*, London, 1972, p. 124.
11 Thomas Hobbes, *Leviathan*, London, 1957, p. 49.
12 Karl Marx, 'Theses on Feuerbach' in C.J. Arthur (ed.), *The German Ideology*, London, 1974, p. 122.
13 Parrinder, op.cit.
14 Jacques Derrida, 'Structure, Sign, and Play in the Discourse of the Human Sciences' in *Writing and Difference*, (tr. Alan Bass), London, 1978, pp. 278-293.
15 Ferdinand de Saussure, *Course in General Linguistics*, (tr. Wade Baskin), New York, 1959, p. 113.
16 Michel Foucault, *The History of Sexuality, Volume One: An Introduction*, (tr. Robert Hurley), Harmondsworth, 1981, p. 157.

17 Colin MacCabe, 'Theory and Film: Principles of Realism and Pleasure', *Screen*, Vol. 17, No. 3 (Autumn 1976), p. 18.

18 Sigmund Freud, *The Ego and the Id*, Standard Edition, (ed. J. Strachey), London 1953-1974, Vol. 19, p. 33.

19 Sigmund Freud, *Some Neurotic Mechanisms in Jealousy, Paranoia and Homosexuality*, in Standard Edition, Vol. 18, p. 225.

20 Ibid., p. 226.

21 Sigmund Freud, *Psychoanalytic Notes on an Autobiographical Account of a Case of Paranoia (Dementia Paranoises)*, in Standard Edition, Vol. 12, p. 63.

22 Sigmund Freud, *Notes upon a Case of Obsessional Neurosis*, in Standard Edition, Vol. 10, p. 166.

23 Ibid., p. 167.

24 'The number three has been confirmed from many sides as a symbol of the male genitals', *The Interpretation of Dreams*, in Standard Edition, Vol. 5, p. 358); for an attempt to establish 'in the zero number the suturing stand-in for the lack' and the number series itself as 'metonomy of the zero', see Jacques-Alain Miller, 'Suture (elements of the logic of the Signifier)', *Screen*, Vol. 18 No. 4 (Winter 1977/78), pp. 24-34, and cf. the title (and contents) of Mike Westlake's novel, *One Zero and the Night Controller*, London, 1980; 'A quite recent symbol of the male organ in dreams deserves mention: the airship' (*The Interpretation of Dreams*, in Standard Edition, Vol. 5, p. 356), for the disaster which overcame the largest British airship, the R 101, at Beauvais in France, see Norris McWhirter, *Guinness Book of Records*, Enfield, 1979, p. 149.

25 Fredric Jameson, 'Class and Allegory in Contemporary Mass Culture: *Dog Day Afternoon* as a Political Film', *Screen Education*, No. 30 (Spring 1979), pp. 75-92, p. 88.

26 Ibid.

27 Sigmund Freud, *Creative Writers and Day-Dreaming*, in Standard Edition, Vol. 9, p. 153.

28 Sigmund Freud, *Introductory Lectures on Psychoanalysis*, in Standard Edition, Vol. 16, p. 376.

29 Jacques Lacan, *The Four Fundamental Concepts of Psycho-Analysis*, (tr. Alan Sheridan) London, 1977, p. 275.

30 Norman Bryson, *Vision and Painting*, London, 1983, p. 154.

Notes on Contributors

Bill Alexander was one of the Commanders of the British Battalion of the International Brigades; he is the author of the history of the British who fought for the Spanish Republic, *British Volunteers for Liberty: Spain 1936-1939*, which was published in 1982.

Deirdre Beddoe is Principal Lecturer in History and Art History at the Polytechnic of Wales at Pontypridd. She is author of *Welsh Convict Woman: A Study of Women Transported From Wales to Australia, 1787-1852* (1979) and *Discovering Women's History, A Practical Manual* (1984).

Alan Brown has done research on Shelley; his interest in Orwell and the school curriculum stems from his work as a teacher preparing students for O and A Level exams.

Beatrix Campbell works as a journalist for *City Limits*; she is the author (with Anna Coote) of *Sweet Freedom* (1982) and of *Wigan Pier Revisited* (1984), as well as a contributor to a large number of publications, including *Marxism Today* and *New Statesman*.

Andy Croft teaches at the University of Leeds in the Adult and Continuing Education Department; he has contributed to a range of journals including *New Socialist* and *London Magazine*, and has also written introductions to a number of reprints of socialist novels, *May Day* and *Last Cage Down* amongst them.

Antony Easthope teaches English and Cultural studies at Manchester Polytechnic. His book, *Poetry as Discourse*, was published in 1983 and he has also written for journals which include *New Left Review*, *Critical Quarterly*, *New Literary History* and *Radical Philosophy*.

Malcolm Evans is Senior Lecturer in the Department of Language and Literature at the Polytechnic of North London; he is author of *Signifying Nothing: Truth's True Contents in Shakespeare's Text* (forthcoming) and has contributed articles to *Shakespeare Quarterly*, *Glyph* and *Shakespeare Jahrbuch*.

Stuart Hall is Professor of Sociology at the Open University. Co-author of *Resistance Through Rituals* (1976) and *Policing the Crisis* (1978), he is also co-editor of *The Politics of Thatcherism* (1983) and a regular contributor to a wide range of publications, including *Marxism Today* and *New Socialist*.

Lynette Hunter has published *G.K. Chesterton: Explorations in Allegory* (1979), *Rhetorical Stance in Modern Literature* (1984) and *George Orwell, The Search for A Voice* (1984); she teaches at the Institute for Advanced Studies in the Humanities, Edinburgh University.

Alaric Jacob worked as a foreign correspondent for thirteen years, and was a war correspondent on every major front during the Second World War; later he joined the external news services of the BBC. His books reflect this life-long involvement in foreign affairs and include *A Traveller's War, A Window in Moscow* and *Scenes From A Bourgeois Life*.

Christopher Norris lectures at the University of Wales Institute of Science and Technology at Cardiff. He is author of *William Empson and the Philosophy of Literary Criticism* (1978), *Deconstruction: Theory and Practice* (1982) and *The Deconstructive Turn* (1983), and editor of *Shostakovich: The Man and his Music* (1982).

Stephen Sedley is a QC specialising in civil rights cases; his publications include an anthology of British folksongs and a volume of Spanish prison poetry in translation.

Robert Stradling is Senior Lecturer in History at University College, Cardiff. He is author of *Europe and the Decline of Spain* (1981) and has published articles in the scholarly journals of England, Spain and the Netherlands.